W9-BPM-746

The 108 Skills
of
Natural Born
Leaders

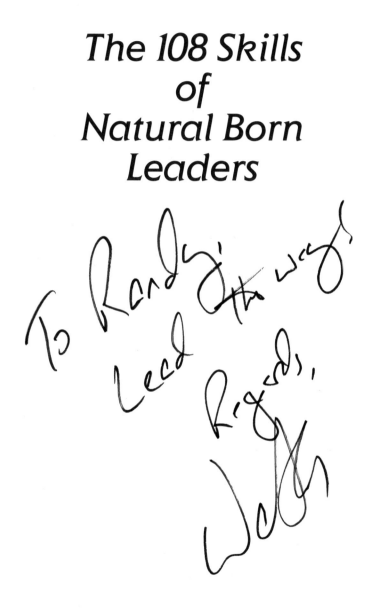

To Randy; the ways
lead

Regards,
Warren

The 108 Skills
of
Natural Born
Leaders

Warren Blank

AMACOM
American Management Association

New York · Atlanta · Boston · Chicago · Kansas City · San Francisco · Washington, D.C.
Brussels · Mexico City · Tokyo · Toronto

Special discounts on bulk quantities of AMACOM books are available to corporations, professional associations, and other organizations. For details, contact Special Sales Department, AMACOM, a division of American Management Association, 1601 Broadway, New York, NY 10019.
Tel.: 212-903-8316. Fax: 212-903-8083.
Web site: www.amacombooks.org

This publication is designed to provide accurate and authoritative information in regard to the subject matter covered. It is sold with the understanding that the publisher is not engaged in rendering legal, accounting, or other professional service. If legal advice or other expert assistance is required, the services of a competent professional person should be sought.

Library of Congress Cataloging-in-Publication Data

Blank, Warren.
   The 108 skills of natural born leaders / Warren Blank.
      p.   cm.
   Includes bibliographical references and index.
   ISBN 0-8144-0646-7
   1. Leadership—Case studies.   I. Title: One hundred eight skills of natural born leaders.   II. Title.

HD57.7 .B567   2001
658.4'092—dc21   00-065046

Printing number

10

Contents

Part III
Leadership Influence Skills

Acknowledgments

Many people helped me formulate the ideas in this book. I am particularly grateful to all the thousands of participants in my leadership training courses who have shown me positive models of leadership excellence and helped me clarify the skills of natural born leaders.

Adrienne Hickey, AMACOM executive editor, provided positive support throughout the project. Christina McLaughlin and the rest of the AMACOM staff made important contributions to improve the manuscript. Joe Mangino, Bill Hinkle, and Beverly Hanger offered several useful suggestions on early drafts. I owe an extra special thanks to Aaron Brown for the many insights he generously offered.

My mother, Helen Blank, served as a model of dedication to always do the best in life. My teacher and friend, Maharishi Mahesh Yogi, helped remind me that the real source of leadership lies within.

And, more than anyone else, my wife, Mary Ann, clarified my thinking and expanded my heart during every stage of this project.

Introduction

It is never too late to become what you want to be. This book is about becoming a more skillful leader. It's designed to provide you with the tools to be what people label a "natural born leader."

The need for leaders has always been important, and it has never been more urgent. The constant, accelerating, unpredictable change in today's competitive environment demands more and better leadership. People at all organizational levels and in all sectors want to be inspired. They want direction through the chaos created by uncertainty. People want to commit to important results that serve themselves and others. These needs define the locus of leadership. Those perceived to be "born leaders" fulfill these needs. Such natural born leaders offer courses of action through uncertain waters and create commitment toward destinations that make a difference.

The traditional view holds that natural born leaders are rare commodities. I call this the "right stuff" myth. It implies that only a few people own the abilities and have the necessary ingredients, the elusive "right stuff," to be leaders. If this is true, then we might as well pack it in and stop wasting all the time, money, and effort spent to improve leadership. We should simply acknowledge that most people just do not have these special ingredients. We should direct people to keep their heads down, hope that a few "real leaders" will come along, and muddle our way through.

I propose an alternate view: Anyone can be a leader. My experience working with hundreds of organizations and with thousands of executives, managers, supervisors, and employee groups indicates that a set of specific skills define what people commonly label as a natural born leader. This book identifies these skills. The book provides an individual assessment for people to measure their current level of competence. The book suggests ways to practice skill development. To the extent that individuals achieve greater mastery, they will be more effective leaders and earn the designation "natural born leaders."

My perspective changes the landscape for leadership development. It overcomes the limiting and, I believe, inaccurate mind-set that only a few have the right stuff to be leaders. Those who choose to step up to the leader role can take responsibility to develop their leadership ability. This book provides a leader success template. It offers a basis for meaningful leader action and a way to continually enhance leadership effectiveness.

The skill development choices provided in this book offer organizations a more potent method to develop leadership capacity. Many organizations suffer from what I call the "faulty plumbing and wiring leadership limit." That is, their organizational culture restricts leaders and leadership development. The deep fabric of organizational life, its internal plumbing and wiring, fails to provide sufficient rewards for leadership initiative or, worse, outright punishes those who take the risk of leader initiative in either formal or informal ways. Warren Bennis, the well-known leadership and organizational expert, first articulated this notion by suggesting an "unconscious conspiracy" in which organizations create hidden obstacles that make it extremely difficult to lead.

This book provides organizations with a performance development process that can be institutionalized to enhance leadership development and effectiveness. The formalization of this process results in rewiring and refitting the hidden forces that now limit leadership. The formalization process gives everyone a chance to fulfill their natural ability to lead, make a difference, and contribute to organizational success.

The Journey

Helen Keller once said, "There is no royal road to the summit, each person must zigzag their own way." The journey toward developing your natural born leader skills begins by understanding the natural born leader phenomenon. Chapter 1 describes this phenomenon and outlines the skills associated with being a natural born leader. Three broad natural born leader skill categories are described: foundational leadership skills, leadership direction skills, and leadership influence skills.

Chapter 2 takes you on the next step along the leadership development journey. It provides a natural born leader skill assessment. The assessment provides feedback on how you match up to the portrait of a natural born leader. It measures your strengths and areas that need improvement.

The next stage of the journey involves selecting the skills you want to work on in each broad category and then committing to skill development. The goal is to try to improve each day in measurable ways and perform a little better tomorrow than you did today.

The next three chapters describe the foundational natural born leader skills. These skills form the footing upon which you stand to be seen as a natural born leader. These skills are prerequisites for leadership effectiveness. Three pillars make up the foundational skills. Chapter 3 describes the self-awareness skills that define who you are as a leader. Chapter 4 defines the skills that leaders use to build rapport. Chapter 5 explains how leaders clarify expectations.

Chapters 6, 7, and 8 describe the natural born leader direction skills. Leaders identify issues, concerns, and opportunities that require leadership action. Chapter 6 specifically defines the skills leaders use to "map the territory" to recognize those needs. Leaders translate their mapping results into a course of action. Chapter 7 outlines the skills that leaders apply to chart a course of leadership direction. Leaders multiply themselves by cultivating leadership in others. Chapter 8 describes the skills leaders deploy to develop others as leaders.

Leaders gain willing followers, which requires their application of influence skills. Leaders establish their capacity to influence by building a base to gain commitment. Chapter 9 details the skills leaders use to build their base so that others will support them when they offer a leadership direction. Leaders use specific skills to influence people. Chapter 10 tells you how leaders apply these skills to gain willing followers. Chapter 11 describes the skills leaders use to establish an environment that fosters a willingness to follow. Leaders live within a larger organizational context. They create a motivating environment to support their leadership efforts.

Beginning Your Journey

You do not have to master every skill or develop them all at once. Many people who are labeled as "natural born leaders" have mastered only some of the skills. Perhaps no single person who achieves "natural born leader" status gains complete mastery of all the skills. Select a starting place that works for you after you take the assessment in Chapter 2. You will be attributed natural born leader status when you demonstrate your ability in even a subset of the skills. As you work on your skills, you will enlarge and enrich your leadership capacity, become more confident, and gain more consistent recognition as a "natural born leader."

"There are no secrets to success," commented General Colin L. Powell. "It is the result of preparation, hard work, learning from failure." The 108 skills of natural born leaders are not secrets, either. Leaders throughout history have demonstrated their ability to apply these skills, though some of the skills are newer. Deeper insights into how people, groups, and organizational dynamics operate have transformed our understanding of how leaders direct people, guide organizations, and influence followers.

Whether the skills are ancient or current, you can increase your success as one called a "natural born leader" by knowing your current skill competency level, working hard, and continually using your experience to take you to the next level. Luck is the place where preparation and opportunity meet. Skills come from learning, practice, and mastery.

Good luck and good skills!

1

The Natural Born Leader Phenomenon

She's just a natural born leader.
He was born to lead.
Some people are always leaders; they were just born that way.

Have you heard people make such comments? Have you made such statements yourself?

A select group of people seem to have that "certain something" that elevates them above the pack and enables them to be what we call "natural born leaders." Such unique individuals emerge in every situation in which they find themselves. Many distinguish themselves at an early age. Perhaps you have noticed a child at the playground who "naturally" organizes the lunch break games or rallies the neighborhood kids for a summertime project. Such children have no formal leadership training, but they step up to lead the other kids. You may have witnessed a teen, a young adult, or a person just starting a professional career who "innately" knew what to do and stepped up when no one else seemed willing or able to lead. And you probably have observed people in your career at all organizational levels who have "naturally" moved a group, division, or company forward despite the challenge or difficulty.

Natural born leaders are said to exist in all fields. Consider some individuals perceived as born to lead in industry: Jack Welch of General Electric Company (GE), Andy Grove of Intel Corp., John Chambers of Cisco Systems, Sam Walton of Wal-Mart, Mary Kay Ash of Mary Kay Inc., Warren E. Buffett of Berkshire Hathaway, Akio Morita of Sony Corporation, and the father of mass production, Henry Ford. Think of Franklin Delano Roosevelt, Winston Churchill, Charles de Gaulle, or Margaret Thatcher, all appraised as natural born leaders in the political arena. The natural born leader label also goes to military men such as H. Norman Schwarzkopf and Colin Powell of Desert Storm and George Patton and British field marshal Bernard Law Montgomery during World War II.

The natural born leader notion is hard to discount. When people demonstrate dramatic initiative, when they easily figure out what needs to be done, and when they effectively influence others, we assume they are "born to lead."

At some level, we *want* to believe in natural born leaders. The notion fulfills our romantic need for heroes. We desire larger-than-life characters to inspire us. We want to know there are some people who can bear any burden, overcome any obstacle, win any fight, and succeed in any situation. The idea that such people exist offers a sense of security, provides a degree of hope, and sets a model for us to honor and strive for. In our quiet, inward moments, we all know our limitations. We take comfort in the notion that somewhere out there, natural born leaders exist who can guide us beyond our limitations.

The Natural Born Leader: Fact or Fantasy?

The dictionary defines the word *natural* as "found in nature; without man-made changes; real, not artificial or manufactured; innate, not acquired." To be a "natural" means you were born that way. It is in the genes, programmed by your DNA. We readily observe the results of the genetic program in a "natural" redhead, in someone who is "naturally" slender, or in those whose skin is "naturally" sensitive to sunlight.

Does this same genetic predisposition apply to a leader? Are some people "naturally" born to lead?

I argue no. No one is born a leader. No one is genetically programmed or innately structured as a leader. In my book *The Nine Natural Laws of Leadership*, I explain that a leader is a person who gains willing followers.[1] Individuals in any situation and at any time throughout history were leaders *because* they attracted willing followers. No other description or definition clearly defines the essence of a leader. Leaders gain followers when they provide a direction and utilize influence methods that attract others to willingly support them and their direction. Leading, or the process of directing and influencing others to willingly follow, is based on a set of skills.

I propose that some people are labeled natural born leaders because they *effortlessly, spontaneously, consistently,* and *frequently* demonstrate the specific skills that cause others to willingly follow.

Leading is not an innate function of the leader alone or independent of the followers. To be a leader is contingent on the follower's assessment of the leader, the follower's interpretation of the leader's direction, and the interaction between the leader and follower. Followers are the leader's allies whose support, in effect, "makes" the leader. If no one follows, there is no leader.

Consider the space shuttle *Challenger* disaster. Engineers at lower levels of NASA felt the O-rings, a specific type of seal on the craft, could fail and render the shuttle unsafe. They tried to convince NASA senior management that the launch should be postponed. Senior management did not agree. Tragically, the engineers proved to be correct. Think of what happened here very carefully. These engineers had the right idea and were pointing in the right direction. Yet they did not have the authority to make the final decision. And they could not gain the support (that is, influence) senior management to delay the launch. Without followers, a person with an idea, plan, strategy, or vision, even if it is correct, is simply someone trying to provide a direction. Leadership occurs when others willingly follow that direction.

The natural born leader label is an attribution made to those who master the skill set related to gaining willing followers. No one is born with these skills. The natural born leader label actually describes exceptional or master leaders, those who effortlessly, spontaneously, consistently, and frequently demonstrate the skill set.

Some people are, of course, born with abilities that enable them to master leadership skills more effectively. In *Living with Our Genes*, Dean Hamer and Peter Copeland explain how behavioral aptitudes, personality preferences, and individual temperaments are programmed into our genes.[2] Such genetic capacities affect our aptitudes. Consider the child who brilliantly plays the piano without any training. Picture the athlete who rarely practices yet glides across the playing field with total grace. Think of those who almost automatically have a knack for the language, concepts, and practices of engineering, medicine, the law, or some other complex discipline. Such individuals have an innate ability that allows them to perform and excel naturally in their field.

Yet, unlike innate physical features, such as blue eyes or large hands, an innate behavioral aptitude, temperament, or preference does not guarantee the behavior will be actualized. People need opportunity, encouragement, and training. The goddess Athena was birthed from Zeus's head as a full-grown woman warrior. Humans are not born fully formed as a pianist, athlete, engineer, or leader. Some may have an inherited ability to more easily learn a second language. For example, some people may have the capacity to learn more than one language. Only those given a chance can become bilingual. Skill learning and skill development are necessary. Like a musical instrument, genes do not determine what music is played. Genes simply define the range of what can possibly be played.

True greatness, or skill mastery, requires skill practice. The superlative golfer, Tiger Woods, obviously has innate talent for the sport. However, his dad put a golf club in his hands at the age of three. Woods works tirelessly to hone his golfing skills. Imagine where Tiger Woods might be today if his father did not encourage him to play golf or had actually forbidden him to ever play any sports.

You Can't Do Anything about Your Genes

Some people seem to be born with a "leg up" in this world. They passed through the gene pool dispensary and got the prized DNA associated with greater likelihood of performance effectiveness. Yet your inborn capacities do not make a difference anymore. Because you are reading this book at this moment in time, you have already been through the gene dispensary. Your innate ability was programmed a long time ago. Whatever you naturally got at birth has already placed you somewhere on the innate-capacities continuum. The ready-made, from-the-factory set of preferences programmed into your individual DNA master source code cannot be changed.

You got what you got. Until science develops a do-it-yourself, home-use, gene-splicing kit, the innate, natural characteristics and temperament you have cannot be altered.

What you were born with only outlines the possibility, the potential to perform. And while it may set boundaries, you also have the natural ability to respond to opportunities that nurture your potential so you can achieve greater results. You may not become anything you want to be, but it is possible to be all that you are.

Everyone Has a Natural Born Capacity to Lead

To put it very plainly, then, no one is born a leader. However, everyone has a natural born capacity to lead because it is natural for people to respond to nurture. People have an innate ability to learn and grow. Anyone can be a leader because anyone can attract others to willingly follow. All people can enhance their ability by learning the skills of the best and most exceptional leaders. As your skill level grows, evolves, and blossoms, you can gain more followers more effortlessly, spontaneously, consistently, and frequently. More and more people will attribute natural born leader status to you.

You were born as someone. Becoming a leader is a choice. What you know can always change. What you are, based on predetermined innate limits, may not. You can develop as a leader by acquiring knowledge of the skills and an understanding of your capabilities, and by making the choice to change. You can mold your abilities by skill learning, practice, and feedback. You can make a conscious and intentional choice to upgrade yourself so you more closely resemble the portrait we attribute to natural born leaders and you become a more effective leader.

The Portrait of a Natural Born Leader

One hundred and eight skills paint the portrait of a natural born leader. The skills are not flavors of the month. They are the facts of the leader's life. They describe the actionable propositions that define the leader process. No single person completely mirrors every brushstroke in the picture. People match the portrait in varying degrees and demonstrate some skills more effectively than others.

Look at a few of the corporate chieftains in *Fortune* magazine's "America's Most Admired Companies" list. "Combative" describes General Electric's CEO Jack Welch. "Prankster and unabashedly affectionate" pertains to Southwest Airlines head Herb Kelleher. "Scathing" describes Microsoft boss Bill Gates. Each of these company captains has totally committed followers who ardently support them. Yet each demonstrates different skill mastery and in different ways.[3]

Some fit the natural born leader profile based on mastery of skills important in specific circumstances and with certain followers. For example, when rapport matters, those who can build trust more easily achieve exceptional leader status. If change, chaos, and uncertainty characterize the competitive environment, those who take decisive action more effortlessly emerge as exemplary leaders. When a motivating environment creates greater success, those who skillfully foster more open communication and participative decision making are perceived to be natural born leaders.

Everybody already has developed skills in some areas because everyone has gained willing followers in some situations. To expand your abilities and your effectiveness as a leader you must know the 108 skills. To operate in a wider circle of influence you must assess current skill competence. To attain the natural born leader label even more fully you must constantly practice towards mastery.

The 108 skills of natural born leaders are grouped into three categories. Each category is made up of three sets of skills.

The Skills of Natural Born Leaders

Category	Skill Sets
Foundational skills	Expand self-awareness Build rapport Clarify expectations
Leadership direction skills	Map the territory to identify the need to lead Chart a course of leadership action Develop others as leaders
Leadership influence skills	Build the base to gain commitment Influence others to willingly follow Create a motivating environment

Foundational Skills

The foundational skills are prerequisites for all other skills. Mastery of the foundational skills provides the necessary firm footing to have more impact, be more effective, and achieve greater leader success. Vince Lombardi once said that success comes from those who are "brilliant at the basics." For master leaders, the basics are self-awareness, a capacity to build rapport, and an ability to clarify expectations.

Leadership Direction Skills

Leaders provide direction through uncertainty. Leaders lead when people do not know what to do. People do not need to be led when they can detect obstacles and they know how to overcome them. Leaders must emerge when problems blindside people and when people cannot resolve the problems they face. People do not need to be led when they recognize an opportunity and are able to exploit it. Leaders step up in response to opportunities others miss and when people do not know how to take advantage of possibilities.

People need direction when the organizational structure cannot or does not provide it. No organization can create a perfect bureaucracy. Established organizational systems may not offer useful guidance in the face of dramatic change. Existing policies and procedures may create rather than resolve difficulties. Unforeseen obstacles and opportunities always arise no matter how good "the corporate plan" or how well thought out the "management schedule."

Exceptional leaders "map the territory" to identify the need to lead. They chart a course of action to meet the need. No single leader can identify all the needs and chart every course of action. Those who lead, especially on a broad, global scale, and those who direct large groups and organizations must multiply themselves. They develop others as leaders.

Leadership Influence Skills

Expert leaders have to influence people to willingly follow. *Willingness* is the operative word. Recall the scene in Steven Spielberg's film *Saving Private Ryan*. Captain Miller, played by Tom Hanks, is assigned a group of men to find Private Ryan and bring him home. As they search for Ryan, the platoon encounters an enemy machine gun nest. They successfully take it out, but one of their men is killed. The GIs want to murder a captured German soldier out of revenge. Captain Miller directs his men to let the captured German go. One disgruntled soldier, Private Reiben, rebels in frustration over Miller's decision.

Reiben declares, "I'm through with this mission," and begins to walk away. The platoon sergeant confronts Reiben, and threatens to shoot him if he doesn't "get in line." All the soldiers start shouting as the tension mounts to a breaking point as no solution seems apparent. Captain Miller finally speaks. "What's the pool up to on me?" he asks. Silence engulfs the group. The soldiers had created a betting pool regarding Miller's profession before joining the Army. Miller tells the men that he is a schoolteacher. He explains how that fact did not seem important in the battle zone. He goes on to clarify his feelings about being a soldier, about fighting for his own life and his desire to protect his men. Miller then tells Reiben he can leave. Miller clarifies that he will fulfill his mission to find Private Ryan so that he can get home to his wife. Miller walks off, alone, to bury the men killed during the battle. Without a word, the entire platoon, including Reiben, joins him.

Miller could have ordered Reiben to "fall in line" and "do what I say because I am in charge." He could have told the sergeant to execute the soldier for desertion. Miller focused on gaining willing support.

Exceptional leaders gain commitment rather than rely on command and compliance. They create a desire in followers rather than demand that subordinates fulfill requirements. They inspire rather than require. Those who offer a direction, at whatever level, become leaders when others willingly follow.

Nirmala Palsamy is a practicing nurse who heads the Village Health Nurse Association in the Indian state of Tamil Nadu. Her story, reported by Meenakshi Ganguly in *Time* magazine, illustrates how until others follow, no leadership occurs. Palsamy, and nurses like her, offer contraceptive information and suggestions as they scoot around on mopeds to visit their patients. Concerns about population growth caused the Indian government to pass mandates regarding enforced sterilization. Nurses were offered financial incentives to encourage the policy. For years, Palsamy was opposed to birth quotas in her state. She got little support and was even told by her superiors that she would be "suspended" if she openly challenged the policy. Finally, in 1992, her message got through to the new head of the Tamil Nadu family-welfare program, S. Ramasundaram. Palsamy convinced Ramasundaram that birth-control targets caused distrust in mothers toward nurses, which resulted in resistance to state policy. Population growth dramatically decreased in the area after Ramasundaram followed Palsamy's advice of no government interference.[4]

Palsamy's story demonstrates the challenge that master leaders face: No one has to willingly follow another.

Master leaders build a base that creates the conditions necessary to gain follower commitment. They influence others to embrace a particular course of action. They also know how the overall context affects their efforts to gain followers. They create a motivating environment that reinforces and energizes follower commitment.

Tell Me Something I Don't Know

"It's what you learn after you know it all that counts."
—John Wooden, former UCLA basketball coach

You will probably recognize many of the skills as you read through this book. I would be surprised if you did not know many of them! The skills describe what master leaders do, how they think, and what they are. Sir Isaac Newton didn't invent gravity. He identified and explained it. The 108 skills identify and explain why we attribute to such people natural born leader status. The skills do not prescribe what leaders should be. The skills bring to light the defining characteristics of the master leader portrait rather than attempt to create a new picture.

Knowing is not doing. Everybody knows it is important to listen. Few demonstrate good listening skills. Many can drive a car. Few can maneuver a Formula One race car at 200 miles per hour around the track in the Indianapolis 500. To gain natural born leader status, a person must know what to do *and* do it *and* ultimately perform in an effortless, spontaneous manner. Being a natural born leader requires frequent and consistent application of these skills during the difficult times that demand leadership action. Apathy, arrogance, and self-deception kill leadership potential.

Chapter 2 offers a way to gauge your ability to translate knowing into doing. The chapter contains a self-assessment to give you a glimpse into the mirror that compares your picture with the portrait of a natural born leader. Subsequent chapters provide a description of the natural born leader skills and action choices on how to perform those skills.

Unset Your Mind and Maximize Your Natural Born Leadership Skills

We must unset our mind about the romantic notion that only some people are natural born leaders. More and better leaders are needed at every organizational level. Global leaders direct with a wide-angle lens of awareness. They direct entire organizations or a network of organizations. Global leaders have as their horizon the larger-scale endeavors that affect great numbers of people for long time periods. Such people typically get the unique "natural born leader" label.

However, the focus on the few who operate at the global level and the belief that only some of us are born leaders actually limits leadership in organizations. Most leadership really occurs at the local level. Local leaders recognize a need and take action during the day-to-day work demands and within bounded time frames. They influence others to follow in small groups and in one-on-one interactions. Organizations succeed when many leaders take the fight into the trenches, use tactical maneuvers, and provide specific action steps that point toward specific gains.

The romantic notion that only some people are natural born leaders disempowers people at every level. It disheartens those who are trying to grow and develop their natural talents to lead. It also gives people an excuse not to try to lead or develop their skills. If only some are "born to lead," then you can shrug and simply say, "I can't be a leader." This hamstrings the person, the group, the organization, and the society as a whole.

Are Managers Leaders?

The 108 skills describe leaders, not managers. Managers perform tasks similar to leaders, but being a manager does not make someone a leader. In *The Nine Natural Laws of Leadership,* I compare the leader and manager roles and describe the key distinctions between leaders and managers.

I explain that managers are *given* their role within the organization. They are expected to direct subordinates to fulfill their job requirements and accomplish their assigned responsibilities. Managers ensure subordinates comply with established procedures, rules, policies, and regulations. Manager action is based on defined responsibility, established authority, and required accountability. Managers are expected to get things done "by the book." Managers work through challenges to achieve established outcomes and are expected to carry out the job as long as they have it.

Being a good manager is tough. Good managers must hold their subordinates accountable to accomplish their prescribed duties and motivate them to complete assigned tasks. Managers know how difficult it is to keep subordinates focused on job priorities and complete requirements on deadline. All good managers deserve credit for meeting the challenges inherent in getting things done through their employees.

In contrast, leaders *take* their role. They direct followers when established procedures do not work, when there are no procedures, and when uncharted opportunities arise. Leaders live in a world of uncertainty, guiding others to follow when others don't know what to do. Leaders direct followers to take advantage of opportunities and overcome obstacles that occur outside the prescribed tasks and duties of job requirements. Good managers frequently and willingly step into the uncertain arena of leadership action because they perceive the need to lead. They know that "the book" can never cover all contingencies, so they take the risk of initiative to provide leadership direction.

Leading is a different kind of challenge. For leaders, the

difficulty lies in the reality that they cannot fall back on the "by the book" standard for their direction. Leaders must chart a course through untested terrain. Thus, leaders live in a madhouse of change. And because they must attract followers, they must rely on a different source of influence. The differences can be stated simply as follows:

Manager Influence versus Leader Influence

Managers	Leaders
Influence derives from formal authority.	Influence derives from the interaction between the leader and followers.
Rely on the line relationship, which is defined by the organizational hierarchy.	Rely on a relationship of rapport, trust, and recognized credibility.
Influence is based on position (superior) to position (subordinate) power.	Influence is based on person-to-person power.
Influence comes from the right to command and demand, require and force compliance.	Influence comes from commitment, desire, and the ability to inspire and collaborate with followers.
Influence comes from control and can involve force.	Influence transcends control and derives from the quality of interaction.
Can only use their authority "down" the organizational ladder to direct subordinates.	Can exert influence in any direction: up, across, down, and outside the organizational hierarchy.

Leaders rely on reciprocal influence in which they are willing to listen, understand, and be responsive to followers. Leader influence requires a coactive exchange in which leaders can meet followers at their level and take them in the direction the leader wants to go. Good managers use their authority with fairness and are willing to accept the responsibility of being in charge and hold others accountable. Good managers become leaders when they seek first to gain commitment.

Managers can rely on "unity of command," the principle that one person, based on place in the hierarchy, has to be in charge. Multiple leaders can and do emerge at every organizational level when they gain willing followers. Good managers use their hierarchical position when necessary. Good managers do not rigidly require always being "in charge." Good managers contribute to leadership by willingly following others who offer leader direction.

Taking a manager position involves accepting the risk of not meeting organizational requirements. Managers accept the risk of not being able to juggle the multiple, competing demands created by directing diverse subordinates, serving one's boss, and completing specific manager tasks. Leaders take the risk of not gaining followers or not leading them to success.

Managers face organizational limits such as inadequate resource allocation from their boss and systemic constraints such as restrictive policies and procedures. Good managers may not be assigned or able to hire the kind of employees who really want to work or have the skills to accomplish their assigned tasks. Managers may not get compliance from their subordinates but have the right to demand it. They can use organizational procedures to enforce obedience. However, an obstinate subordinate who knows how to "work the system" can make life miserable for a manager who tries to hold the person accountable. Leaders must attract followers. Leaders face the limit that no one has to *willingly* follow another.

Management originates from externally derived sources: organizational standards and procedures. Managers can justify their actions based on "the manual" or policies. Leadership originates in consciousness, or how the leader processes information. Leaders rely on their state of awareness—their internal, subjective reality about what they feel matters and requires attention.

Developing Your Skills as a Natural Born Leader

The people we label as natural born leaders have mastered the 108 identifiable skills that define the portrait. Some mix of nature and nurture defines where you are now. How much is nature and how much is nurture is a matter of speculative debate. As of right now, you can understand, practice, and master the skills. That fact does not come from speculation.

To train athletes we make them run. To train leaders we must help people learn how leading really works. It involves using the natural ability we all have to learn and grow and improve as well as tapping into deeper levels. You will improve as you find the connections between yourself and these skills. You will be more effective as you understand where you are now and you embrace and commit to develop your skills.

The journey toward natural born leader status begins by seeking percentage improvement. Focus on making a degree of change each day in the direction of mastery of all 108 skills. The scale to which you enhance your ability to implement these skills is up to you. It takes some courage to sincerely attempt to transform one's self. You must be willing to admit the need for improvement. You must put in the time and effort to make changes. You have to accept that you may not get as far as you care to in a certain time period on a particular skill. Real courage is not about overcoming the fear of failure. Real courage exists in accepting the possibility of not succeeding and taking action anyway. Nonleaders succumb. Exceptional leaders overcome.

True leadership mastery comes from true change in yourself. Some people create the impression of change. A natural born redhead can dye his hair. Someone with naturally blue eyes can wear contacts so her eyes look brown. Cosmetic changes may improve one's appearance. We also know those changes are not real. You have natural born leader ability because you were born with the ability to make real improvements.

One Skill Away from Excellence

Imagine a mountain climber who is one step away from the summit. Picture a writer who is one chapter away from finishing a brilliant story. Consider a musician who is one refrain away from playing a brilliant song. What would you say to these people if they wanted to stop? Let me encourage you to work toward that next skill that could help you reach the summit in terms of leadership effectiveness.

Your skills will improve in a sequential process. As you become more proficient at the foundational skills, such as rapport building, you will be more successful applying the direction skills, such as developing others as leaders. Skills in these two areas will help you with your influence skills, such as creating a more motivating environment. In a step-by-step fashion, progress at each level helps you more smoothly incorporate subsequent skills. Your skills will also improve in a simultaneous fashion. For example, by developing your mapping skills, you will simultaneously develop skills related to charting a course and building a base of commitment.

This paradoxical nature of leadership skill development, which is both sequential and simultaneous, is partly why many leadership training efforts fail. They try to force development into a lockstep method. They fail to allow the learner to take ownership for progress by jumping to areas that are simultaneously being stimulated.

Begin Where You Are

The only way to predict the future is to have the power to shape the future. You have the power to endlessly shape and reshape yourself. Basketball coach Pat Riley stated in his book *The Winner Within*, "Excellence is the gradual result of always wanting to do better."[5] Your current skill set and competency format represent a pattern of experience and preference. What makes it useful to you today? Do you need to upgrade? Can you succeed in the future with your current skill set? What limiting factors can you transcend more easily? Which will require significant effort? Follow your interests and focus on what you can improve. If you try to do what you cannot do you will fail.

Are You Worthy of the Natural Born Leader Label?

Any of the 108 skills can be mastered with the intent to manipulate. Some people perform the skills only to pander to potential followers. Those we perceive as the best natural born leaders direct others based on life-supporting values. Followers support those they believe represent their values. The values you choose are determined by you. Author and athlete Mariah Burton Nelson has said, "If people look up to you, you need to become the kind of person worth looking up to."

Endnotes

1. Warren Blank, *The Nine Natural Laws of Leadership* (New York: AMA-COM, 1995).
2. Dean Hamer and Peter Copeland, *Living with Our Genes* (New York: Doubleday Books, 1998).
3. Geoffrey Colvin, "America's Most Admired Companies," *Fortune* (February 21, 2000), pp. 108–112.
4. Meenakshi Ganguly, "Speaking Her Mind," *Time* Special Environmental Issue (April–May 2000), p. 47.
5. Pat Riley, *The Winner Within* (New York: Berkley Publishing Group, 1994), p. 182.

2

Self-Assessment: The 108 Skills of Natural Born Leaders

This assessment measures how well you apply the 108 skills of natural born leaders now. The assessment is a guide to enhance your leadership effectiveness. Your scores clarify the specific skills that define your success. They also identify those skills that need improvement to help you become a more powerful leader. The assessment is not a test that has right or wrong answers. View it as a checkup that helps you determine your current status.

Respond to each statement in terms of how *others* would rate you. This is important because, as emphasized in Chapter 1, the natural born leader label is an attribution given to leaders from their followers. You need to consider how others would rate you because they represent potential followers. The follower's evaluation defines your natural born leader status.

Respond to the statements in terms of your general pattern of action. Think of how you typically behave in most situations. Avoid thinking about unique situations when you answer the statements.

Complete the entire assessment and then score yourself. The assessment consists of nine sets of statements; each set of statements correlates to one of the foundational, leadership direction, and influence skills of natural born leaders introduced in Chapter 1. The scoring key provides a scale to determine which skills you need to develop further.

As another option, ask other key individuals to complete the assessment for you based on their interpretation of your skills. They will help verify your perception of your skills.

THE SELF-ASSESSMENT

Instructions

Think of a core group of key people you need to willingly follow your lead. Using the scale from 1 to 6, to what extent would the members of this group agree with each of these statements about how you actually behave?

1 = Very strongly disagree
2 = Strongly disagree
3 = Disagree
4 = Agree
5 = Strongly agree
6 = Very strongly agree

Set One: Self-Awareness

_____ 1. Always approaches work with intensity and focus.
_____ 2. Does not get worn out or rattled even when demands are high.
_____ 3. Uses time effectively, especially in the face of multiple, competing demands.
_____ 4. Learns from all experience.
_____ 5. Seeks feedback from all sources on a regular basis.
_____ 6. Has a strong, positive sense of self; knows and understands him/herself.

Set Two: Capacity to Develop Rapport with People

_____ 7. Easily finds a common ground that creates a bond with others.

_____ 8. Demonstrates sincere empathy toward everyone.

_____ 9. Makes him/herself available and interacts with others in an easy, open manner.

_____10. Expresses appreciation on a regular basis for others' actions and accomplishments.

_____11. Demonstrates rock-solid character, ethics, and principles in all circumstances.

_____12. Creates an atmosphere of trust at all times.

Set Three: Ability to Clarify Expectations

_____13. Establishes clear and agreed-on expectations with others in all situations.

_____14. Always clarifies when people's expectations limit or restrict their thinking and action.

_____15. Explains the organization's expectations whenever people need clarification.

_____16. Relies on facts versus assumptions or inferences to clarify expectations.

_____17. Identifies any and all rumors, clarifies their validity, or finds out if they are true.

_____18. Displays a high level of optimism in all circumstances.

Set Four: Ability to Map the Territory to Identify the Need to Lead

_____19. Analyzes all situations from alternate perspectives to identify issues and concerns.

_____20. Speaks with many different people to recognize issues and concerns that need attention.

_____21. Focuses on both the long and short term, global and local issues.

_____22. Constantly monitors the impact of change.

_____23. Displays refined business acumen in every situation.

_____24. Learns quickly in every situation.

Set Five: Ability to Chart a Course of Leadership Action

_____25. Takes the most important action first to resolve a problem or exploit an opportunity.

_____26. Considers multiple courses of action whenever possible.

_____27. Charts action courses that focus on customers first.

_____28. Offers direction that is doable and makes a difference in all circumstances.

_____29. Demonstrates good citizenship with every leadership decision.

_____30. Always takes decisive action and knows when to abandon a course of action.

Set Six: Ability to Develop Others as Leaders

_____31. Attracts people who have raw talent and who want to develop their skills.

_____32. Coaches and trains all aspects to enhance people's leadership potential.

_____33. Continuously appraises people's skills in all facets of their performance.

_____34. Allows others freedom to identify and resolve issues on their own whenever possible.

_____35. Uses diversity as a strength in all situations.

_____36. Works with individuals at their own pace to develop their leadership skills.

Set Seven: Ability to Build the Base to Gain Commitment

_____37. Builds credibility with every action.

_____38. Takes on tasks and positions that increase the capacity to influence others.

_____39. Shares power with key followers whenever necessary.

_____40. Conspicuously supports and defends key followers whenever necessary.

_____41. Models commitment to effective action and positive results in all circumstances.

_____42. Forms alliances with key followers to enhance the capacity to influence others.

Set Eight: Ability to Influence Others to Willingly Follow

_____43. Always demonstrates how others will benefit if they follow a course of action.

_____44. Communicates all directions with a consistent, precise, and compelling message.

_____45. Always communicates in ways that followers understand and find acceptable.

_____46. Works through any resistance so others accept a course of action.

_____47. Accepts that some people will not follow and continuously works to gain willing followers.

_____48. Uses established relationships to influence others throughout the organization.

Set Nine: Ability to Create a Motivating Environment

_____49. Molds an organizational culture that is strong, adaptive, and vision driven.

_____50. Always creates clear performance standards to increase motivation toward success.

_____51. Clarifies each person's role and encourages everyone to take a leadership role.

_____52. Fosters open communication, allows decision participation, and provides feedback in all interactions with others.

_____53. Resolves conflicts in a mutually satisfactory manner whenever possible.

_____54. Uses the full range of incentives to motivate others.

Scoring Key

Add up your scores for each set of skills and record them in the space provided here.

Set One	_____	Expand Self-Awareness
Set Two	_____	Build Rapport
Set Three	_____	Clarify Expectations
Set Four	_____	Map the Territory to Identify the Need to Lead

Set Five	————	Chart a Course of Leadership Action
Set Six	————	Develop Others as Leaders
Set Seven	————	Build the Base to Gain Commitment
Set Eight	————	Influence Others to Willingly Follow
Set Nine	————	Create a Motivating Environment

Scoring Interpretation

Compare your total in each column with the following scores to determine your status:

Excellent	33–36
Very good	29–32
Good	25–28
Some improvement needed	21–24
Substantial improvement needed	20 or below

Your Action Approach

Continue your exceptional work in any skill area where you scored an "excellent" in the self-assessment. Skim through the chapters dealing with those skills. Pick out one or two skills that you feel may need some fine-tuning. Try out a few of the suggestions offered to enhance these skills.

Consider ways to sharpen your skills in the areas where you scored "very good" or "good." Review those chapters to find the specific skills that you feel deserve more attention. Select several of the choices to develop those skills and work on them whenever possible.

Take action to improve in any skill area where you scored "some improvement needed." Read those chapters carefully. Evaluate which skills demand the most attention right away. Systematically work to improve each skill as soon as possible by applying several of the suggestions offered.

Create an immediate development plan if your score indicates "substantial improvement needed" for any skill area. Study those chapters with intense focus. Select those skills you clearly recognize as needing work. Seek support from others to help you on your path to improvement. Eliminate any external barriers that may impede your application of those skills. For example, let's assume you have a low score on Set Seven, "Build the Base to Gain Commitment." Barriers may exist to forming alliances (statement 42) because you work in a field office and the key allies you need work in headquarters. Find a way to take an assignment at headquarters for even a short time period. Or accept the constraints on developing this particular skill and work to offset it with increased effectiveness on another skill. For example, you might work on building your credibility with those at your location who can serve as links to key allies in headquarters.

Remember that the journey begins with percentage improvements. Make some degree of change each day.

I
FOUNDATIONAL SKILLS

3

Expand Self-Awareness

Awareness guides action. Self-awareness means you are clear about what you do with your time, attention, and actions. Self-awareness represents the subtlest natural born leader skill. Self-awareness is fundamental to leadership growth. Any skill deficiency has its roots in bounded awareness, limited "wakefulness," and restricted consciousness or information processing.

Dee Hock, founder and CEO emeritus of Visa International, explains that those who seek to lead spend 50 percent of their time leading themselves. In other words, they know their strengths, weaknesses, and assumptions. They understand their motives and recognize what deserves attention. They realize they have a range of choices and know when and why they should take action. They know their tendencies and how they take expression in their life.

Self-awareness is totally internal. Only you can access your inner awareness. More important, each of us can access our internal state and enhance our self-awareness. We have the power to turn our attention inward and know our "inner self" more fully.

Exceptional leaders look within first to enrich, enlighten, and expand themselves. They know they cannot really control anyone else. They use self-awareness to control themselves and ultimately have greater influence upon others.

People are less likely to follow those who have significant

blind spots. Potential followers balk at those who behave with arrogant conceit. With more self-awareness, we are more self-responsible. That is, we are more "able to respond." With greater self-awareness, we are more self-accountable. That is, we can be "counted on" by others.

Self-awareness propels leaders forward with the adaptability necessary to listen and learn and the versatility and eagerness to try new things. The more self-aware a leader, the greater possibility exists for successful use of time, focus of attention, and performance of action. Even the most powerful person experiences the discomfort created by a lack of awareness. Think about sitting at a keyboard frustrated because you don't know why the system crashed. We can only overcome computer illiteracy, or any lack of literacy, with a clear cognizance of the discomfort it causes and a heightened sense of what action can overcome the problem.

Jesse Jackson once said, "As I develop and serve, be patient. God is not finished with me yet." Each of us has more capacity than we have used. We have greater promise than we have achieved. We have untapped potential that we can draw upon by continually increasing awareness of who we are, what we want, and what we desire to become. Self-awareness helps you capitalize on your personal assets, overcome your personal liabilities, and continually stay fresh, vital, and awake.

The quality of direction that leaders provide originates in their internal self-reference points, their assumptions, values, and beliefs. Leaders can lead or mislead, be expansive or restrictive, inclusive or exclusive, just or unjust. Dag Hammarskjöld, former United Nations secretary general, once said, "The more faithfully you listen to the voice within you, the better you will hear what is sounding outside. And only those who listen can speak." Self-awareness depends on listening to our inner voice.

Self-awareness skills also provide the ability to more effectively handle the stress and strain of leadership. Followers are attracted to those who remain cool under fire, calm in the face of crisis, and collected when chaos reigns. That capacity comes with greater self-awareness. The natural born leader label goes to those with the skills to know who they are and the capacity to know how to cope with the challenges of leading.

Mastery of the skills in this section will enable you to:

+ Understand your intentions, inner motivation, and preferences.
+ Respond to stress and use time more effectively.
+ Create more balance in your life.
+ Continuously learn to improve your leadership capacity.
+ Use both your rational and intuitive capacities.
+ Operate with a broader perspective regarding your role as a leader.

1. Get Quiet and Listen

Who is doing the leading? What intentions lie behind the direction that leaders offer and the methods they use to influence? What factors guide the leader's focus of attention and judgement? The answers to these questions define the first and most important skill mastered by those we label as our *best* natural born leader models.

Leadership ultimately begins as an inside job. The leader's course of action and methods of influencing other people reflect the "leader within," the internal reference points that define the leader's inner self. In the final analysis, the kind of leadership you create comes from who you are at your deepest core. Only you have access to that place and complete control over that place.

The best leaders get quiet and listen to clarify their inner reference points. They continuously examine their beliefs, values, and assumptions. They analyze the decision rules they use to assign meaning to life. They carefully consider why they commit their energy to particular actions. Exceptional leaders turn within to figure out the fundamental forces that form the basis of who they are.

The best leaders know the differences between the small self and the big self. To illustrate this subtle but important distinction, imagine you are standing on the bank of a river on a sweltering hot summer day. You jump into the cool river and swim across. When you climb out on the other side, you feel like a "completely different" and "new" person. Yet you are actually the same person. Your small self, the continuously changing aspect of yourself, was hot and now it is cool. It was dull and now it is alert. It felt uncomfortable and now it is refreshed. It was irritable and now it feels delight. It was lethargic and now it is eager and willing to engage in energetic action. The transformation of mind, body, emotion, and perspective in this experience occurred at the small-self level. That self always varies. That self changes its identity in response to life's transitory and mercurial events.

At a deeper level, your "big" self, the internal identity that jumped into the river and climbed out on the other side, has not changed. The big self exists within as a nonchanging individuality. It ultimately defines what you do, why you do it, and who you are. Exceptional leaders consciously get quiet and listen to "self-refer" and look within to understand the big self.

The personality traits we associate with quality leaders include being authentic, principled, confident, compassionate, courageous, resolute, ethical, steady, and trustworthy. These are actually traits that describe high-quality human beings. We want leaders to fulfill this image. Yet we also believe such qualities should describe a spouse, parent, coworker, boss, doctor, lawyer, parent, teacher, coach, sibling, politician, baker, butcher, and bus driver! Such characteristics transcend the differences of national identity, cultural values, social mores, and religious dictums. They reflect the universal higher self that everyone aspires to become. These characteristics define the type of person we want to lead us.

You begin the journey to develop your natural born leader capacities by acknowledging that you, your inner self, ultimately does the leading. You must get quiet and learn to observe and listen so you can clarify what kind of leader you are and what kind of leader you want to become.

Take a few minutes every day to get quiet and listen. Review your actions and clarify the motives that directed you. Reconstruct how and why your attention went in one direction or another. Recount the decision rules you used to make choices. Recognize what guided you to take initiative and what may have held you back.

Make the distinction between what matters because it matters to you and because it matters to others. Without this awareness, behavior actually resembles life as a puppet. Someone else (or some institution) pulls the strings. In the most extreme case, action directed from outside means you are moving mindlessly along a path without any internal compass to guide you.

Get quiet and listen to define your internal reference points. Some people function only to support themselves or a selected, restrictive, and exclusive group. They may justify their actions as acceptable when resources are limited. They may argue, "There isn't enough for everyone, so we must control whatever is available for ourselves and our inner circle." This explains how and why people use divisive tactics within organizations and in politics. It explains how and why cruel and oppressive leaders exist. Such leaders chart a course of action that reflects only their selected, restrictive, and exclusive values, beliefs, and assumptions. Followers latch on and support such leaders because they identify with and hold those same exclusive reference points. This reveals that leader and followers are reflections of each other. How else can we explain the rise to power of an Adolf Hitler or a Slobodan Milosevic? These cruel and destructive men had ardent followers. They and their followers believed that their point of view was "the truth." They believed their cause must be championed because they were "right" and others were "wrong."

Consider your reference point range. Does it satisfy you? Is it expansive and inclusive enough for you? Only you can make that decision. One of the mistakes made in leadership training courses or leadership books occurs when the trainer or author tells the participants or readers what their reference points and values should be. I do not believe it is my place to do that for you. I absolutely do believe that leading depends on making those decisions. I also believe that you can make more skillful decisions with greater self-awareness. I believe our most enlightened natural born leaders operated from the most expansive, inclusive, and positive reference points.

Get quiet and listen for a few minutes a day to identify that transcendent place where you perceive your world without the limited boundaries of ego, family, culture, society, or state. Consider those "truths" that never change. Define those "truths" that go beyond localized and limited reference points. Locate the expansive, confident self within you that feels both independent and interconnected with your surroundings.

Get quiet and listen to realize that the only thing we really control 100 percent in this lifetime is who we are. We can only fully command what we choose as our internal reference points, not the external conditions. We can only absolutely determine what choices we are willing to make, not the results we will get. We can only decide what we choose to become, not what others will become.

Get quiet and listen to create an automatic reinforcement dynamic that promotes change, growth, and improvement. Once you become aware of your inner reference points, you contact the self that is doing the referring. You are free of small-self-referral boundaries. And that means you are truly free. From that state you offer a more enlightened model of leadership and attract a higher quality of followers.

David Lilienthal was an adviser to presidents from Franklin Delano Roosevelt through Jimmy Carter. He was head of the Tennessee Valley Authority and the Atomic Energy Commission. He started a small firm called Development and Resources Corp. to bring power, water, and communications to the developing world. Lilienthal had a desire to wire the world. He described the kind of person he believed would change the world: "The manager-leader of the future should combine in one personality the robust, realistic quality of the man of action with the insight of the artist, the religious leader, the poet, who explains man to himself. The man of action alone or the man of contemplation alone will not be enough; these two qualities together are required."[1]

The reality of natural born leading, then, is a state of contemplation-action or "being-doing." Your inner being—who you are—drives what you do as a leader. Get quiet and listen to define your inner being. By doing that, you become clear about the true nature of your being. You can then do a better job as a leader.

2. Live with Passion and Direct It with Precision

"She leads with passion. . . . He has a passionate commitment to that cause." Have you heard people make such statements about leaders they admire? The best leaders live with passion. Passion motivates them beyond the normal, routine, and ordinary. It drives them to stand out as "born to lead." Passion creates the leader's intensity and zest. It energizes the leader toward a direction or issue. Passion can also distort, create a limiting fixation, generate a foolish frenzy, or misguide thinking and action. Passion can overrule clarity and become an enemy against purpose. Consider how Henry Ford's passion drove Ford Motor Company to a 57 percent market share in 1925. That same quality caused him to be unwilling to alter his product style. By 1926, Ford's market share dropped to 34 percent. Exceptional leaders control the power of passion with precision. They use their intensity and guide and monitor it with a laserlike focus.

Define your passion, the game that pushes you to work in your optimal challenge zone. The best and most committed people are always motivated by passion. Money, status, and position are important, but they are actually only ways to keep score. What do you ardently desire? What would be the single most important task you would undertake if you could do only one thing with this life? What project would you tackle simply to do it? Define your passion, then pursue it relentlessly.

Use precision to clarify your passion. You cannot work effectively with a generalized cloud of hope. Think on paper. Write your thoughts out so you can see them manifest in front of your eyes. Create the most accurate, complete, and vivid description possible. Root out generalizations. Translate "I want to run a great computer company" into a more precise statement: "I want to guide 10,000 people who produce computer data storage devices that never fail." Redirect vague statements into action processes. For example, "I want to help people" becomes a more precise, laser-focused statement when you define your goal: "I want to build safe haven hospices for the elderly."

Further direct your passion with precision through action plans. General George S. Patton's life passion was to lead a group of brave men into a desperate battle against a mortal enemy. He translated that passion into careful and constant study about the details of how great battles had been won. He analyzed the precise approaches used by the specific enemies he faced. He further translated his passion into specific battle plans that enabled him to achieve great victories.

Martha Stewart's life passion for stylish entertaining and living transformed her from the head of a catering business to an amazing entrepreneur. Her media and entertainment company, Martha Stewart Living Omnimedia Inc., made $11.7 million in net profits in 1999 on revenues of $232 million. She is the editor of *Martha Stewart Living* magazine with a circulation of 2.3 million. She appears on an hour-long syndicated TV show seen by 1.6 million people daily, and she is a regular on CBS's *The Early Show* and a frequent guest on the *The Late Show with David Letterman.* Stewart's can-do-anything-and-everything attitude demonstrates her passion and precision in action.

List the specifics of what you need to know, do, and become to turn your passion into action and results. Then identify the key information you must gather to realize your passion. Put peripheral data aside to be considered when needed. Talk with specific people who may enable you to fulfill your passion. Acquire the specific resources needed to get the job done. Observe what has worked for others and outline precise ways those methods could work for you. Validate with data any points of comparison. Again, think the process through on paper. Write your ideas with cogent phrases and use words that clearly convey meaning. Sloppy, indirect, multimeaning language confuses and misdirects.

Keep your passion lively and focused to avoid becoming overzealous. Patton's intense passion also caused him to inappropriately slap and denigrate a young GI after a difficult battle. He was so incensed at what he felt was the soldier's cowardice that he lost perspective. Patton's slap caused him to lose the respect of soldiers and his senior officers. Martha Stewart's subordinates and coworkers have complained openly in the media that she is a compulsive overachiever, known for a tendency to run over people. Her 1998 unauthorized biography, *Just Desserts* by Jerry Oppenheimer, reveals how her driving ambition shattered her marriage, strained her relationships with her daughter and family, and destroyed friendships.[2]

To avoid such pitfalls, use a part of your "passion-energy" as a tool for frequent reflection and careful reexamination. Recapitulation, the act of consciously and intentionally "revisiting" an act, either to improve upon it for next time or to let it go, is an effective technique to refine your passion. Surround yourself with people of like mind who can give you honest feedback (see skill 9). Ask them to give you precise information on when and how you need to focus your passion.

Living with passion and directing it with precision requires significant amounts of hard work over extended periods of time. That is why we label those who master this skill natural born leaders. They invest the time and effort into performing these actions. Give yourself the time needed. Be passionate about making the time necessary.

3. Achieve Success over Stress

Think of the image that comes to mind of those you label natural born leaders. They are vital, adaptable, and stable. They remain cool under pressure, calm under fire. They stay levelheaded when others get rattled. They operate at room temperature when conditions get too hot or too cold. The best leaders achieve success over stress. They know how to effectively handle the wear and tear of life. They intentionally and consistently apply techniques that increase physical stamina, enhance mental clarity, and improve emotional stability. Many stress management methods exist. I have achieved great results with Transcendental Meditation. It is simple and it works. Find what works for you so that you can increase your skillful ability to gain success over stress.

Assess your level of physical stamina. Feeling overly tired in the late morning or afternoon may indicate the need to upgrade your fitness routine. The physical body recovers more quickly from the strain of stress when it is regularly strengthened and stretched. Schedule at least ten or fifteen minutes every day for some physical activity. Take a brisk walk after lunch and dinner to increase cardiovascular efficiency. Do some simple bending and stretching every day to remain limber. Learn and use basic yoga postures. Try some simple breathing techniques to simultaneously relax and energize yourself.

Join a gym or work out with a home weight or strength-building system if you are really ambitious about exercise. Monitor your response to any increased exercise routine. You will not overcome the impact of stress by exercising to the point of exhaustion. Too much activity can overtax the body, especially as it ages. Get a regular physical to ensure all your internal systems and vital signs score in the appropriate range. Read *Body, Mind, and Sport: The Mind/Body Guide to Lifelong Fitness and Your Personal Best* by Dr. John Douillard to learn how to monitor your body's response to exercise.[3]

Pay attention to diet. Food fuels the body. No single diet prescription is appropriate for everyone. Regulate your food choices based on how you feel after you eat. If certain foods energize you, then eat them. Let your body signal you about what works and doesn't work. If you feel dull or discomforted after eating certain foods or food combinations, you need to make changes. Experiment with alternate food choices.

Food creates energy based on digestion. Monitor your elimination process. Being "stopped up" signals weakness in the digestive fires. Again, alter your diet by testing your response to how your body assimilates different foods and combinations. Try a digestive enzyme that promotes the body's automatic processes. Eat more fiber. Drink more water. Ask your doctor or a healthcare professional for information about how different foods affect your particular body type. Make changes gradually with a vigilant eye on how your body responds to different food choices.

Audit your level of mental clarity and stability. Stress can be self-induced by worry, unnecessary fear, or an inability to maintain proper perspective. Leading often requires living under heavy time pressure and making tough decisions. People lose clarity, or "choke," because they are unable to call upon established, previously learned response methods. People overreact and then force their actions. Or they "under respond" because their mind "locks up." Mental stress causes people to act like beginners again. They make awkward statements where they used to be articulate. They are unable to perform tasks that were once carried out flawlessly. Many political pundits believe Al Gore's poor performance in the second 2000 presidential debate was an under-response due to his overconcern about appearing to be condescending towards his opponent George W. Bush.

Put worry in its place. Make a list of concerns that fog your mental clarity. Evaluate which situations require action and then do something about them. Consider which worries and fears simply represent ways you spin your mental wheels. That is, you cannot do anything about certain situations, but you worry and fret about them anyway. When such mind blurbs pop up, turn the energy you expend on anxiety into an active response. Turn your attention to something more productive when worry grips your mind.

Conduct a "perspective audit." Ask yourself how important an issue will be five years or even five months from now. Translate the findings from your audit into alternative choices you can make when your perspective goes haywire. Realize that the mind can sometimes run on its own and spin you into a stressful state. You can take control of your mind and direct it to where you want it to go. You simply have to decide to move your mental energy in another direction.

Consider your rest routine. The body needs an appropriate balance of rest and activity. Your degree of success over stress can be measured by how you feel when you wake up in the morning. Ideally, we should wake up without an alarm clock. We should feel refreshed, rejuvenated, and energized to begin the day. To move closer to that ideal, monitor your time to bed and wake-up response. Experiment with going to bed earlier and getting up earlier. Set a goal to get the same number of sleep hours every day for two weeks. That means you must avoid using the weekends to catch up after burning the candle at both ends during workdays. Make the decision to take a break at regular intervals. Schedule a few minutes each day to simply relax away from the phone, computer, or paperwork on your desk.

Review your lifestyle choices. Include activities that are fun, engaging, and simply make you feel good. Such activities alleviate stress. Stay alive in every sense of the word by doing things that make you feel lively.

Review your work-style mentality. Always expect excellence from yourself. And recognize that being perfect is not always possible. Beating yourself up over imperfect action or results creates a vicious stress-creating cycle: frustration, forced extra effort, poor results, more frustration, it goes on. Review the lessons from skill 7 to move beyond stress-induced perfectionism.

Try a scientifically validated health-creating/stress-reduction technique such as Transcendental Meditation (TM). Research on TM shows it offers a significant amount of deep rest without any effort, belief, or special trappings. TM also improves mental clarity, reduces the tendency for worry, and improves interpersonal interactions. Learn TM and do it for six months. The impact is immediate. It only takes twenty minutes twice a day.

All these stress management methods require action. Some approaches, such as diet reform or exercise, demand discipline that makes stress management difficult. That is why we attribute natural born leader status to those who gain success over stress. They demonstrate the discipline. Start where you are and get moving. Over time, it will take less discipline because the results become self-reinforcing. You will become less stressed, which will make it easier to stay focused on your stress management routine.

4. Leverage Time

Everybody has the same amount of time each day. We all have the same number of days every week. Each month has the same number of days and each year the same number of months for us all. Those we label natural born leaders know how to leverage their time. They get things done in the time they have. They realize no one actually saves time, spends time, loses time, or can make up for lost time. They live their time by taking control of their life. Time is not money; time is life. If you waste your money, you can always make some more. If you waste your time, you lose it forever. To leverage time you begin by knowing how you live it and then work systematically to take effective action over those parts of your life that you can control.

Start by conducting a time audit. For a full two-week period, write down what you actually do after every thirty-minute period. Review the audit to determine habits that undermine your using time in ways that satisfy your needs. Do key demands of your job and personal life fall second to less important, time-consuming actions? For example, suppose your audit reveals that you do not accomplish anything of real value after a regularly scheduled daily meeting. Perhaps you putter around the office or move papers on your desk for fifteen or twenty minutes in an unfocused manner before getting started on important work. You may not have realized this time was not lived effectively. That is, although you were doing "something" during the time, the audit uncovers how that "something" was actually unproductive behavior. The audit might also reveal when and how you get distracted from things that matter. For example, imagine that several times during the week you get sidetracked from important projects by the telephone with nonessential calls. Your audit helps you realize how frequently such intrusions get in the way of completing critical work.

Armed with the results of your audit, begin to consciously take control over your life. Redirect your actions. Leverage your time so you live your life rather than have it slip away with each clock tick.

Determine your top priorities. Identify what you *must* do—the requirements for your job or family that must be fulfilled. Then define what you *want* to do. Outline the actions that energize you. Clarify what you like to do to achieve your personal and professional goals. Create a schedule to complete top-priority "musts" and "wants" first. That might mean you begin work on the priority items immediately after your morning meeting, which your audit revealed was wasted time. This would add fifteen to twenty minutes of productive time for getting your important things done. Do the "putter" work after you complete a key portion of top-priority work. A focus on top-priority work requires that you not answer the phone during time scheduled for such projects. Let your assistant or voice-mail system log your calls so you can return them later.

The important jobs are often big jobs that can take hours. Master leaders know they rarely have huge blocks of uninterrupted time. Rather, they make "Swiss cheese" of the important tasks. They cut holes in the big job by breaking it down into many little jobs. For example, you can "Swiss cheese" the time-consuming job of building rapport (see Chapter 4) with a five-minute "Hello, how are you?" discussion. You can cut holes into the big job of mapping the territory to identify the need to lead (see Chapter Six) with a ten-minute walk through your organization.

Make a daily "to do" list on paper. Write down the tasks that must be accomplished to achieve your top priorities. Scratch each completed task off the list to reinforce your sense of accomplishment.

Schedule for the "time robbers." Recognize what is controllable and what's not within your control. A senior manager once told me that 80 percent of his time every day was eaten up by events he could not plan for or anticipate. Assume that 80 percent figure is absolutely accurate. How could this manager possibly gain control of his life when so many factors robbed his time? My recommendation was, "Schedule only 20 percent of your day." I suggested he leverage his time by keeping 80 percent of the day open and ready for the uncontrollable time robbers. Such preemptive preparation or planning for interruptions is the only way to respond if your day is riddled with time robbers. Put your energy into what you can control and take your chances with the rest.

Block out time every day on your calendar for a "meeting with yourself." Use this time to review important correspondence or return phone calls or e-mails.

Take a moment several times a day and ask yourself, "Given what I truly want to accomplish today as a leader, what will be the best use of my time right now?" Whatever your answer, do it immediately. Recognize that means you must really do it. For example, suppose you realized the most important use of your time was to leave work to go home and rest because your stress level was over the top. To truly gain control of your life at that time, you must get out of your office and go home. By asking, "What is the best use of my time right now?" on a regular basis you begin to leverage your time more productively. As you remain true to yourself and follow through, you will be more productive in how you live this time of your life.

5. Juggle Professional and Personal Demands

A full life results from living 200 percent of what it has to offer. Exceptional leaders care about career success, goal attainment, and making a difference for their organization. They also focus on family, friends, personal interests, and nonwork activities that matter. Diversity of interests comes into play here. Some people live for their work. They fulfill their personal life by leading others. Most do not put all their eggs in one basket. Decide the balance you want and serve the needs that matter to you.

Assess your current juggling act. Constant fatigue and lack
of energy may mean you overfocus on work, especially if your
annual physical checkup reveals you are healthy and your doctor remarks, "There is no medical reason you should be tired."
Of course, there is a reason. It may be that something important
is missing in your life. You may feel blue or downright de-
pressed, or become cynical, impatient, irritable, or angry over
the small things because you lack balance between personal and
professional demands.

Achieve greater balance by applying your great capacity for
achievement. Think of it. Is your capacity to plan, organize, and
follow through a key reason for your professional success?
Apply that great capacity to how you live the personal side of
life. Schedule quality and focused time for the nonwork-related
friends or events that matter.

Consider the comment in Dean Kim B. Clark's commencement address to the Harvard Business School class of
2000. "There is no success in business that can compensate
for failure at home, and think of that as the most important
investment in your lives. The most important work you do in
your whole lives will be in your home."

6. Remain Flexible in the Face of Difficulty

Leading demands living in a world of challenge. It is easy
to be adaptable and resilient in the good times. The difficult
times demand flexibility. We do not attribute natural born
leader status to those whose behavioral resilience fades when
hard times crop up. When such people lock up or their mental
stability gets shaken and they lash out with emotion, we do not
view them as master leaders.

Those we label natural born leaders do not lock up. They
remain flexible in the face of FUD: fear, uncertainty, and doubt.
FUD defines a form of "anticipation energy" that drains flexibility. Natural born leader status does not make one immune
to challenges. It does mean the leader overcomes the negative

anticipation about what might happen. The best leaders know that FUD restricts their behavioral resiliency. They are keenly aware of difficulties, dangers, and possible downfalls. They know that FUD does not resolve these issues or help prepare for action. FUD simply wastes the precious energy necessary to be flexible.

Effective leaders maintain a flexible response mode. They skillfully recover from setbacks. They perform their best in crises and are their humblest in prosperity.

Review your FUD factor. When does it grip you? Does a pattern exist? Break out of the lock that creates FUD. First, self-refer (i.e., listen to your inner reference points, as discussed in skill 1) and recognize FUD as an unacceptable position. Change the channel. Redirect your attention power to more constructive activities. Focus on doing something, anything. List five or even ten choices that would be more useful than locking up. Pick one and do it. Talk to trusted colleagues about choices they use to overcome inflexibility under similar conditions. Apply a suggestion they make.

Monitor your tendency when confronted with difficulty. Rage may work if you want to scare people, but it doesn't attract others to willingly follow. It rarely focuses consciousness on effective solutions. When you feel the internal fires of rage heating up, step away from the situation. Walk off the emotion. Have a cool drink of water to calm the inner fires. If your temperature does start to rise, get mad at being mad. Use the energy that might cause you to lash out as a motivator to become more flexible.

There are difficulties "out there" that happen in the environment. We easily can note a leaf falling from a tree or rain pouring on a roof. In the same sense you need to consciously make note of a difficult event when it happens and the fact that it creates a problem. Stay present. Getting lost in a mire of "Oh, my gosh, this is terrible" takes you on a downward spiral toward FUD.

Fall back on your already-established skills. In the military, when the pressure of battle escalates, soldiers survive not by suddenly becoming courageous. They survive by falling back on their training. They stay present and apply the skills they learned during boot camp. Ask yourself, "What skill can I use now to address this difficulty?" Ratchet up your skills to achieve success over stress (skill 3) so you have the resiliency to overcome difficulty.

7. Use Failure as a Growth Tool

Master leaders recognize that there are no failures. There is only feedback. No one ever fails. People simply get results that they label as failures. We attribute natural born leader status to those who find value in every experience, especially when they do not get the results they want. Failure is actually the opportunity to begin again with more intelligence.

Nobody wins all the time. The meaning of winning, however, depends on how people keep score. The best leaders do not get mired in scoring their results as negative, ineffective, or disappointing. They find the meaningful lesson, learn it, and move on. They overcome the tendency to spend any energy resisting failure. Resistance only deepens dependence on the thing being resisted. Exceptional leaders free themselves from the belief that they "failed" by using the experience as a learning event.

Pat Riley, the highly successful professional basketball coach, has said, "You have no choice over how you lose, but you do have a choice over how you come back and prepare to win again." The best leaders maintain a focus on the goal and they learn from the entire experience of moving toward the goal, regardless of the bumps along the way.

Start developing this skill by taking full responsibility for your experience. Consider what "taking responsibility" means. Recall a specific place at a specific time when you did not get the results you wanted. Recognize that you had some key choices. You could have simply accepted where you were and done nothing. People who make this choice fall down as a result of the failure. You could have blamed someone else for the outcome. People who make this choice become the victim. You could have simply complained about it. This is the "whiner response." You could have run away from the outcome—the escape choice. Or you could commit to changing yourself by using the experience as a learning event. This response describes what it means to take full responsibility.

Fail often to succeed sooner. Think of a degree of failure as a prerequisite to achievement. Effective salespeople know they typically make one sale for every ten calls. Each time they do not make a sale, successful salespeople believe, "Great, I got one of those rejections out of the way." Get your failures out of the way by learning from them all. Use each one to eliminate the need to go that route again.

Monitor the common tendency to turn an undesirable outcome into "the story of my life." We do not attribute natural born leader status to people who institutionalize failure by constantly telling the story of how they "botched," "bombed," "crashed," and "blew it." When you do not get the result you want, tell a positive story about the outcome rather than turning it into a tragic tale. Describe the challenge. Detail the actions you took. Identify the twist that led to the outcome you did not intend. State your disappointment if you must. Then say what you learned from it. Make the event a morality tale like Aesop's Fables. These stories were written to instruct in an amusing and delightful way. Conclude your story with an affirmation such as, "This event was necessary because I *needed* to learn something." As Aesop concluded in the story of the hound chasing the hare, "Necessity is our strongest weapon." Failure occurs as a necessary tool for growth.

8. Focus on Lifelong Learning

Those we label natural born leaders are the best learners. They continuously upgrade their capacity. They constantly focus on skill enhancement. They find ways to practice skill development. They know that perfect practice, that is, practice with effective guidance, makes perfect, so they learn from other successful leaders. Woodrow Wilson said, "I not only use all the brains I have, but all I can borrow." An eagerness to learn and willingness to listen are critical ingredients of self-development. Master leaders live by the maxim that the road to success is always under construction.

You are already demonstrating your desire to continuously learn by working through these 108 skills. Translate the information you glean from this book into a specific plan for skill development. Work on one skill or a subset of similar skills. Focus on mastery of that single skill or subset so that it is a part of your automatic repertoire. Then move on to another. Avoid trying to do too much at once. That just makes it harder.

Practice, practice, practice. Professional entertainers and athletes are paid enormous sums of money to perform for a few minutes a day or a few hours a week. The good ones use the rest of their time to practice. Practice means just that—practice. Don't try developing a skill when the most senior person in your organization visits your office or your career is on the line. Practice in less crucial circumstances. Practice with trusted friends and colleagues. Practice in low-risk situations when you are not pressured for time. Give yourself the luxury to make multiple attempts that do not turn into career-limiting moves.

Engage a "buddy" to work with you on specific skills. Programs such as Weight Watchers are effective because people commit to helping each other. Explain to people that you are trying to improve a specific skill or modify a specific behavior. Most people will support your efforts if they know your intention is to learn. Focus on small changes at first. Small changes come more easily. A 1 percent change every day for a hundred days yields a 100 percent transformation in just over three months.

Make lifelong learning entertaining. Read biographies of people you believe are natural born leaders as a self-development tool. Watch a video that portrays a character you believe illustrates natural born leader skills. Review specific scenes several times to gain a deep understanding of what the character said and did to demonstrate expert leadership.

9. Seek 360-Degree Feedback

Those we label natural born leaders take feedback from all sources. They use all 360 degrees of input to evaluate their performance. They want to know how their boss views their efforts. They rely on peers for feedback on ways to improve. They listen to those outside their organization for ideas. They seek out subordinates to gain valuable insights. They realize that others may have been in the same place they are now so they use their experience to help them move forward. Eleanor Roosevelt once said, "Learn from the mistakes of others. You can't live long enough to make them all yourself."

Hunt for feedback every day. Ask people above, below, across, and outside your organization for input on how you are doing. Seek feedback to confirm that you are on the right track. Ask for reinforcement to clarify points for improvement. Take the pain that sometimes accompanies getting corrective feedback to help secure your power to grow.

Commit to unadulterated excellence no matter how arduous the task. Get feedback on how well you measure up to that standard. Establish an unyielding commitment to improve no matter what the obstacles. Inquire on ways to make improvements.

Seek feedback that opens up the "blind spots" about your behavior. Blind spots represent behaviors that are known to others but not known to us. Everyone has such restrictions to their perception. A manager in a large equipment manufacturing organization was unaware that his attempts at humor came across as condescending. He didn't even recognize the lack of laughter as indicative of how unfunny he was. It took some direct feedback to shine the light on this blind spot. As is usually the case with blind spots, the manager was completely surprised about how people felt. Compare your perception with that of others on particular behaviors. Tell them how you interpreted your action. Ask them for alternate interpretations or insights—how did they perceive your actions? By asking others for ways you could improve you'll remove the veil that conceals your blind spots.

Seek feedback that indicates whether you should simply do more of what you are doing. That is, you might be on the right track but need to "up" your frequency. One manager got positive marks from subordinates when she talked with them about long-term organizational plans. They wanted their manager to spend more time explaining business plans. It was easy for the manager to meet this need once she got feedback about it.

Ask for "feed forward" information as well, to determine what you need to do differently in the future. That is, ask others to preview what you may need to do in response to upcoming events.

Accept any feedback you get as valid. People will shut down if you argue against their perception. Always get specifics. Ask for examples to understand the particular behavior that caused someone to assess your performance in a certain way. Inquire about what others perceive as effective and ineffective actions. Ask them to show or tell you what you could have done differently.

10. Use Your Whole Brain

Master leaders know how their brain works and how to use it more effectively. Our gene imprint dictates different forms of brain dominance. Some brains tend to be more logical, rational, and orderly. This tendency indicates left-brain dominance. Others prefer more intuitive, creative, and nonsequential mind work. They are right-brain dominant. Traditional organizations favor left-brain thinking. Marketing types can use flair, drama, and color. Finance, accounting, engineering, R&D, and legal all have their roots in rationality. Traditional organizational actions such as planning, organizing, scheduling, and controlling are based in left-brain thinking. Yet everyone has two sides of the brain. In the 1976 *Harvard Business Review* article "Planning on the Left Side and Managing on the Right," Henry Mintzberg revealed that effective managers rely heavily on both "gut feel" and clearheaded logic.[4] Neurophysiologists indicate that increased coherence between the left and right parts of the brain is associated with higher levels of mental functioning. Master leaders maximize their brainpower with whole brain thinking.

Determine your brain dominance tendency. Take a quick snapshot right now by answering five simple questions:

1. Are you a) left-handed or b) right-handed?
2. Are you more likely to a) take a step-by-step approach to scheduling your activity or b) just let things unfold?
3. Do you generally make decisions based on a) hard measures or b) hunches?
4. Do you believe it is more important to be a) reliable or b) imaginative?
5. Do you typically ask for a) very specific instructions or b) a general overview?

The "a" answers suggest left-brain dominance. The "b" answers imply right-brain dominance. Are you more left, more right, or do you already utilize a mix of thinking? To get a more complete brain dominance assessment, take a valid and reliable assessment such as the Herrmann Brain Dominance Index created by Ned Herrmann. Once you know your tendency, work toward more balance in your thinking approach.

Many of the subsequent skills in this book foster left-brain thinking. Consider the following additional techniques to get the gray matter moving on the right side of the brain:

♦ *Practice generating ten more ideas after you think you have the "right" one.* Then generate ten more! Do not be constrained by "reality" in this process. Creativity expert Charles "Chic" Thompson, author of *What a Great Idea!*, and others explain that sparks of insight fly when people simply push for lots of ideas.[5] Work this approach with others to help you maximize right-brained thinking. Their ideas will get your brain going when your thinking locks up.

♦ *Argue both sides of the issue.*

♦ *Ask people in another area of expertise for their view.*

♦ *Work on a problem or issue for a while and then get away from it.* Let it "stew" in consciousness. Creativity writers such as Peter Russell, author of *The Brain Book,* often recommend this technique.[6] They argue the brain has "self-organizing" power. It organizes new ideas and integrates thoughts on its own when given the chance to work away from a problem.

♦ *Pair opposites to stretch your thinking into "illogical" areas.* For example, consider how to reduce costs and increase service. Wal-Mart does this with the nice, friendly person who greets you when you walk into the store. That warm welcome and offer, "Would you like a cart?" provides good customer service. The greeter is also watching out for shoplifters.

♦ *Use logical models in the "wrong" way to analyze a problem.* A cost-benefit analysis compares resources needed with results achieved; it's a solid and logical approach. Consider how resources *limit* your ability to get results. Consider what you do *not* need to achieve results. This "crazy" kind of thinking might fire off some neurons across the two brain hemispheres and give you a unique insight.

♦ *Use a metaphor to understand an issue.* For example, how is catching a big fish like running an effective meeting? Work this metaphor with me. What bait do you need to get people to the meeting and keep them attentive? How do you reel in the group when it goes off track? What kind of a boat (facility) do you need to keep people comfortable during the fishing trip (meeting)? When should someone else grab the rudder (lead the discussion)? What actions must you take to untangle the rigging (deal with conflict)? How do you get the fish into the boat after you catch it (ensure that people follow through on actions)?

♦ *Catch yourself if you shut down the right-side "brainware."* Premature judgment restricts the creative flow. Know when you have to make a decision, and avoid judging ideas or information for as long as possible. Avoid what Chic Thompson calls "killer phrases" such as "Yeah, but . . . ," "We tried that before," "That's not relevant," or "Be practical!" Such comments overtake the mind like a sedative. They put your right brain to sleep. Check yourself when your logical side makes such statements.

Turn them around and instead of saying "Yes, but . . ." say, "Yes, and . . ." to keep ideas moving. Phrase your comments constructively. Ask, "How can we try that again in a better way?" to reconsider alternatives. Ask, "How could that be relevant?" or "In what ways does that help us?" to invoke more whole brain thinking.

11. Know Your Personality Gene Code

Everyone is born with a personality style and set of preferences or gene code. The code may make it easier or more difficult to understand, learn, and effectively apply the 108 skills. Those who know their code gain insights that support their skill mastery efforts. They compensate for areas that limit them. For example, leaders who score as introverts can team up with more extroverted types to help them build relationships. Leaders whose gene code restricts their intuitive thinking can consciously practice using right-brain thinking techniques.

Take a battery of valid and reliable tests that measure attributes essential to leaders. Two well-known instruments are the Myers-Briggs Type Indicator (MBTI) and the FIRO-B (Fundamental Interpersonal Relations Orientation-Behavior) instrument.Talk with your HR department on how to access these tests.

In addition, use measures that assess your motivational style. Some measures clarify the extent to which achievement, power, or relationships drive you. The work of Howard Gardner reveals that our genes also structure different kinds of intelligence.[7] For example, people can be word smart, picture smart, music smart, body smart, logic smart, people smart, and self-smart. Talk with someone in your HR department about taking such tests to determine your personality and motivational style. You may need a trained expert to interpret your scores. Use the results to monitor yourself as you work on all the skills in this book.

12. Be an Ocean

The ocean is ever stable and silent at its depth. The ocean is also ever-changing and active on its surface. Waves at sea represent energy that moves through the water, yet the water actually remains in the same place. Waves that originate from the deepest, most stable, and quiet part of the ocean are bigger and more powerful. All rivers rush toward the ocean.

Natural born leaders remain inwardly silent while engaged in dynamic activity. They create waves of various magnitudes that move people and organizations. They draw people to them and nourish all who come.

To be an ocean means to see the world in yourself rather than yourself in the world. It means you realize "the world is as you are." It means you live with a sense that you are the producer, director, and actor on the great stage called life. When you are an ocean, you play out your part to achieve the best and most positive outcomes for "what's out there" because it reflects "what's in here." You operate from an expansive, all-encompassing level of self-awareness.

A great teacher once told his students to fill a sieve with water. A few laughed and said, "It cannot be done," and left. A few students poured water into the sieve but got discouraged when it immediately drained out. One student sat quietly for a long time looking at the sieve. She then got up and threw the sieve into the ocean. "Now it's full of water," she exclaimed. The teacher smiled at his masterful student. "We achieve success in life," he commented, "not when we try to fill ourselves up but when we see ourselves as fullness to be shared with others."

To be an ocean represents a meta-skill of self-awareness. The skill is acquired by mastery of all the other skills discussed in this chapter. Like wisdom, it emerges spontaneously as the result of an accumulation of knowledge and action. It often comes quietly to infuse our awareness with a sense of calm and absolute clarity about what to do and how to do it.

Endnotes

1. Joshua Cooper Ramo, "A Two-Man Network," *Time* (January 24, 2000), p. 50.
2. Jerry Oppenheimer, *Martha Stewart—Just Desserts: The Unauthorized Biography* (New York: William Morrow and Co., 1997).
3. John Douillard, *Body, Mind, and Sport* (New York: Crown, 1995).
4. Henry Mintzberg, "Planning on the Left Side and Managing on the Right," *Harvard Business Review* (July–August 1976).
5. Charles Thompson, *What a Great Idea!* (New York: HarperCollins Publishers, 1992), p. 83.
6. Peter Russell, *The Brain Book* (New York: E. P. Dutton, 1979).
7. Howard Gardner, *Frames of Mind* (New York: Basic Books, 1985).

4

Build Rapport

Rapport describes the affinity one person has with another. Rapport is a big reason some people gain the natural born leader attribution. When rapport is high, others admire you and see in you what they want to become. They perceive in you the best that they can be.

Rapport binds people to the leader like a magic glue. It creates the interpersonal bond and sense of unity that is basic if a leader wants to gain willing followers. Think of your own experience. Who were you more willing to follow—a person you respected, admired, and had an affinity with, or someone who made you feel uncomfortable?

Rapport has always been important for leaders. Today, it is paramount. Loyalty has been deeply strained or even destroyed in many companies. Connecting with customers (both internal and external) and partnering are two of today's keywords for corporate success. Janice Gjertsen, manager of business development at AOL's Digital City in New York, states, "We are in the relationship era." The best leaders build rapport to reacquire the allegiance necessary for success, to create customer connections and partnerships, and to fulfill the needs of the relationship era.

Getting to know people, displaying good manners, and being pleasant are techniques or "technical" people skills. Rapport is an emotional skill. When you build rapport, people feel you are on their side; that's because when you have real rapport, you are! Rapport is that identification process that links followers to a leader. Natural born leader status goes to those who master the skills that establish rapport.

Mastery of the skills discussed in this section will enable you to:

+ Establish a common ground with others.
+ Demonstrate empathy to others.
+ Understand and respond to others more appropriately.
+ Fulfill others' relationship needs.
+ Be someone others admire and trust.

13. Establish Common Ground

Rapport building begins with skillful creation of common ground. Common ground unites, links, and connects leaders and followers. Common ground fosters the feeling of familiarity within followers toward the leader. Followers sense, "She is like me; we share an identity. I can support her direction."

Common ground establishes the thread of shared reality necessary to attract followers to a leader. Think about your decision to vote for a presidential candidate. Consider your judgment regarding whose ideas sound most reasonable in a meeting and your choice of which people you seek out for direction with your job challenges. We more frequently favor the person with whom we feel most comfortable. We go to the person we feel is more like us. We seek out those who share our concerns.

Focus on finding common ground with others. Inquire about factors that have had an important impact on them. Find out about others' favorite activities. Seek out life experiences others feel were important. At each turn, identify the shared reality that forms the unity of common ground. Intentionally listen for the links between your background and theirs. Explore another person's interests looking for ones you both share.

Accept that some people prefer not to disclose personal

information. When you sense this is the case, turn your attention to professional information. Search for insights about what people like about their job and make a connection with what you like about yours. Ask people about their professional goals and relate similar goals of your own. Find out why a person chose a certain career path and then share your story. Ask that person what she believes is important for the organization and then relate what matters to you.

Understand that people will disclose information to you in concert with your willingness to disclose with them. The degree to which you are open affects the other person's degree of openness. For some people, you will have to share your background, interests, activities, and goals first to set the stage for them to provide you with similar information.

Common ground building takes time. Make the time. When your schedule is tight, do it in small chunks. Spend just a few minutes finding out about someone's job or career interest. Describe a similar interest to them. Follow up later with a more substantive discussion. Over a few weeks, you can forge significant links of common ground with people.

14. Walk in Another's Shoes

Effective leaders walk in another's shoes to create genuine empathy: the ability to understand experience from the other person's perspective. Followers need to know the leader can relate to their feelings, concerns, and desires. Skillful walking in another's shoes means showing people you truly know them at their level and can relate to the events of their lives. The best leaders walk in another's shoes to demonstrate by behavior and to communicate in words that the other's feelings and beliefs are important and valid.

Herb Kelleher, CEO of Southwest Airlines, demonstrates skillful walking in another's shoes in visible ways. He goes out on the ramp and loads luggage with his baggage handlers. He serves peanuts alongside flight attendants when he takes a Southwest flight. He boards the plane in the same sequence all

Southwest passengers use, the number on his boarding card. He takes whatever seat is open, even if it is a middle seat. And, if there is no room in the overhead bin for his carry-on bag, he has it checked and waits for it at baggage claim.

Develop your capacity to "walk in another's shoes" by living their experience. Try Herb Kelleher's approach and perform tasks with people. Work your assistant's job for a day. Ride the trucks with the delivery personnel. Work a position on the production line. Sit at a computer terminal with a software engineer. The more fully you really understand someone else's experience, the more likely you will be able to demonstrate empathy. In fact, the very act of working with other people illustrates an effort on your part to walk in their shoes. I am always struck by how infrequently some managers make the time to get out into the work areas of their employees. The simple act of sitting next to a plant facility operator reveals a willingness to walk in the other person's shoes.

Communicate empathy by acknowledging people's concerns or point of view. Phrases such as "Yes, that's a problem for you," or "You're right," send a signal that you can relate to their situation.

Take a moment to simply look, soak in, and consider what it must be like to live in another's world. Run a mental simulation of another person's day. Imagine them getting up and commuting to work. Ask yourself what it must be like for them to take mass transit or drive through traffic from their home. Think about how they get their workday started and the initial tasks they must perform. Review what it would be like to work in their group or at their job location. Think about how they must feel at the end of their day. Most people are so wrapped up in their own experience, they never contemplate the minute-by-minute reality of others.

Elliott Masie, publisher of *TechLearn Trends*, a web newsletter, has offered an e-Lab called "Time to Walk in the Shoes of e-Learners!"[1] The online lab allows attendees a chance to take an hour or more to experience an e-learning program. Masie clarifies the importance of walking in another's shoes with his comments that buyers, designers, and developers of e-learning rarely experience others' classes, so they do not understand the helping and hindering factors in this new medium.

Genuine empathy, by definition, originates from a sincere place. A plastic display of empathy cracks rapport. Going along with others simply to show "I am one of you" doesn't really work. People can sense true empathy. Robert Kennedy displayed a remarkable level of sincere empathy in his actions and words and by his emotional response to others. Kennedy was born to enormous wealth and status. Yet observers often witnessed how deeply he connected with people. He was visibly moved when he visited impoverished neighborhoods. He openly displayed his concern for the plight of the poor and the difficulties of the downtrodden. Kennedy spoke to the people with a kind and meaningful, tender tone. He held and comforted the children. He responded to their concerns with a look and a word of encouragement that said, "I understand."

Refer back to the "get quiet and listen" skill (skill 1, Chapter 3) to get in touch with your real intentions regarding walking in another's shoes. It is better not to try to be empathetic if you do not feel it. Empathy is not a skill you can develop with a "fake it until you make it" approach. It must come from a sincere intention to walk in the other's shoes and it must be applied with skillful attention on the other person's real needs.

15. Listen with Active Ears

Exceptional leaders listen. They pay careful attention to what others say. Think of these words: "Pay attention." A cost of awareness must be incurred to listen. The best leaders pay this price to show others they are interested and understand them. Listening with "active ears" means your ears and awareness are focused and alert to the other person. Listening demonstrates respect. Listening also helps you respond more accurately. Followers are attracted to those who actively listen. Active listening also helps you determine where and how followers need direction and how to meet a follower's needs.

Listening is one of those common-sense behaviors that is

not so common. Few people skillfully listen. People actually hear only about 50 percent of what is communicated. They only really listen to about 25 percent of the message. They only understand about 12 percent of what is said. They actually believe only about 6 percent of what others say. Most important, people only remember about 3 percent of what they are being told.[2] These figures are shocking and also disappointing. Yet they reveal that it should not be too difficult to distinguish oneself as high on the listening skill meter. Since most people do not listen very well, any significant display of listening on your part will move you way up the scale.

A host of techniques demonstrate how you can become an active listener. Make eye contact; it communicates sincere interest in the follower. Ask for additional information; it demonstrates that you want to really know what followers have on their mind. Restate or paraphrase key points. This technique ensures you understood what the follower meant. It also lets them know you actually heard what was said. Summarize both the content and intent of the message. Content refers to what was said, the facts. Intent refers to the deeper meaning, the feeling behind what is communicated.

For example, a person may make a statement to express concerns about meeting a difficult deadline to serve a customer. Summarizing the "content" means saying, "You are concerned that you won't make the deadline." Summarizing the "intent" means uncovering the implied feeling: "That bothers you because you don't want to disappoint the customer."

Structure your environment to avoid distractions. Move away from your desk. Put down whatever is in your hand. Face the person. Hold your calls if possible.

Some people make it difficult for us to listen. They speak very slowly. They circle around an idea without making a point. They go off subject and talk about irrelevant information. Or they simply want to dump on you and complain. Avoid the common mistakes that chill conversation and crack rapport. Such mistakes include:

♦ Finishing the other person's sentences
♦ Getting impatient and cutting the speaker off

+ Daydreaming about something else
+ Faking attention
+ Simply avoiding the speaker

Instead, intervene in a positive way. Respond in ways that overcome the other person's limits while also demonstrating that you are a good listener. When addressing the slow speaker, make comments such as, "You're making your points very deliberately. Do you need some more time to think about this before we talk?" or, "We need to set a time limit for this discussion since we are both very busy."

Respond to those who circle around ideas with a comment such as, "You have raised several issues. What is the most important point you want to make?" or, "You have mentioned several ideas that demonstrate your concern. Let's get back to [state the key issue]." Ask probing questions to direct the person to the important concerns.

Ward off those who just want to download complaints or "dump" on you. Make comments such as, "You obviously have some serious concerns. Do you just need to talk about this or do you want some advice? I would be happy to offer some suggestions. I think that would be more useful for us both." Ask complainers to offer solutions rather than let them simply ramble and gripe.

Hold your fire when you hear something upsetting. Get as much information as possible before you respond. Or indicate your need to think about the issue and get back to the person. Reinforce your "success over stress" skills (skill 3, Chapter 3) to remain stable in the face of upsetting information.

No one is too good a listener. Everyone behaves as "listening challenged" at some time or other. Observe your strong and weak listening experiences. Identify the patterns where you fail to keep your active ears open. Work on refining those patterns. Remember, most people are terrible listeners. Even a small percentage improvement in listening will help you build rapport.

16. Be Accessible and Approachable

Building rapport requires giving people access to you and helping them feel comfortable when they are with you. The best leaders find ways to be available and meet with people who need their time.

Face-to-face contact in the office always communicates availability. Establish real availability with a "true" open door policy. Create the conditions for people to pop in with an idea, concern, or simply a desire to talk. Set specific time periods in which your door is truly "open." Close the door when you need time to work and do not want to be disturbed.

Telephone and e-mail contacts are also important. It cracks rapport when days pass before we get a response to a phone call or e-mail communication. It sends a message, "You do not matter enough even to be acknowledged." Even a simple, "I'm swamped right now and would like to talk. Could we get together at (mention a specific time)?" keeps the rapport corridor open.

Make the contact meaningful. Replace ritual politeness with authentic interaction. Put others at ease by communicating that you are at ease. Make the first few minutes count. Find an informal place to sit or talk together when possible. Greet people with a smile and handshake. Start the conversation by asking a question or sharing some important piece of information. Listen to what others have to say and let them guide the conversation once they get on their issue.

Offer focused time rather than just putting in time with your physical presence. Pay attention to your tone of voice. Does it communicate warmth, or does it suggest an unwillingness to give your time and be approachable? Rushed or clipped speech may be heard as, "I'm too busy to really listen." If the topic involves a tough issue, respond with a more serious demeanor. If you are swamped, explain that and offer to get together at another time. Make an appointment and write it down. Follow up without fail. People will accept that you have to stop a conversation, provided you do get back to them. Consider the meaning of this statement: "He will always give you time and make you feel welcome when he has it. If not, he'll get back to you." If people are able to say this about you, your effectiveness on accessibility and approachability is high.

Thank people for coming by as a way to reinforce this skill. Review the key points of the conversation. Pick up on those points in subsequent conversations to demonstrate that the interactions are meaningful to you.

Shy or introverted people have a harder time with approachability. If you fall into this category, practice this skill in safe settings. Set a goal to work on your approachability with two people a week. Taking small steps, spend ten minutes here or there letting yourself "come out" with others. Consider that others may be just as shy and introverted as you are. That means you share some common ground! You may use this a basis for starting a conversation and being more approachable. Have you ever been at a boring cocktail party when someone says to you, "These parties can be so boring"? Did that icebreaker create a bond and make it easier to speak with them?

Some people limit their approachability by creating an air of mystery about them. Such behavior may be dramatic and enticing to watch in a movie or read about in a story. In real life, being an enigma makes people feel uncomfortable and creates a barrier to approachability. Recognize that rapport building is one prerequisite to effectively influencing potential followers and that being mysterious does not build rapport.

Disclose appropriate information about yourself. Confide your thinking about appropriate topics to "let people in," so they can know who you are and what you care about. Test your "air of mystery" quotient. Pay attention to others' responses. Do they physically back up when you approach? Do they seem shaky when you talk with them? Do they get tongue-tied around you? Do they seem unable to maintain eye contact? These may be signals that others feel you are inaccessible and unapproachable.

I can easily recognize people who have eliminated mystery and mastered rapport through approachability and accessibility when I walk with them through their office or work area. As we stroll along, I notice how people's faces light up. I hear people offer an easy "Hello." I notice people walk up to the person without hesitation. I hear them eagerly ask a question or offer an insight about work.

Building rapport through accessibility and approachability requires time. You have to make a decision regarding the amount of time you want to spend on this skill. The other rapport-building skills may be more manageable for you. However, recognize that if you give this skill little or no time, you make it difficult to apply the other skills. Revisit skill 4 (as discussed in Chapter 3) and leverage more of your time in the approachable and accessible world.

17. Develop Remote Leadership Capacity

Remote leadership capacity refers to building rapport with those not in your immediate environment. Remote leadership is an increasing challenge. Many people now perform their jobs from their homes. The global economy has driven many companies to expand internationally and create overseas units that are located several time zones away. The remote leadership reality will probably only get more intense, but it is not a totally new experience. Multiple office locations have been commonplace for years. Generals typically direct their troops from headquarters' bunkers. The best leaders have always been able to build remote rapport.

Begin with an analysis of your personal need for "face-time" with key followers. Examine the extent to which you like to spend time interacting with people face-to-face—that is, to press the flesh and look into their eyes. Estimate when and how face-time makes work more dynamic and enjoyable for you. Consider also the extent to which you like face-time as a way to keep tabs on others, hold the reins, and make sure people do what you want, the way you want it. Apply this exercise with fierce clarity to avoid any blind spots.

Next, assess the level of "biological interaction" actually necessary for job success in your area. Compare the practical realities of your personal needs and the demands of the job given the geographical dispersion you live in now. In some cases, face-time is a must in order to do effective work. In other cases, you may lament the limits of face-time simply because of your personal needs. If your personal need for "in your face" work is high, it may cause you to suffer if most of your contacts are at remote locations. You may force yourself to travel to the point of burnout simply to see people and have a chance to meet with them face-to-face when the job does not demand it. You may also become miserable because you cannot meet your need to be with people.

Realize also that in a high-level remote reality you *cannot* keep very tight, direct tabs on people. Recognize, too, that people can often sense another's intent. Think for a moment about what happens when your need for face-time with other people results in overly tight control. Most people do not respond well to being held down under someone else's thumb. You limit your capacity to build rapport and attract willing followers with such action.

Armed with information about your needs and the job demands, you must use your judgment. Find a place that is realistic on the continuum of personal need and real job demands. That place allows you to spend face-time with people to get the job done and improve your credibility in their eyes without racking up more frequent flier miles than you can ever use. It also ensures results without slapping down the heavy hand of control. There are no perfect prescriptions for finding this balance; you must find the balance that works for you. To help yourself, ask others you trust how they cope with the dilemma.

Rely on e-mail, cell phones, and other devices to stay connected. In his book *The Circle of Innovation*, Tom Peters argues that no businessperson is more than six-tenths of a second away from another as measured by the speed of light.[3] A variety of communication devices enable you to work independent of time and location to continuously build rapport. Establish designated phone talk time. Set the tone that these discussions are about rapport building. Include personal disclosure about your own work-related issues. Establish a set time and method for Internet interaction. Use your Internet service provider's "connection wizard" function for instant e-mail chats. Ten minutes of such phone or Internet schmoozing can satisfy at least some degree of your personal need for interaction and build rapport with others.

Create an appointment "chat room" for online interaction.

Many online conference products such as Hot Office and Lotus QuickPlace are available to involve multiple people in a remote interaction. In his web newsletter, Elliot Masie describes many applications for real-time (i.e., live) online meetings. An example was a live, moderated, interactive cardiac procedures session that involved more than 7,000 cardiologists from three countries who interacted via satellite in a high-intensity discussion about heart surgery.[4] Your business meeting needs may not involve such a large audience, but there are many other applications for online conferencing that might be relevant for your business. They include product rollout meetings or employee orientation or customer service meetings.

Although the Internet may never match the water cooler as a zone for personal interaction, especially for those with a high need for personal contact, you have to ask yourself if other choices, such as constant travel, are realistic. Realize also that relationship rules are no different in Internet space than anywhere else. A certain level of trust must be established to make interactions, even online interactions, meaningful.

Obviously, the computer, cell phone, fax, or pager can become an albatross. These communications devices may drive you to "over connect," such that you cannot escape to even relax with family and friends. You may become overburdened with so much connection capacity that you cannot even respond to all the voice mail, e-mail, fax, and pager messages you receive. Discuss these very real limitations with others (i.e., those you give your pager or cell phone numbers or e-mail address to) to establish meaningful limits. Continuously evaluate those limits. Give and get feedback to ensure that communication devices remain a real benefit as opposed to a burnout factor.

18. Size People Up

Exceptional leaders size people up to gauge where others are coming from and how to respond to them. Sizing people up helps to reveal what others care about and believe is important.

It helps the leader understand the "how and why" behind other people's responses. By effectively sizing someone up, leaders know how to clarify expectations (see Chapter 5) more quickly and completely. It also makes it easier to determine when and how the leader can work with others to identify a meaningful leadership direction (see Chapter 6) and chart a meaningful course of action for them (see Chapter 7). The best leaders can more effectively develop others' skills (see Chapter 8) once they have successfully sized them up. Leaders are more able to influence people (see Chapter 10) and create a motivating environment (see Chapter 11) when they have effectively sized up what matters to people.

Exceptional leaders size people up to decide the extent to which people can be depended on as committed followers. It helps them know who can be trusted to carry out their leadership direction. Recall the line from Mario Puzo's *The Godfather*: "Is he a Sicilian?" Don Corleone would ask. The question helped the Don size people up to determine, "Does the person do business according to our code?"

Your starting place to develop this skill is to understand yourself. What matters to you? What are your preferences? What is your frame of reference? You can then compare your strengths, weaknesses, and personality traits with others and determine where other people stand in relation to what is important to you. That helps determine the extent to which you can depend on them or not.

To learn how to size people up, read books and articles that offer insights into human behavior and factors that drive action. Practice observing people. View your next meeting like a movie. Watch people's behavior and how they interact. Look for patterns that indicate preferences that might be telling insights into how people really think and feel.

Pay particular attention to how people react in stressful or challenging times. A friend of mine told me once, "Go camping with people if you want to know what they're really like." He argued that people reveal themselves pretty clearly after being in the wild for a few days. They display their true colors after a rainy night or two sleeping on the ground. Their real emotions come out when they wake up and have to find a way to make a fire for a hot cup of coffee.

It might be hard to get to observe many people on a camping trip, but you can pay close attention during tough situations at work. For example, pay attention late in the day after a group has been working together in a crowded conference room on a difficult issue. Put on your "size people up" observer glasses when they have to rework a project for the third or fourth time. Watch the response after someone gets promoted or leaves the company for a better job. Notice how people function when they must do something new or unfamiliar.

Catalogue your impressions and then test them. Suppose you notice someone who appears to get testy after several hours in a meeting. Pay attention to when and how that person behaves in the next meeting. Share your observations with trusted colleagues once you have defined your intentions regarding sizing people up. Ask people to comment on your sense of others. Ask for specifics in cases where your sizing-up assessment differs from theirs.

Avoid making premature decisions, however. Give people a chance to show themselves in a variety of situations. Be willing to let people surprise you. Your initial sizing-up impressions may not accurately describe a person's true range of behaviors. People can change. Overcome the false attribution error. That is, suppose you decide that someone is arrogant and insensitive, then you observe this same person displaying concern and caring. You may be inclined to discount these behaviors as simply flukes because they are different from what you expect from this person. Be willing to test whether new, different, or alternate information actually reveals a richer range of a person's behavior.

Consider this: Being a natural born leader is also an attribution, an impression others have of you. You are reading this book to develop and demonstrate the skills associated with that perception. As your skills grow, you probably expect others to recognize your improved capacity. You need to offer that same flexibility while you size others up.

19. Apply the Platinum Rule

Rapport results from the way leaders respond to followers. The Golden Rule says, "Do unto others as you would have them do unto you." This rule indicates rapport building is "leader centered" rather than "follower focused." The "platinum rule" of relationships offers a more powerful rapport building approach: "Do unto others as they would be done unto." The best leaders build rapport by meeting followers at their level.

Think about the other person's career choice as one way to apply the platinum rule. I generally have more rapport building success by encouraging R&D professionals, engineers, and attorneys to analyze everything in great detail and focus on the facts and statistics. They typically prefer this approach. They chose their fields because the work allows them to fulfill this inclination to analyze information. I may prefer something different. However, it helps me create rapport with such groups when I accept and respond to them based on their preferences. My experience also reveals that most marketing and salespeople respond more readily to people issues. Again, I may prefer another approach. To build rapport, it is more useful to embrace and reciprocate in terms of their preferences.

Implement the platinum rule with the straightforward approach. Ask people, "How would you like to be treated in this situation?" Effective active listening will help you get a clear answer. The direct approach may not work with some people. In these cases take an indirect tack. Observe follower responses. Do they respond more easily if allowed to speak up in their own time or by being asked for their opinions? Do they favor lots of information or just the broad-brush approach? Respond to them in kind.

Skillful application of this rule works like a magic tonic. Think of your own experience. How did your best boss, co-worker, or staff member respond to you? Was it solely on their terms? Or did they met you at your level and create "platinum-quality rapport"?

20. Tune in to MMFG-AM

MMFG-AM stands for "make me feel good about myself." Everyone enjoys the sense that they make a difference. Everyone wants to know that their work and accomplishments matter. Mark Twain said, "I can live for two months on a good compliment."

Master leaders build rapport when they tune in to their followers' need for appreciation and recognition. People often complain to me that they only get attention when things go wrong. Recognition for work is a key motivator and rapport builder.

Shari Holloway, desk supervisor for American Airlines at the Raleigh-Durham (RDU) airport, frequently models this skill. I fly in and out of RDU several times per month. I frequently observe Shari while I'm waiting on line to check in for my flight. She moves from ticket agent to ticket agent to offer help and an encouraging word. She openly thanks her staff when they provide good service. I once asked a counter agent how Shari's comments made her feel. "It means a lot to me," she replied, "especially when things get crazy during busy travel days. Shari is great," the agent commented.

Find ways to acknowledge others. Recognize the little things. This gesture goes a long way. Thank the person who always gets paperwork in on time. Express gratitude to the person who speaks up in a meeting when others simply sit and say nothing. Find a way to laud any action that contributes to project success. In their popular book *The One Minute Manager,* Ken Blanchard and Spencer Johnson call this "catch people doing something right."[5] Set a goal to consciously recognize people who simply do their jobs the way they should.

Use multiple ways to tune in to MMFG-AM. Send a handwritten note. Post a "Great Job!" notice on someone's door. Ask the entire staff to offer their applause at a meeting. As with all these rapport building skills, timing and frequency are critical. Immediate is better. I recommend showing a little more appreciation than you might be comfortable with at first, then you can always cut back once you've made the point. It is also good practice to verify individual differences regarding your appreciation efforts. Some people do not like to be singled out in public. Others would get embarrassed by a poster on their door. Ask people how they would like to be appreciated. Observe people's reactions when they receive appreciation. Appreciation efforts do not work if they simply embarrass someone.

21. Display a Sense of Humor

The best leaders keep the world in perspective. They see the bright side of things. They can find humor in most circumstances. They can laugh at the absurdity life often offers. Humor eases tension and takes the bite out of tough situations. A sense of humor draws followers to the leader. It helps followers feel safe and energizes and activates their minds.

Humor also plays a larger role as an essential element of effective living. Health professionals agree that those with a sense of humor have a greater sense of being and belonging. That feeling gets communicated and creates the rapport that attracts others to the leader.

Some people say that humor must be limited within the serious business of work. Yet people laugh most often about the things that are most serious to them. Think of all the jokes you have heard about money, taxes, and even death.

Stay within your style and focus on topics that delight you. This means overcoming the limiting belief that "I'm not funny." Everyone gets a tickle out of something. For example, bring to mind the somber image of Alan Greenspan. Imagine him saying, "Inflation is what lets you live in a more expensive neighborhood without having to move." Share what tickles you and let people see your sense of humor. Don't worry about never getting jokes, not remembering funny stories, or not spinning a good yarn. You don't have to tell jokes to demonstrate your sense of humor. You do not have to try to be funny. You do not have to be a great raconteur. Just talk about topics that interest you and reveal your sense of playfulness.

I knew a corporate attorney who everyone thought had absolutely no sense of humor. I found out the attorney was an avid Red Sox baseball fan. Since I enjoy baseball too, I asked him about the Red Sox once. He went on for twenty minutes about his love for the team. Several of his comments were about humorous incidents at Red Sox games. I laughed loud and hard at some of his comments. Respond to others' quips and cleverness. Your sense of humor is conveyed when you engage other people and react to them. Simply restating what someone else said, with a different tone or with a link to another idea, can cause a chuckle or create a second round of humor.

What if your attempt at humor bombs? Acknowledge the bomb. Have at hand a few ready-made recovery lines to stop the flop. George Bush certainly never created the impression that he was one of American politics' stand-up funnymen. Yet he demonstrated a good sense of humor when he flubbed a line during his 1988 presidential campaign. Bush said, "We've had triumphs. We've made mistakes. We've had sex." "Sex" was the tongue-tied replacement for "setbacks." Bush recovered easily from his flub by saying, "I feel like the javelin thrower who won the toss and elected to receive." When you do bomb, and everyone does, say or do something rather than try to ignore the bomb. Try a deadpan stare that says, "That was awful." Use a shake of the head that communicates, "What was I thinking?" Point a finger at your head to acknowledge, "What was going on up here?"

Of course, a funny ad-lib can be offensive when someone is truly upset. One-liners can appear flippant. Partisan political comments crack rapport. And, of course, you don't need to be told that off-color, derogatory, or sarcastic comments do not demonstrate humor. Use of humor, like all the skills in this book, requires self-awareness and sensitivity.

22. Demonstrate Rock-Solid Integrity

Rapport defines the affinity people feel for you. With rapport, people see in you the best of what they want to be. Integrity means character, ethics, and principles. Master leaders model rock-solid integrity to demonstrate the highest standards of behavior. They illustrate the best that others want to become.

Get in touch with your ethical framework. Don't do anything you would not want your family to read about in the newspaper. Clarify for yourself and to others the key decision rules you use. Review the ethics code for your profession and take visible action to illustrate your commitment to the code.

Identify the single value that is so important to you and that you believe is so fundamental to a happy and meaningful life that you would teach it to your children. Model that value in every action. Integrity comes spontaneously when you live your ideals.

Establish a set of principles for difficult situations. Life does push us into the gray areas. Trade-offs may have to be made. Integrity about which side of the fence you decide to fall toward in a challenging situation requires a predefined set of decision rules.

Recognize that your integrity comes from within. It is totally within your control. Consider the case of Mitsubishi Motors Corp. In August 2000, the company admitted it hid consumer complaints about vehicle defects from the Japanese government for more than twenty years. No defect coverups occurred in the United States because the U.S. National Highway Traffic Safety Administration demands different reporting procedures. In other words, someone in the company made a decision to fudge the issue in Japan because they could get away with it. Integrity is a choice we get to make every day. Apply skill 1—your "get quiet and listen" skill—and examine your inner reference points when deciding about the choices you make.

23. Build Trust

Rapport can probably be summed up with one word: *trust.* In today's more complex, changing, chaotic world, rapport results from more trust, not less. We offer the distinction of being a natural born leader to those who skillfully build trust with every action they take and with every word they speak every day.

Use every interaction as a "moment of trust." Do what you say you will do. Consistency creates trust. Make a promise and keep it. Don't make promises you cannot keep. Take in a confidence and vow to absolutely never betray it. Do not gossip. Accept responsibility for your actions and results. Do not make excuses. Trust grows when people "own up" and accept accountability for their actions. Assess your communications and make sure you send consistent signals. Mixed messages create doubts about trustworthiness. Extend your trust of others a little further. Being trusted creates trust. Be more open with information to demonstrate you trust others. Secrecy says, "I do not trust you." Relationships are reciprocal. Trust begets trust.

Accept that trust always involves risk. People let go of their genetically programmed "fight or flight" response when they think, "I trust you." In that state, a set of assumptions about safety, security, and dependency stand as givens. People's attention then goes to other concerns and issues because they believe trust is in place. However, new information may change those assumptions. A difficult demand or unexpected alternative may challenge established trust. Discuss this reality with people up-front. Come to an agreement about how you and they should interact in such circumstances. You can then avoid trust problems. The very conversation also models your trustworthiness because you demonstrate your desire to protect and respect others.

Perhaps the most important and simplest way to build trust is to tell the truth. The truth builds trust. It is also easier to remember the truth.

Endnotes

1. Elliott Masie, "Time to Walk in the Shoes of e-Learners!" Online. *TechLearn Trends #188, www.techlearn.com/trends* (October 16, 2000).
2. Madelyn Burley-Allen, *Listening: The Forgotten Skill,* Second Edition (New York: John Wiley & Sons, Inc., 1995), pp. 2–3.
3. Tom Peters, *The Circle of Innovation: You Can't Shrink Your Way to Greatness* (New York: Alfred A. Knopf, Inc., 1997).
4. Masie, Online, *TechLearn Trends* (October 19, 2000).
5. Ken Blanchard and Spencer Johnson, *The One Minute Manager* (New York: William Morrow and Company, Inc., 1982), p. 39.

5

Clarify Expectations

People are more willing to follow those who provide clear and positive expectations. People also follow leaders who understand and meet their expectations.

In *First, Break All the Rules,* Marcus Buckingham and Curt Coffman describe the twenty-five years of extensive organizational effectiveness research conducted by the Gallup Organization. Buckingham and Coffman reveal the number-one factor associated with high levels of organizational profitability, productivity, retention of good employees, and customer satisfaction: People know what is expected of them at work.[1]

The June 21, 1999 issue of *Fortune* magazine[2] reported the reasons thirty-eight CEOs failed. These top executives represented large companies including American Express, Compaq, Continental Airlines, Scott Paper, Quaker Oats, Kodak, Rubbermaid, IBM, AT&T, Kmart, Kellogg, and Westinghouse. The failed chieftains were either "pushed out, had their company bought, or left a company that had lost its way." The two most frequently cited reasons the executives came up short can be translated as a failure to meet expectations. Bad earnings news hurt thirty of the thirty-eight CEOs (79 percent). The "lifer syndrome" (i.e., they stayed too long with the company) doomed twenty (53 percent) of the thirty-eight executives. The third most frequently cited reason for failure revealed a failure to meet the expectation of rapport that followers have for their leaders. Seventeen of the thirty-eight CEOs (45 percent) were derailed by people problems.

Consider your own experience. Have you ever walked away from a meeting with the discomforting thought, "I am not sure what I am supposed to do"? Have you ever been given a directive to perform a task that was unclear to you? What is your response when someone sets a negative tone or suggests there is no way to succeed? Contrast those experiences with the times when someone gave you a clear sense of purpose. Compare your reaction when you got precise and positive directions about a sense of high possibility. In which circumstances did you come away thinking, "That person knows how to lead"? Natural born leader status goes to those who skillfully clarify expectations.

Mastery of the skills in this section will enable you to:

♦ Find out what others expect.
♦ Explain your expectations to others.
♦ Create mutually agreed-on expectations.
♦ Clarify organizational expectations.
♦ Overcome limiting expectations.
♦ Set positive expectations.

24. Establish Mutually Agreed-On Expectations

Master leaders know that expectations drive perception and influence behavior. People get what they expect. People expect leaders to meet their expectations. Exceptional leaders understand follower expectations. They clarify their own expectations. And they find a way to create mutually agreed-on and shared expectations.

Conduct expectation clarification sessions. Meet with people one-on-one or in small groups. Assess your level of rapport with them to determine which approach would be best for different people. Ask people to explain their expectations of you.

Find out their expectations about situations you face together. Give and get specifics. For example, if someone says, "I am concerned about the changes in budget," ask, "What have you heard?" or "What specific concerns do you have?"

Mike Abrashoff demonstrated one skillful way to identify other people's expectations as described in *Fast Company*.[3] When he became captain of the U.S.S. *Benfold* in June 1997, Abrashoff conducted one-on-one interviews with every sailor on the ship, asking them a series of questions: Where are you from? Why did you join the Navy? What are your goals in the Navy? What do you like most about the *Benfold*? What do you like least? What things would you change if you could? This type of information offers a wide range of insight into follower expectations.

Use expectation-clarification sessions to tell people what you expect of them. Lay out specifics regarding your expectations of each person and the group. Outline behaviors that meet your expectations. Clarify the standards you expect people will use to guide their actions. Define the results you expect as well.

Seek shared expectations. Focus on areas where your expectations overlap with others. For example, suppose you and others expect important changes in online business. Build on that shared expectation to create a mutually agreed-upon response to activities that involve online business.

It is equally important to clarify expectations that cannot be met. You may not be able to fulfill certain hopes people have. For example, the shift foremen in a large chemical plant presented their expectations to the plant manager regarding training. They wanted more leadership and team training programs offered for the entire 800-person group of operators. The foremen had been trained in these areas and gained benefit. They felt operators should receive the same training so that everyone was on the same page. The plant manager knew that the existing budget could not allow offering the training to 800 people. He put his cards on the table. The group discussed ways the need could be met. A mutually agreed-upon decision was reached. A few key operators would be included in the remaining, already-scheduled foremen courses. Budget numbers would be restructured for the next training cycle to include more operators. The shift foremen understood and accepted the budget realities. They felt positive about the plant manager's willingness to move toward meeting their expectations.

Be open about what's what when you present expectations. Minimize the lag time in conveying "bad news" or "reality" news. That is, tell people as soon as you can about difficult issues. Avoid the mistake of trying to protect people from bad news. If you do not clarify the difficult issues now, consider this: How does waiting serve you? What do you think the reaction will be when you ultimately do deliver bad news to people? I rarely find people are less unhappy simply because they found out later. I also find it cracks rapport to wait. That is, it creates a degree of mistrust when people realize someone actually knew about the bad news all along and did not tell them.

It takes some guts to talk hard realities. It means you have to deal with some discomfort and disappointment. Clarify that reality when you present the tough issues. Let people know that you understand the topic will be difficult for everyone. This builds rapport. It also says, "We need to work on this together," which creates an expectation regarding how you feel about the contribution others can make.

Define your limits. Meeting others' expectations does not mean letting them dump on you. The best leaders do not become sponges that soak up everyone else's responsibilities. Clarify inappropriate expectations, then ask, "What would you like us to do?" This powerful question puts the ball back in their court while simultaneously indicating your willingness to help. The comeback may be, "I want you to do it." If that's the case, remind people of your limits. Ask again, "What would you like us to do?" It might take three or four repetitions of this phrase to get the message across that you are not a dumping ground.

Clarify accountability regarding meeting expectations. Let people know how they can count on you to fulfill expectations. Point out how, when, and why you need to count on them, too. Jack Welch, GE's CEO, applies this technique very powerfully.

He takes notes during meetings about who is expected to do what. He concludes the meetings by reviewing these expectations with each person. He follows up to assess progress toward meeting expectations. Welch's behavior sends a powerful accountability message to others.

25. Root Out Limiting Expectations

Exceptional leaders know that people who have limiting expectations restrict their thinking and actions. Leaders also know that expectations stem from people's belief systems. Beliefs develop as internally consistent sets of filters in our awareness. Those who adopt limiting beliefs do not see them as such. They consider their limiting beliefs as valid. Successful leaders root out these limiting expectations and challenge their reality.

Identify expectations that you feel limit action and outcomes. Acknowledge the reality of limited expectations. That is, concede that another's expectations have validity based on that person's knowledge, experience, assumptions, and values. Give people the chance to justify their limiting expectations and get specific information. Ask, "Why do you say that?" Summarize your understanding of their point of view by saying, "The way you describe it, that is true," or, "I agree with your expectations given the way you look at the situation." Your acknowledgment paves the way for them to be receptive to another perspective.

Challenge what you perceive as their limiting expectation. Ask them to consider how their expectations actually serve them. Suggest other ways to interpret the situation, and offer your point of view as an alternative versus an actuality. Ask people to consider the benefits of your more positive expectation in contrast with their own. Use a soft hand when necessary. The habit of limiting expectations may be rooted in fear. People resist facing fear. Rework your rapport skills to improve your chances of moving people to the doorstep of their fears. Demonstrate your ability to walk in another's shoes (skill 14) and to listen with active ears (skill 15), two skills discussed in Chapter 4.

Another technique is to engage a group to address the limiting expectations held by an individual or subset of people. The collective consciousness of ten people may be more convincing than your singular efforts.

It may be necessary to "let the data speak" in order to overcome limiting expectations. Use hard evidence. For example, consider retail e-commerce. In its early days, many experts held the belief that online retail shopping would not become a major channel for businesses. Several limiting "realities" existed. Credit card security would be difficult to maintain given the penchant for hackers to break into the network. Shoppers would not be comfortable with a point-and-click experience for items they typically preferred to physically examine. The shipping logistics for retail sales of single items would be a nightmare. Skeptics agreed that online retail shopping sounded nice, but it would not really be doable on a massive scale. Then another reality emerged. In 1999, during Thanksgiving and New Year's, an estimated 26.4 million Americans shopped online. They spent $5 billion online, or more than triple the amount spent during Christmas 1998, which analysts had christened the first e-holiday. Once enough people started pointing and clicking their way to online malls, the limiting expectations faded away. Sometimes you may have to wait until you get such hard evidence to overcome a limiting expectation. Clarify to others that if they have to wait for verification on every issue, they may miss the boat.

26. Explain Organizational Expectations

Successful leaders serve as linking mechanisms between the larger expectations of the organization and how others comprehend them. The best leaders become boundary spanners who explain expectations between different hierarchical levels and across organizational functions. They offer clarity when people are confused about what the organization expects.

Continually listen for comments and concerns that reveal people do not understand the organization's expectations. One red flag indicator you can listen for is when you hear people making remarks such as, "Do you know what we're supposed to do?" Use your "listen with active ears" skill (skill 15) to get as much information as possible about exactly what expectations are unclear. Identify the extent of people's uncertainty. Is the problem centered only within a specific group or does everyone have the same uncertainty? Does the lack of clarity relate to all elements of a situation or just some? Answers to these questions may reveal a severed line of communication. You may be able to ward off unclear expectations in the future by repairing that line.

Find out whatever you can to clarify the organization's expectations. Talk to those in your high rapport group and ask them to share what they know. Review organizational documents, memos, or publications. I consulted with a medium-size computer firm in the U.K. that was purchased by one of the big U.S. players in the industry. Uncertainty was rampant, as it usually is when such changes occur. In a meeting, the group revealed a variety of "what do they want from us" concerns. They were unsure about the U.S.–based company's expectations. One manager then reported key information she obtained in a document published by the takeover company that outlined key issues regarding its strategy. The document was available to everyone, but no one else had taken the time to read it. She cleared up several important issues.

Taking the initiative to master this skill takes time and effort. Decide how important this skill is for success in your organization. Consider the degree of change the organization has experienced recently. If it is high, organizational expectations will invariably be unclear for many people. Your emergence as a skillful boundary spanner could then catapult you forward as someone many perceive as a natural born leader.

27. Use Fact-Based Thinking

Master leaders rely on factual information as one important method to set meaningful expectations. They know that expectations float around in people's minds as the integration of assumptions, inferences, values, beliefs, and factual information. That means "soft data" often dominates expectations. Effective leaders rely on fact-based thinking to firm up and clarify expectations.

Gather your facts and direct others to bring facts to the table when you conduct expectation-setting sessions. Verify the extent to which others believe the facts. Use data that people understand and can translate into meaningful expectations. Accept that people can lie with statistics. Reinforce your rapport skills to let people know your intention is to be fair and honest with data you use. Challenge others to operate with that same standard of integrity.

Expectation clarification should not become a debating contest designed to score points. I watched with great dismay a C-Span broadcast of a Federal Election Commission session. The commissioner's agenda involved the appropriation of $12.5 million for the 2000 Reform Party presidential campaign. Both John Hagelin and Pat Buchanan sought the funds after the Reform Party had split during its convention in Long Beach. Hagelin and Buchanan both claimed they had captured the "real" party nomination. My disappointment arose during the forty minutes of discussion among the election board members. My impression was the participants were more interested in presenting clever arguments than in solving the problem. The third-party candidate issue faded into the background as several members pontificated about tangential points.

28. Name the Game

Skillful leaders know that some people do not play fair. Some people pay lip service to agreed-on expectations. They say they agree to a particular expectation, then they do not follow through. A vicious cycle then occurs. New expectations are set. The expectation is disregarded, indicating agreement was again lip service. The process begins again. The problem becomes more acute when some people resort to deceit when setting expectations. They agree to an expectation but covertly take alternate action. Leaders cannot command and demand that others follow through on expectations. Leaders do not have the formal authority a manager can use to require subordinate compliance. Even managers cannot depend on compliance when they interact with a peer, or someone up the organizational ladder, or someone in another part of the organization.

The best leaders confront lip-service responses and deceitful behavior by using the "name the game" skill. They expose the lack of fairness. The reveal the dishonesty or deceit by labeling it for what it is. For example, you can say, "We set a mutually agreed-upon expectation yesterday in our meeting. You did not follow through. You have done this before." You can take an even bolder step and state, "It seems as if you are simply paying lip service to the process." Or you can say, "We set an expectation that you would do A and you turned around and did B. This is not the first time this has happened. You have not been totally up-front."

Confronting people with "name the game" brings covert tactics into the open in an attempt to break the pattern. People may deny that their action indicates lip service or deceit; they may offer excuses or alternate explanations for their actions. Challenge these attempts to wiggle away into the covert corner. Establish another, specific shared expectation. State that no more excuses or explanations for a lack of follow-through are acceptable. Explain that a lack of follow-through or any alternate action will demonstrate lip service or a lack of honesty.

It takes courage to "name the game." You have to be willing to confront the covert tactics and you have to remain steady. Work on your "success over stress" skill (skill 3, covered in Chapter 3) to reinforce your sense of balance. Recognize that the "name the game" strategy has limits. No matter how skillful you are, you cannot get everyone to play fair. Some people will always resort to dishonorable tactics. Other prescriptions to the contrary, some people are highly successful and do not seek a win-win result. Call upon your "get quiet and listen" skill (skill 1) to remind yourself of the kind of leader you want to be.

29. Work the Grapevine

The informal communication network, or grapevine, offers a quick and often reliable method for leaders to broadcast their expectations. Identify key people who serve as grapevine "nodes." These are the "central processing units" that others go to for information. They are the people who enjoy spreading information. Assess the quality of your relationship with these people. They will relay your expectations more effectively when rapport is high. Sound out your expectations to them. Then let the magic of the grapevine work its way up and down the corporate corridors.

Test the grapevine's accuracy. Position yourself to receive an expectation you placed in the grapevine. Identify when and how an expectation did not get communicated as accurately as possible. Spend a little more time and use more specific facts when you use the grapevine again.

30. "Netware" Your Expectations

Today's leaders have the Internet as another tool to clarify expectations. E-mail and websites can be used to set and explain expectations.

Create an expectation e-mail format that others understand. E-mail has become a double-edged sword. Its swiftness and ease of use have been offset by its overuse. Some managers I know get hundreds of e-mails every day. Avoid having your expectation e-mails become just another difficult detail. Work with others to discuss when and how you could send expectation-setting e-mails that they would welcome. For example, agree on a specific subject line that clearly flags the expectation e-mail. Decide on a schedule for such e-mails (e.g., daily, weekly, twice a month). Make your messages easy and quick to read by using bullet points. Determine if several versions of the messages should exist, such as a general e-mail for global distribution and specific e-mails for certain tasks.

If possible, develop an expectation website within your group or organization. Create a site that includes information categories people can search to clarify expectations. Use the website to report key decisions made in meetings, upcoming issues that are still being formulated, or new information about customers, suppliers, or internal personnel changes. Establish a "Do you know the answer?" section where people can post questions and request information that is not time-sensitive about a particular expectation they want clarified. Involve others in creating the website to ensure it serves the needs of everyone in your group or organization who will use it.

31. Unravel Rumors

Rumors wreak havoc on organizations. Rumors represent unsubstantiated information that spreads like wildfire through the "rumor mill." Rumors frequently take on a negative tone. Think about it. Rumors are unproven information. People often create a worst case about such information. They become fearful and spin the most negative tale. Skillful leaders understand these realities about rumors. They clarify expectations by unraveling rumors.

Conduct a rumor mill discussion. Conclude regularly scheduled meetings with the question, "What rumors do you hear within the organization?" Make this a formal part of each meeting. The question opens the door to rumor unraveling.

Differentiate rumors from reality. Remember, a rumor by definition is unsubstantiated information. Some rumors are actually true, however. Couched as "rumors," they remain speculative. People then can fail to take action because, after all, "it's just a rumor." Other rumors are not valid. If they remain in the rumor mill they can confuse or simply become a waste of time. Tell people what you know about the truth or lack of validity about rumors.

Take the initiative to unravel rumors when you are not sure if they are accurate. Beat the bushes to find out. When your best efforts cannot resolve a rumor, make that clear to every-one. Statements such as, "As of now, it is still speculative. No one really knows," may at least keep the rumor mill from get-ting out of hand.

Confront the rumormongers. Some people just like to rat-tle on about this rumor or that. Speak with them about the consequences of their actions. Ask for their help in limiting the negative effect of rampant rumors.

32. Clarify the Action-Results Connection

Master leaders know that expectations may not be met be-cause people do not clearly recognize the connection between their behaviors and the outcomes those behaviors produce. Some people have good intentions. They fail to meet expecta-tions because they do not know what specific behaviors are needed to accomplish a task. Also, some simply do not expect that their actions can create negative results because they do not fully recognize the action-results connection.

Clarify the behavior-outcomes loop. Draw a diagram that links a list of specific actions with the results they create. Dem-onstrate how action A creates result B. Ask people who do not seem to understand the action-results connection to explain their behavior. Ask them to define what they did. Get specifics. Ask them to describe their outcomes. Review their description of behavior and outcomes to reinforce the action-results links they do recognize. Clarify the links they overlooked. Let people know your stance on outcomes and accountability.

It may seem unnecessary to do all this work. The action-results loops should be totally obvious. That is not always the case. Consider the enigma of the natural born leader. The real-ity is that certain people perform specific skills (the actions) that cause others to label them natural born leaders (the result). If these links were obvious to all, then everyone could be per-ceived as a natural born leader.

33. Display Unsinkable Optimism

Those we label natural born leaders inspire and motivate others to willingly follow. Part of that willingness comes from the positive expectations and "can do" approach of the leader. Unsinkable optimism is not a mindless expectation. The best leaders truly do see the possibility in every problem. They also know that optimism pays. In a *Psychology Today* article, authors Christopher Peterson and Fiona Lee report an analysis of political speeches.[4] They found that 80 percent of the time the more optimistic candidate won the election. This finding proved true even when initial starting points in political polls were taken into account. Skillful leaders may not always make it to the mountaintop, but their optimistic eye always sees a win in some part of the journey.

Optimism enables. In the early 1980s, Lee Iacocca restarted Chrysler and drove it back to financial and market success. Yes, he had help. The government loans kept the company on the roadway. However, Iacocca also displayed supreme optimism that the company could come back. Winston Churchill offered the same model during the darkest days of World War II when he communicated to all that England could still win the war. In his book *Leading the Revolution*, Gary Hamel outlines his rules to reinvent a company.[5] Number one on the list: Set unreasonable expectations. That means operate with the optimism that bold aspirations are doable.

An optimistic approach begins with self-awareness. Review your skill level regarding success over stress (skill 3), your ability to remain flexible in the face of difficulty (skill 6), and your ability to use failure as a growth tool (skill 7). It will be difficult to proceed with optimism without some mastery in these areas.

Decide to approach every activity with a "can do" spirit. Consider the alternative. Little value exists in starting with the thought, "I cannot do this."

Set an expectation that your optimism is unshakable. This approach will more likely enlist others' support, especially when the trials of leading get tough. Communicate your can-do approach as often as possible. Sometimes people just need to hear you say that they can win; it helps them to win. No matter what else, you can always communicate unsinkable optimism by saying, "I know we will do our best."

When setbacks occur, explain that the results were unique and inconsistent, not long-lasting and expected. For example, say, "This rarely ever happens" after people falter rather than, "This always happens to us." Describe the setback as specific rather than global. Say, "This only affects us in a small area," as opposed to, "This will undermine everything." Account for the problem as external, based on factors beyond anyone's control, versus internal and the result of individual failures. Comment that "the market shifted" instead of saying, "We're just screw-ups." The Peterson and Lee study cited previously offers these as key methods to communicate optimism.[6]

Avoid negative, cynical, doubting, and disgruntled people and information. It sometimes takes a lot of treading just to keep your head above water. Being bombarded with negativity won't help you remain optimistic. Turn off the negative news shows. Walk away from the constant complainers. Take in positive messages to stay positive.

34. Throw Light on Organizational Shadows

Organizations have issues that do not get discussed, just as individuals have secrets they keep to themselves. These issues, or shadows, fall over the organization and obscure clarity. Organizational shadows come in the form of unquestioned assumptions about strategy, tactics, goals, or other managerial actions. Shadows also exist as topics that no one talks about in the open.

For example, one corporation had a top manager who was a high-volume producer but was extremely abrasive. Everyone experienced or observed this manager's wrathful language and actions. He cast a shadow of discomfort over meetings and offended people with his individual attacks. Yet no one addressed the problem publicly. Even the company president let it slide because "the guy can make the numbers."

As another example, a specific government unit had a high profile on Capitol Hill. Congress was very sensitive to the actions of this agency. Historically, those who got credit for politically important results rocketed ahead in their careers. People sought out jobs in this group with the clear intent to use it as a career stepping stone. Many people operated with obvious Machiavellian tactics. They did whatever it took to get ahead even if it hurt others. They also worked to limit others' ability to succeed. Everyone was aware of these behaviors. Everyone also knew such actions did not truly support the organization's mission. Yet the subject was taboo except behind closed doors or in whispered conversations. I was even informed by the organization's internal consultants not to address the issue because it would only "create problems." Organizational shadows cast a pall of muddled or negative expectations. Skillful leaders throw light on these shadows.

Look for symptoms of organizational shadows. What topics are never discussed openly? When are people discouraged from asking questions? What information is carefully guarded? When and how are people excluded? What subjects get harsh stares when raised? When and how does denial replace reality? Where does one positive value, such as being a producer, become a lever to allow a negative value, such as being abrasive, to exist? How do groups collude to accept negative tactics such as Machiavellian behaviors?

Pick a small spot to shine the light. Confronting the lack of clear expectations created by some organizational shadows can be difficult and downright risky. We even have a phrase for such action: whistle-blowing. Start by tackling something doable. Reinforce your rapport with key allies who share your view about the darkening influence of organizational shadows. Recognize that despite the fact that natural light travels at 186,000 miles per second, your spotlight on the shadow may take a long time to dispel the darkness.

Work on your self-awareness skills. Try to "get quiet and listen" (skill 1) to your inner voice to reinforce the kind of leader you want to be. Reinforce your skill to achieve success over stress (skill 3) to handle the wear and tear of shining the light. Realize that the "big" leaders in life mastered these skills. Imagine the broad beam of light cast by Branch Rickey, the Brooklyn Dodgers general manager, when he integrated professional baseball in 1947. Picture the illumination brought by Shell Oil Company's former CEO Phil Carroll and other corporate chieftains who instituted diversity training in their companies in the 1990s.

35. Expect the Unexpected

Despite all their best efforts, even those we perceive as natural born leaders cannot anticipate every eventuality. Stuff happens. Events occur that no one could have anticipated. Sometimes the unexpected is good. Sometimes it is bad. The best leaders retain a part of their awareness in readiness for the uncertain, the unexpected, and the unpredictability of life.

Create an internal reminder that the unexpected may occur. Assume you have done the best you can with all the other skills for clarifying expectations. Now take this next step. Remember that "something else will come up." That simple point in consciousness may be enough to prepare you for the unexpected.

Ratchet up your external "attention power." Keep your senses highly tuned to the unexpected. You already do this in specific situations. For example, recall a drive in a dense fog on a dark night on an unfamiliar road. You operated with every sense heightened in this circumstance. Every image that crossed the windshield got a second look. Every sound that emanated from the car or environment received an even more careful attunement of your ear. Every sensation in the car's ride was felt at a deeper level. Use your attention power to expect the unexpected in the same way you ensure your safety and continued journey weaving along a darkened road. Heightened awareness and greater receptivity lead to better choices.

Endnotes

1. Marcus Buckingham and Curt Coffman, *First, Break All the Rules: What the World's Greatest Managers Do Differently* (New York: Simon and Schuster, 1999).
2. R. Charon and G. Colvin, "Why CEOs Fail," *Fortune* (June 21, 1999), pp. 68–71.
3. "Fast Pack 2000," *Fast Company* (March 2000), p. 247.
4. Christopher Peterson and Fiona Lee, "Reading Between the Lines," *Psychology Today* (September–October 2000), p. 50.
5. Gary Hamel, *Leading the Revolution* (Boston: Harvard Business School Press, August 2000).
6. Peterson and Lee, op. cit.

II

LEADERSHIP DIRECTION SKILLS

6

Map the Territory: Identify the Need for Leadership Direction

Uncertainty creeps into organizational action every day in numerous ways. Master leaders recognize these uncertainties through their "mapping the territory" skills. Mapping enables leaders to determine where they are and where they need to be. They identify the need to lead by continually getting input. They constantly challenge ideas, beliefs, and assumptions that others consider as pat realities.

Mapping skills resemble how a scout surveys the landscape to determine where to go. The best leaders scout out the business terrain to get a firsthand look at unforeseen obstacles and unrecognized opportunities. Think of times when you visited a different part of the office or went out to a field location. Perhaps you immediately noticed an issue or concern that others had missed. You demonstrated the important skill of mapping.

Mapping describes the detective work leaders do to figure out what is going on and find ways to make things better. Consider economist Barbara Ward, who wrote books and articles and spoke on worldwide poverty. Ward's mapping led her to believe that poverty in the Third World had threatening implications for the entire planet. Ward helped shape the United Nations 1972 environmental conference in Stockholm.[1] President Lyndon Johnson claimed he used Ward's 1962 study, *The Rich Nations and the Poor Nations*, as his "bible" on the subject.[2]

Mapping skills directly contrast with the complacency approach that says, "I know what's going on, so why should I bother looking or listening to people?" Mapping failures stand behind many business bombs. In 1976, Digital Equipment Corporation CEO Ken Olsen thought no one would want a computer in the home. Olsen missed the PC revolution and ultimately got fired for it. American car manufacturers did not believe their gas-guzzling cars could possibly be replaced by nimble, high-miles-per-gallon Japanese vehicles. It took the early 1970s oil embargo to wake them up.

Mapping applies to leaders in all types of circumstances. Consider how military generals would ride to the top of a ridge to determine the best attack approach. Recall a manager who walks through the plant every day to see how things are going. Think of how politicians travel through cities and states to talk to constituents about issues and concerns. Today's competitive realities (call it the age of instability) make mapping even more crucial. Mapping helps leaders recognize trends and understand the forces of change. James P. Kelly, CEO of United Parcel Service, Inc. (UPS), models such mapping behavior. In the mid-1990s he recognized the sales channel possibilities of the Internet. He reformed UPS to meet the vast array of logistics systems for dot-com customers. By January 2000, UPS handled 55 percent of all Internet purchases compared to 32 percent for the U.S. Postal Service and 10 percent for FedEx Corp.

Mapping the territory helps the best leaders get to root causes of problems and identify the possibilities inherent in situations. We attribute natural born leader status to those who effortlessly and spontaneously demonstrate mapping skills.

Mastery of the skills in this section will enable you to:

+ Recognize problems and opportunities that require leadership direction.
+ Expand your information base to ensure maximum awareness of concerns and issues.

- Recognize long-term and short-term, localized and "big picture" trends and changes.
- Root out core problems and identify possibilities.
- Improve your business acumen and more quickly understand situations.

36. Go into the GAP: Gain Another Perspective

Providing direction does not start with knowing what to do. It starts with knowing what is going on. The ability to clearly understand a situation is a prerequisite to recognizing the best course of action. Exceptional leaders go into the GAP—that is, they "gain another perspective"—to figure out what is going on. By gaining another perspective, they recognize cues and patterns and pick up the telltale signs that enable them to say, "This is the way to go."

Jenny J. Ming, president of Old Navy, makes going into the GAP part of her regular routine. She frequently travels to trendsetting cities to figure out which fashions will appeal to fickle teens. On a trip to London she observed how teens were wearing darker shaded blue jeans. She decided to darken the Old Navy's stonewash line. Old Navy now sells a whole selection of dark denim. As of January 2000, Old Navy was the biggest contributor to parent company The Gap Inc.'s overall growth.

The best leaders know that everyone already has a perspective or "map" about issues and concerns. Even those who are new to an organization do not come in with a completely blank slate. They have some information that they believe accurately describes the territory. People rely on their existing perspective to guide their actions. However, unless their perspective provides an up-to-date and complete map, problems and possibilities exist that can blindside an organization.

Consider Meg Whitman, CEO of eBay. Her company's computer systems crashed in 1999 shortly after she joined the company. The problem created a rash of customer complaints.

The company's survival depended on dealing with the issue quickly and effectively. The reasons for the crash were not obvious. No one expected the problem to occur. They would have addressed the issue, if it had been part of the already-recognized map of the territory. Whitman worked 100-hour weeks for a month to go into the GAP. She learned everything she could about what happened and how to fix the problem.

Exceptional leaders use their GAP awareness skill to detect the undetected details, to recognize the unrecognizable, and to illuminate hidden or partially obscured solutions. Skillful leaders operate from the GAP to perceive a different world from what nonleaders or novices are able to perceive. They have the seemingly unexplainable capacity to recognize when and how to lead because the GAP actually helps them perceive situations more effectively.

The best leaders go into the GAP to continually update their map and gain a greater comprehension of the context. GAP awareness compares to setting up a satellite dish to pick up signals. Master leaders tune their satellite dish of consciousness to identify the need to lead.

To go into the GAP, alter your routine. Walk into the building through a different door. Observe the workflow at different times of the day. Watch how the front line operates. Look at how people interact with customers and each other. Spend an hour on the loading dock studying operations. Position yourself in the lobby or at the front end of your operation and observe the comings and goings of customers and clients. Eat lunch at a different time. Take a walk through the hallways to just have a look around. Sit in on meetings you usually don't attend. Analyze documents you typically do not review. Be on the lookout for the sore spots that require leadership.

Show up early to review how things are going before work gets "started." Stay a little later once in a while to find out what happens in the half-hour after the workday is over. A simple alteration of your routine allows you to observe situations and find information your established process might miss. If you observe the same terrain in the same way you will rarely gain different insights.

Steal with your eyes. This process describes the spontaneous, "natural" behavior of intensive-care nurses. Beth Crandall of Klein Associates, an organizational consulting firm, conducted a study on how nurses cared for newborn infants in distress. Crandall's work, described in *Sources of Power: How People Make Decisions*, by Gary Klein, uncovered dozens of stories that suggested the nurses would instantly recognize a problem in its beginning stages such as a baby with a subtle breathing problem or a slight discoloration in skin tone.[3] Crandall explored how the nurses made this determination, and their explanation was typically, "You just know." Crandall dug deeper to understand what enabled the nurses to "just know." She compiled a list of nineteen visual signals, cues the nurses observed firsthand with their own eyes, that provided an early-warning signal such as a slight change in skin color. Half the cues were not in the medical literature.

Develop your skill in this area by consciously practicing careful visual awareness for set periods, say ten to twenty minutes, on a regular basis. Practice looking for signals that you may not fully understand, then find out what they mean. Make note of when and how things "just don't look right." Then further explore to determine what may not be right and how to make it right. This process doesn't equate with snooping; it simply means you want to explore a situation thoroughly to know what is going on.

Effective GAP awareness demands that you get comfortable wandering around different areas of your organization. This has a flip side. People have to be comfortable with you. It may be necessary to do some rapport building and expectation clarification before you venture off on a GAP trip. Let people know what you are up to before your start. Reinforce rapport before you begin; this extra effort can prevent unnecessary anxiety in others.

Being computer literate and Internet ready is another way to go into the GAP. Learn how to access data banks. Schedule search time to browse for key information and results. Do a keyword search on your product or service.

Going into the GAP invokes your observational and analytical capacities because you are looking for and becoming acquainted with issues and instances that offer insights into where you need to lead. You also map the territory and identify the need to lead by involving others.

37. Work Like Walton: Talk to Everybody

Sam Walton, founder of Wal-Mart, the number-one retail company in the world, traveled around the country continually visiting his stores. His goal? Gather information from every and any source. Walton talked to store managers, cashiers, stock clerks, and customers. He queried them about the issues, concerns, and problems they felt affected store success and customer satisfaction. Exceptional leaders identify the need to lead by talking to everybody. They create the best map possible by using everyone and anyone as a source of information.

Improve your skill to "work like Walton" by first analyzing the groups you talk with now. You probably have regularly scheduled meetings and informal discussions with others about concerns and issues. Think about who you systematically favor for information and who you may systematically ignore. Work like Walton by including people you typically leave out. Schedule time on your calendar to ask anybody and everybody about the issues and concerns they face at work. Sam Walton's schedule had him visit three stores a day.

Ask people again and again for information so that you are clear about what needs to be done. Typically when people focus on how to resolve a problem, they generate eight answers for every question they ask. Answers do not give you information. Asking does. Accept that you do not have to know everything to lead and that people will tell you what you do need to know.

Take Vera Katz, the mayor of Portland, Oregon, since 1993. Katz sends surveys to 10,000 citizens. She asks for ratings of the police department, water bureau, environmental services, public transportation, and other city bureaus. The surveys also rate the psyche of Katz's constituents. Katz wants to know if people feel safe walking at night in their neighborhood, in city parks, and in the downtown area. The surveys seek responses about whether the streets are clean enough and if the city speed limits are appropriate. Katz's surveys assess the quality of parks and recreation services and the "livability" of Portland. Results are benchmarked against six other cities. Low scores generate a search for specific things the benchmark cities are doing that Portland is not. Results are mailed to residents and then Mayor Katz hosts a one-hour television show to go over fine points.

The Katz example illustrates the importance of letting others help you identify a need to lead by asking them for information. Mine the consciousness of those around you. Sam Walton had no difficulty asking for input. He claimed he got 99 percent of his ideas from cashiers, customers, and stock clerks. Use every and any source as an additional radar screen to help you identify where and when there is a need for you to lead. Find out what others feel needs attention now. Inquire about problems other people anticipate down the road. Create the spontaneous, uninhibited exchanges that help you find out what others think.

Listen to different age groups. Learn from the people closest to your key customers, suppliers, and operating systems personnel. Talk to the newest people in the company. They could have the freshest ideas because they are less likely to be assimilated into the organization's "way of doing things." Many times new people work at arm's length from headquarters, senior management, and the corporate board room. That makes them ideal sources for information from the "outside" about the "inside." Only a new seed can yield a new crop. Only a new source of information can provide you with information that is new.

Recognize that rapport and expectations must be in place for you and others to feel comfortable gabbing. People will open up more as you improve your rapport and expectation clarification skills.

38. Use Bifocal Consciousness

The best leaders use a bifocal approach to map the territory. They identify the need to lead with an awareness of the present as well as the future. Their eye takes in the big picture and the local details. They sense what is going on for people and things, systems and subsystems.

Consider the bifocal awareness demonstrated in an early stage of the AOL–Time Warner merger. *Time* magazine reported how America Online (AOL) vice chairman Ken Novack and AOL senior vice president Miles Gilburne met with Richard Bressler, former Time Warner CFO.[4] They approached the big reality of this major corporate marriage by hammering out the nitty-gritty details. They outlined a crude combined company vision and posted which key players would fill prominent roles. They took their bifocal view back to AOL's headquarters where senior executives reviewed it "the way archaeologists examine the runic traces of an early civilization."

Look ahead. Speculate about events that may occur one, five, and even ten years down the road. Such action will of course involve conjecture. Give yourself the chance to use some of that hypothetical thinking at least once in a while.

Develop your use of bifocal consciousness by flipping your awareness lens back and forth with questions such as:

- How will this issue play out over the next three weeks, three months, and three years?
- How will this problem play out in the global and the local market?
- What present factors will compound over time that we must stop now?
- What current concerns may work themselves out so that we do not have to take action now?
- How can we use what we have now to be more competitive later?

Focus your bifocal vision down the road to avoid a common mistake. Consider this story of what one senior Time Warner executive thinks today given a decision he made in 1990: In 1990, a Time Warner manager, who sat on the AOL board, approached the Time Warner senior executive. The manager indicated AOL was a small but promising company. AOL desperately needed $5 million in cash. The manager proposed that Time Warner could purchase 11 percent of AOL for that amount. The senior executive dismissed the idea. He argued that using the Internet to distribute digital content would mean everything Time Warner had done for seventy years would be thrown out the window. The $5 million investment in 1990 was worth $15.6 billion in January 2000.[5] That early decision illustrates a lack of down-the-road awareness.

Avoid letting your attention become so mired in details that you ignore the big picture. Consider the story of Roger Stempel, who was fired as General Motors CEO. A brilliant engineer, Stempel focused so much energy on detailed engineering issues, he failed to direct his awareness toward companywide issues. People also fail when they focus consciousness on only one part of their business. Consider this comment made by a grocery manager: "As long as the cash registers ring, I know my store provides good customer service." A year later this manager was fired. He failed to perceive the need to watch the registers *and* observe other factors that affect customer loyalty.

Read any well-written business magazine article from *Fortune, Forbes, Fast Company,* or *BusinessWeek* to practice use of bifocal consciousness. Reporters for these publications invariably offer the current-future, local-global view. Simply reading such stories can remind you and reinforce your efforts to use a bifocal approach.

39. Recognize Trends

Master leaders recognize that trouble comes if they do not know what is coming. They understand that trends represent meaningful forces that have substantial impact. In contrast, fads are passing interests. Exceptional leaders recognize trends to uncover the arenas in which they need to lead.

Consider the changing trend in how people are employed. In 2000, nearly 33 percent of American workers, or 34 million people, are contingency workers, according to *The Motivational*

Manager.[6] This group includes temporary workers, part-timers, consultants, freelancers, and the self-employed. The same source reports that 10 million Americans will have started their own business in 2000.

The best leaders pay attention to underlying needs that manifest in society and create a force that could affect their business. They perceive the nuances and how they form into something substantive. They synthesize information into meaningful patterns to recognize a real movement that deserves attention.

Trend recognition represents a form of leadership literacy. Skillful leaders have the most precise and accurate (read: literate) picture of the ebb and flow of situations. They identify the need to lead with more, not less, awareness and with more, not less, accuracy. They may not know everything at all times. Trend awareness makes leaders more literate about their environment, people's concerns, and systemic factors. It enables them to order chaos into a more coherent reality.

Use various information sources to absorb new information. Establish a specific time period every day (say, thirty minutes) to review industry publications, skim through newspapers, or browse the Web. Have the overt intention in mind to figure out, "What does this information suggest regarding a trend that may be forming?" Read *The Wall Street Journal* sections devoted to trend awareness: "News You Can Use" and "Trends in Business and Finance."

Popular writers such as John Naisbitt (*Megatrends* and *Megatrends 2000*) and Faith Popcorn (*Clicking* and *The Popcorn Report*) make a living understanding trends. Their perceptions, and those of other "trend pickers," can help you understand alternate ways to approach the process and provide suggestions on how to formalize conclusions about trends. Subscribe to newsletters in your field. They typically offer information or suggest patterns that illustrate trends in particular areas. Elliott Masie's *TechLearn Trends* newsletter monitors the evolution of online learning, an important emerging trend for those interested in human resources development. Attend a seminar, listen to a business leader/consultant's audiotape series, and attend regional and national meetings in your profession to gain insights into trends.

40. Monitor the Forces of Change

Change disrupts routines and creates unforeseen opportunities. Change, like the ocean waves, can be a big turbulent force or a small gentle nudge. Change creates the need to lead. The best leaders recognize the two primary forces of change:

+ Demanded change
+ Desired change

Demanded or required change typically comes as an external press. A new government regulation or a threat from a competitor demands attention from those who want to lead an organization. A new organizational policy or procedure or an order from senior management requires a response from those who want to lead a group or unit. I often recognize the demand for change when I meet with senior executives. They speak with a pained look on their faces about how the corporate office has raised their expected sales figures or set a more stringent cost reduction number. Required change typically creates pain and causes difficulty because it demands a response. Something must be done to deal with such changes.

Desired or inspired change comes from within. The same senior executives who feel pain about demanded change can speak with excitement about a manufacturing process change they developed. They can enthusiastically explain the changes they want to make in their web presence or a new customer service approach. Inspired change energizes because it originates from personal motivation about taking a direction.

Effective leaders recognize these two primary change forces like a surfer who watches the waves to catch the good swells and recognizes the dangerous ones. They monitor the change ebb and flow to avert the danger of missing the big wave or being swept under.

The best leaders know change is inevitable. They accept the need to change. They understand they must change or they will be changed. Change monitoring helps leaders tolerate the ambiguity created by its waves and prepares leaders to enjoy the ride.

Monitor the forces of change in your business or industry by getting crystal clear on what must be done, could be done, and should be done. "Must" changes reflect demanded changes you have to meet. Often people put their head below the grass and ignore the musts. Consider how often you have heard people make statements such as, "That's not going to happen to us," or, "We don't need to do anything about that," or, "We can ignore that for now." Change-ready leaders challenge these assumptions.

Clearly identify the must or the demand forces of change that require a response. Outline what is coming at you that you cannot ignore. Identify what will not go away. I often notice how these issues are not put on the table in plain sight. People may know that senior management has given a directive or a competitor's action has occurred. Yet when these points are raised, many simply give an empty stare of nonrecognition.

"Could" changes reflect a response to a combined demand-desired change wave. For example, the AOL–Time Warner merger represented a way for AOL to gain access to what it didn't have but had to have: namely, content such as movies, television, and print publications. The merger similarly gave Time Warner access to what it lacked yet had to have: an already established online distribution network. AOL's Steve Case and Time Warner's Gerald Levin wanted to merge to expand and solidify their respective businesses. They saw the content–digital distribution wave coming and wanted to catch a ride on that change wave. They realized they could meet the demand for change with a move they both desired. Apply this lesson to your own situation. Plot the forces of change that demand you respond and those that motivate you to want to ride on that change wave.

"Should" changes exist as pure desire. They come from an inspired bubble of possibility in the brain or a nagging at the gut that says, "We should go this way." Monitor the waves of change you want to catch. Decide what you think your unit, group, or organization should do because it will make a positive difference. Identify a change that you really believe matters. Determine the changes you want to make because they are the right things to do.

Apply the other skills in this set to recognize the change forces. Go into the GAP regularly looking for forces of change. Gather information from others about forces they perceive as pending. Use your "bifocal consciousness" lens of awareness to note the change waves close to shore that will surely wash across your area very soon. Keep an eye out for change waves in the distance. These are changes that originate from above you, within your organization, or emerge based on environmental conditions. Switch between the local and long-term lens to gain the most complete perspective about change. Observe the trends that will eat you up unless you respond. Pay attention to trends that may pass you by if you do not decide to catch them.

Document the ripple effects to recognize important changes. Identify a list of key change forces that impact your organization today but were not visible one, five, or ten years ago. Analyze the ripple effect to determine if and when it will continue. Review factors that have recently emerged that may affect your organization in the near and somewhat more distant future. Consider how these change-wave trends can be exploited. Analyze the consequences of change in other parts of your industry, related industries, or in your organization that may flow back to your area of expertise.

For example, Cadillac had been the number-one luxury car in America until 1997 when Lincoln drove ahead. By 2000, Mercedes-Benz zoomed into second place and Cadillac dropped into third place. In that same year Lexus, in the number-four spot, moved up close on Caddy's tail. Cadillac's average buyer is age 67, which means the brand's core market is literally dying off. Younger buyers, focused on flair and greater performance, have moved to foreign cars. Cadillac General Manager Michael O'Malley has taken the lead in response to these change force ripples. O'Malley will spend $4.3 billion over the next four years to update and expand the Cadillac line. Four new models, more powerful engines, sportier handling, and edgy styling will define the brand as O'Malley responds to the ripple effect of change on his product.[7]

Pay close attention to common danger signals of change. If something seems too good to be true, it probably is not true. If everybody believes a situation is completely safe, no one will watch for or even recognize some unforeseen hazard that may lurk in the darkness.

Determine which change forces could bring a positive benefit and which will almost certainly destroy some part of the established landscape. Change is not always bad. Consider the benefits created by constant improvements in computer processing capabilities. Yet, if a key customer changes its software package, your group may run into compatibility problems.

Masterful recognition of change forces can transform the impact of change. You can move away from the typical confusion, disorder, and havoc created by change and instead move toward to the place where novelty, surprise, and new patterns of impact emerge and alternate patterns of response are applied. Reinforce your skill for achieving success over stress (skill 3, covered in Chapter 3) to maintain the necessary mind-body stability needed to recognize change forces.

41. Use Strategic Eyesight

Strategic eyesight enables master leaders to recognize and use true competitive advantage: the leverage gained when an internal strength matches up with an external opportunity. Mohandas Gandhi demonstrated strategic eyesight when he made his Salt March in 1930. The preservative properties of salt made it essential to survival in India. The British maintained their dominance over India with laws that made it illegal to manufacture and sell salt without a license. Gandhi recognized that anyone could make salt since it lay openly in large quantities on the beach when the tide went out. His march brought tens of thousands of Indians to the sea. They simply scooped up the salt and sold it. The British arrested them until the jails were filled. But more and more Indians continued to make and sell salt. Gandhi's strategic eyesight saw the opportunity to make salt. He leveraged this opportunity with the knowledge that he could garner enough people to march to the sea. His actions provoked Great Britain to recognize it was losing control over India.

Improve your strategic eyesight by analyzing your group or organization's internal strengths and limitations. Define with brutal honesty what you can really do well and where you fall flat. Consider five key areas when conducting your internal analysis:

1. Operational factors (i.e., the efficiency, speed, and cost-effectiveness of your operations)
2. Product or technical factors (i.e., the product line quality or innovative capacity of your organization)
3. Customer factors (i.e., the relationships and solution capacity available within your organization to meet customer needs)
4. Financial factors (i.e., the level of financial stability in your organization)
5. People factors (i.e., the quality of your workforce's intellectual capital and job-related skills)

Carefully analyze the external opportunities and threats in your competitive environment. Identify the specific capabilities of key rivals. Review what they can do well and where the market offers an unexploited arena for success. Direct your strategic eyesight to five important areas to analyze external factors:

1. Industry changes (i.e., challenges to growth and the basic business model)
2. Globalization (i.e., the impact of global competition and global media)
3. Customer expectations and demographics

4. Government regulation, including current and future legislation
5. Human capital (i.e., the available talent pool)

Focus on those areas where you believe you have leverage, or strengths that can be matched with opportunities. Compare your perceived leverage points with existing competitor strengths and strategies to verify your competitive advantage. The results of this analysis will indicate a need to lead to exploit your competitive advantage. Consider potential problem areas also. Compare internal weaknesses with environmental threats. This diagnosis suggests where you need to lead to overcome serious problems.

Strategic eyesight helps overcome the trap of success that often overtakes organizations. Consider The Walt Disney Company, traditionally known for razor-sharp management. Yet several Disney downfalls have occurred. Disney suffered from box office clunkers and troubling numbers in the consumer-products unit. Poor home video sales in 1999 caused net income to fall 28 percent. When asked how this could have happened, CFO Thomas O. Staggs commented that the company was "a victim of its own success"; things had been going so well that no one wanted to change things.[8] Disney may have been dulled by past success, but the company got a big boost from the wildly popular *Who Wants to Be a Millionaire?* show on the Disney-owned ABC Network. Net income jumped 31 percent as *Millionaire* brought in an estimated $100 million in profit. Disney chief Michael Eisner has refocused his strategic eye. He promises to turn what he calls "the proverbial battleship," although he admits that always takes time.

42. Recognize Root Causes

Exceptional leaders identify the need to lead by getting to the bottom of an issue. Uncertainty often exists in layers. The more obvious "surface" issues conceal the deeper, root cause reality. The best leaders define the most important need. They begin by going back to the seed issues. They use many methods to recognize root causes. They map all the information available about an obstacle or opportunity, then add more information over time.

Create a diagram to depict what you know about an obstacle or opportunity. A simple flowchart is useful to detail information. A cause-and-effect diagram, also known as a fishbone diagram (see Figure 6-1), can also be helpful.

Figure 6.1: Fishbone Diagram

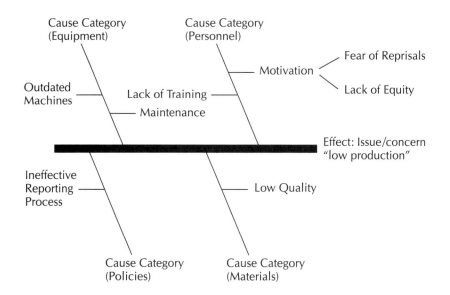

The diagram offers an example to investigate low production (i.e., the effect). Four "cause categories" are suggested: equipment, personnel, policies, and materials. More fundamental causes are suggested for each category: equipment (outdated machines and maintenance); policies (ineffective reporting process); materials (low quality); and personnel (lack of training and motivation). Two more root causes are suggested for motivation: fear of reprisal and lack of equity.

Place the "effect" (i.e., the problem, issue, or concern that requires leadership direction) on the right side of the diagram. Identify general "problem lines" that may be causal. Draw in branches on each problem line and label them as more specific causes. Continue to create auxiliary branches to further clarify additional causes. For each branch in the diagram ask, "Why did that problem happen?" Take the analysis as far back as you can to clarify the root cause. Review the diagram for causes that repeat.

Avoid going down a cause-and-effect line that is totally beyond your control. For example, falling sales may be driven by an interest rate hike at the Federal Reserve Board. Unless you are Alan Greenspan, you cannot do much about that turn of events.

Test the biases that people have. For example, a finance person may believe the root cause of a problem is lack of funds. An engineer would immediately focus on design. A marketer would conclude the fundamental problem was a lack of advertising. The human resources person would say the real cause was limitations in the recruitment system. Push people past their established area of expertise. For example, ask the finance person how a change in design may be the root cause.

Root cause analysis can take time and can be frustrating for those impatient for results. Take your time and avoid the speedboat approach. Moving too quickly often results in a great solution for the wrong problem.

43. Sense Possibilities

> *The problem is never how to get new, innovative*
> *thoughts into your mind, but how to get old ones out.*
>
> —Dee Hock, founder of Visa International

We attribute natural born leader status to those who can sense possibilities while others are stuck in outdated thinking. In 1975, Gerald Levin wanted the conservative Time Inc. board to shell out $7.5 million for a slot on the very first communications satellite. Levin, working for a marginal division called Home Box Office, needed to go space-side so he had the means to broadcast home movies into American living rooms nationwide. Skeptics complained that cable TV guys don't know anything about "space" and dismissed the satellite HBO concept as "nuts." Levin sensed the possibility of satellite distribution. He convinced the board to follow him. Almost overnight, HBO became the cash machine that shows a new movie every Saturday night and is "not TV, it's HBO."[9]

We revere those who see the opportunity where others only perceive problems. Followers latch on to those who can assimilate uncertainty in any situation and translate it into a meaningful direction. Those who can recognize prospects emerge as people others want to support.

Develop your possibility sense by reviewing what "is," then focus your awareness on "what else could be?" Challenge the restrictive aspects of the status quo. Test the extent to which the current state actually meets current demands. Frederick Smith, head of FedEx Corp., plans to reinvent home delivery of parcels. United Parcel Service (UPS) and the U.S. Postal Service (USPS) have offered home delivery for years. Smith senses new opportunities. His bright white trucks and neatly dressed driver-delivery personnel provide scheduled home delivery appointments within a one-hour window. Deliveries are made evenings until 8 P.M. and on Saturdays to make it more convenient for customers. Packages can have customized instructions such as, "Put it on the back porch," or, "Leave it with my neighbor, Mr. Parsons, in the brick house next door."

Engage others with possibility questions. For example, ask, "If this *could* work, how would we do it?" "If we *did* know how to deal with this problem, what would we know?" Possibility questions sound curious at first. Yet they work because they jump-start the mind. They allow people to let go of what they "know is true" and move into a more expansive thinking mode.

Focus on the "how" as well as why. "How" questions get people thinking about action. For example, "How do we improve contacts with our Internet customers?" generates possibilities. "Why" questions direct thinking toward purpose, meaning, and the ways things occur. For example, "Why do our contacts with our Internet customers have to improve?" or, "Why are we getting so many complaints from Internet customers?" Sense possibilities from both the how and why perspectives. Let the situation guide which questions you need to ask. "Why did the production run fail?" is not appropriate *after* the run has failed. The question focuses on blame, which typically makes people defensive. Defensiveness produces a labyrinth of explanation, justification, and excuses. Instead, sense the possibilities by asking, "How do we catch up?" Then ask, "Why do production runs fail?" when working with operators in planning sessions on ways to limit mistakes or improve quality.

44. Display Refined Business Acumen

A genius is a talented person who does his homework.
—Thomas Edison

It is difficult to identify the need to lead with restricted business acumen. The best leaders understand their industry and market. They understand their competition. They know the product mix. They have a good handle on the functional operations within their organization. They stay up-to-date on technical developments in their field. You display business acumen through your use of language and how you relate information to standard models in a particular area. Recognize that this effort requires a long-term development plan.

Start immediately to increase your business acumen skill. Analyze where you are now. Rank-order important areas of business acumen in terms of where you feel least competent. Select a specific aspect of a "least competent" area where you can most easily and quickly gain expertise. For example, it may only take you a few weeks to read a college introductory accounting text to increase your acumen manyfold in "the language of business." Attend a technical meeting for an hour as a way to increase your knowledge in a particular area. Armed with overviews in these subject areas, you can display greater acumen almost immediately. Further study will continue your progress.

Create your own self-study business school program. Set up a schedule to read one industry publication each week. Organize a monthly visit to a different area of the company where you spend several hours on-site to learn that part of the business. Read one book a month to get deep-level details about a functional area such as finance or production management or spend some time reading up on legal issues affecting your business or industry. Set up a lunch meeting every week with a colleague in a different functional area. Have your contacts outline the key issues and concerns they face. Each week, learn two financial ratios, two sales techniques, two production principles, or two Internet-based issues and how they apply to your organization and industry. Take an online learning class in an area of interest. This self-development tool offers the flexibility to study expert content from your desk within your time schedule.

Practice using your newly learned vocabulary and application of models and theories. Because you may fumble and initially use a term incorrectly practice in low-risk situations with people you trust. This provides a safe environment to grow your confidence until you feel conversant enough on a topic to address a wider audience.

Business acumen often takes time to develop, so stay with it for the long haul. True business acumen demands "seasoning." Ultimately you have to be in the trenches to develop this skill. Reading books and talking to others can only take you so far. Many organizations routinely assign personnel to different areas to help them develop a well-rounded appreciation for the business. Influence senior management to provide this opportunity in your organization if it does not already exist.

Accept your limits also. You will never become a total expert in every area. Focus on getting a broad sense of the major issues. Go deeply into the areas that you enjoy the most. Your own interests can help direct you to areas where you will most effectively identify the need to lead.

45. Be a Quick Study

In *Fortune* magazine, author Patricia Sellers reported how Carly Fiorina became CEO at Hewlett-Packard Company.[10] Fiorina's candidacy faced what seemed like a major handicap. She had never worked in the computer industry. Yet she sold herself to the board by clarifying her "ability to pick up quickly the essence of what's important." Fiorina demonstrated this ability as a division president at Lucent Technologies. Fiorina proved her quick study skills at HP. She placed number one in the 1998, 1999, and 2000 *Fortune* 50 Most Powerful Women in American Business poll. Debby Hopkins also had to learn fast when she became a senior vice president and CFO at Boeing in 1998, before moving on to her current role as executive vice president and CFO at Lucent. Hopkins had no aircraft industry experience and no formal business school degree. "You have to know how to do a lot of things," Hopkins commented. She obviously did it quickly. Hopkins rated number six in the *Fortune* powerful women poll in 1999 and second in 2000.

Ask the experts to brief you. I recently consulted with a group of attorneys in a large legal organization. I am no expert at the law and have only minor experience working with offices of legal counsel. I asked the person who engaged me to outline the key issues facing the group. She provided a seven-page, single-spaced e-mail. The document was brilliantly descriptive. It provided just the right window I needed to quickly understand the group's concerns.

Look for patterns that help you "get" what's going on. Analyze the relationships between sets of problems. Seek the complementary factors that exist among issues. Learning theory indicates these are ways to improve learning speed and memory.

To be a quick study demands that you demonstrate what you learned. Create unique labels to help you recognize and remember information. The seven-page, single-spaced e-mail I got about the attorney group helped me understand the situation. It also created a burden since it was a lot of information to digest. And it contained a fair amount of "legalese." While reading the document, I thought about descriptive labels to help organize the information in my mind. Elephants, rabbits, and foxes popped out at me. Elephants were big cases that could go on for years in both the investigation and trial phase.

They involved many attorneys. Rabbits were the multitude of trials that had to be resolved quickly due to statutory requirements. Many small sets of attorneys raced through such cases. Foxes were cases involving crafty crooks who had to be chased for long periods through many legal twists and turns. Attorneys who worked on foxes hunted them over rough terrain because of voluminous amounts of evidence, the need to use informers, and the demand to cut deals to catch the key offenders. In talking with the attorney group, I mentally used these vivid labels as reminders. The technique worked. Feedback from the group included statements such as, "He really understood our issues," and, "I was surprised; he knew what was going on and he isn't a lawyer."

Summarize your observations on paper as soon as possible. Create a "this is what I saw and heard" list. Simple information bullets will suffice. The act of writing things out will also help you recognize and remember information. Send your bullet list summary to key people with a request for comments. Ask, "Does this capture the important issues?" and, "What else is essential?" You will know this works when you get a return message that says, "You got it!"

Endnotes

1. Frederic Golden, "A Century of Heroes," *Time* Special Environmental Issue (April–May 2000), p. 54.
2. Barbara Ward, *The Rich Nations and the Poor Nations* (New York: W. W. Norton & Co., 1962).
3. Gary Klein, *Sources of Power: How People Make Decisions* (Boston: MIT Press, 1998).
4. Daniel Okrent, "Happily Ever After?" *Time* (January 24, 2000), pp. 39–43.
5. Ibid.
6. *The Motivational Manager*, a Lawrence Ragan Communications, Inc., newsletter, 2000.
7. David Welch, "Cadillac Hits the Gas," *BusinessWeek* (September 4, 2000), p. 50.

8. Ronald Grover and David Polek, "Millionaire Buys Disney Time," *BusinessWeek* (June 26, 2000), pp. 141–144.
9. Joshua Cooper Ramo, "A Two Man Network," *Time* (January 24, 2000), pp. 46–50.
10. Patricia Sellers. "These Women Rule," *Fortune* (October 25, 1999), pp. 94–123.

7

Chart a Course of
Leadership Action

The leader's mapping reveals possibilities and problems that the established organizational systems and structures do not address. That is, the existing rules and regulations, processes and procedures do not offer guidance about how to respond. Master leaders chart a course of leadership action through the uncertainties their mapping uncovers.

Look at John Mackey, CEO of Whole Foods Market, Inc. He started the company in 1980 in one funky Austin, Texas, store. By 2000, the nationwide chain of more than 100 stores in twenty-two states had pulled in revenues topping $1.5 billion. Net profits are double the industry average. Mackey created a grocery unlike what most would expect in the supermarket industry. Large-scale grocers operate on super-tight margins. Mackey established an upscale retailer (translation: higher prices for higher quality goods) that only stocks foods that are free of chemicals, hormones, and artificial anything.[1]

That marketing angle, relevant for today's health-conscious and economically more affluent Americans, reveals only part of Mackey's potent direction. He created a huge market for his quality foods business by charting a course that has overcome many traditional supermarket management weaknesses as well. Supermarkets typically suffer from chronic labor problems. At Whole Foods, personnel operate in teams that have the power to approve new hires. Teams can vote people out if they don't meet the team's rigorous standards. Bonuses depend on performance. An open-salary policy means everyone knows what everyone else, including top managers, gets paid. Regular and rigorous reviews evaluate store operations on hundreds of standards.

The best leaders lay out a path to overcome an obstacle or exploit an opportunity. They take the necessary steps others either cannot, will not, or simply do not take. Skillful capacity to chart a leadership course enables people to gain the label natural born leader.

Mastery of the skills in this set will enable you to:

◆ Establish a course that meets the need to lead.
◆ Focus on the most important courses of action.
◆ Consider alternate paths to fulfill the need to lead.
◆ Meet customer demands.
◆ Respond to change.
◆ Chart appropriate, savvy, and doable courses of action.
◆ Be decisive and remain flexible in your choice of direction.

46. Break the Symmetry—Create a New Symmetry

Symmetry defines the established patterns of order that exist in any system. Organizations create symmetry through rules, policies, regulations, and procedures. These control mechanisms help the organization achieve the predictability necessary to direct masses of people and conduct organizational business. Managers are charged to direct others so that the established symmetry holds.

No organization can create a perfect system. No set of prescribed guidelines can cover every contingency. Transformation works its way in and strains the established symmetry. Consider your own experience. Think of the impact caused by external forces such as competitor actions, technological improvements, government regulations, or customer needs. Think about the impact of internal forces such as innovative, entrepreneurial ideas, and the consequences created by employee needs for growth.

The most exceptional leaders recognize the need to alter established symmetry based on their mapping activities. They break the established symmetry when its patterns no longer support the organization's action. They chart a course of action that creates a new symmetry in response to a need or opportunity.

Symmetry breaking describes a basic force of nature. It is the creative destruction that transforms a seed into a stem into a leaf into a flower and into the fragrance. Symmetry breaking is fundamental to leadership in any organization to help the organization respond to changes in its map.

Mapping the territory clarifies *where* the established symmetry no longer meets current or future needs. Charting a course defines the new symmetry that responds to your mapping insights. Consider the example of Bruce Burlington. While head of the Food and Drug Administration (FDA) Center for Devices and Radiological Health (CDRH) unit, Burlington recognized the need to break the symmetry. CDRH oversees the manufacture of FDA-approved medical devices such as pacemakers. Congress flatlined Burlington's budget for five years, which meant the CDRH would get no funding increases for that time period. Personnel costs would continue to go up such that by year three the organization would be operating at a loss. Burlington recognized that attrition alone would keep the personnel costs within the flatline limits. However, no new personnel could be hired. The organization would not have enough person-power to oversee the full range of medical devices it presently covered.

Burlington perceived a course of action, a new symmetry. He proposed CDRH drop the low-risk medical devices (approximately 30 percent of the total) from the traditional close scrutiny provided by the organization. In addition, Burlington suggested streamlining established work practices to improve operational efficiency within CDRH. He also indicated CDRH would have to set up new forms of control for the 30 percent of medical devices that would no longer be given direct oversight. An organizationwide change-management training program was designed to help people cope with the massive symmetry breaking Burlington's course created. Two years after charting this path, Burlington reported the positive results of this effort. The CDRH model serves as a standard for other government organizations. Leaders such as Burlington break and remake the symmetry to energize rather than paralyze others.

The best leaders recognize the need for symmetry breaking as organizations grow in numbers of people. Such growth creates bureaucracy, the move toward more rule-based behavior in an effort to control larger numbers of personnel. Left unchecked, the increased bureaucracy can create a restrictive symmetry.

Take the case of Microsoft Corp. *Fortune* magazine writer Joseph Nocera interviewed several people who left the company. The group included some top-level people who were close confidants of Bill Gates himself. One key reason people left was the unceasing march toward bureaucracy. For example, Nathan Myhrvold recalled the "swashbuckling days" when ten people sat together to write the first version of Excel. Yet those who left revealed that Microsoft grew to the point where process was as important as outcome. Decisions became harder to push through. Internal politics became a way of life. Eric Engstrom, an eight-year "Microsofty," lamented how half his time was spent defending turf. Although Microsoft remained entrepreneurial longer than most, according to Sam Jadallah, who worked with the company for twelve years, he complained that running the ship ultimately became more important than plotting the path. Risk taking rapidly disappeared and Jadallah found himself having less fun. Size limited the ability to take initiative, according to many of those who left the software company.[2]

In the earlier days at Microsoft, there was a lot to do and only a small number of people to do it. Anyone could grab on to some piece of a project and run with it. But with thousands of people working a new product launch, such as another iteration of Windows or Office, the range of individual responsibility narrowed. Grabbing extra responsibility would more likely result in a reprimand than a reward.

Every organization creates one kind of symmetry in its march toward bureaucracy. Organizations move toward rule-based action and ultimately, as the Microsoft story reveals, create limits on many positive forces within organizations. Exceptional leaders break the established symmetry of bureaucracy to keep those forces alive.

Chart a course that breaks limiting symmetries. Outline actions that help the organization meet challenges. Include in your action plan a clarification of your assumptions about the need for a new symmetry. Recognize that change for its own sake simply creates stress and resentment. Link your direction and new form of order to your mapping insights as Bruce Burlington did. Clarify how your new course creates a more effective symmetry. For example, Microsoft could consider restructuring itself into smaller groups that are only loosely coupled to the larger bureaucracy so that they re-create the positive elements of a smaller organization.

47. Lead Boldly Where None Dare

Master leaders chart courses of action into the unknown. Such action requires a degree of boldness. A bold course does not necessarily mean an earth-shattering insight about how to move a group or organization ahead. The boldness comes from the fact that no one else dared to think of the action or no one was willing to try. Bold leader action sets a new standard of possibility.

Bold action requires a direction that challenges the current boundary limits in group thinking. The popular acronym BHAG, developed by James C. Collins and Jerry I. Porras in their book *Built to Last,* represents such action. BHAG stands for Big Hairy Audacious Goal. Collins and Porras suggest the boldness of a BHAG stimulates organizational progress and energizes people to action.[3]

To establish a BHAG, consider your organization's current standards of action. Find out the upper level of growth that most people believe the organization *could* achieve this year. Inquire about the limit to increased market share that most people believe is *possible* in one year. A bold direction confronts the reality of these limits. Ask yourself what bold target signifies a dramatic move forward in response to the limits you've uncovered in others' thinking.

Of course, the boldness of a BHAG can also become simply wishful thinking. A quantum leap forward cannot be too far ahead. On the other hand, action that keeps the organization even with its current status or in any way behind is not bold, either. Boldness requires balance. Identify the upper end of boldness and chart a course that offers balance.

Bold action is also needed on more localized leader issues. SMIG (pronounced "smig") might be an appropriate new acronym: Small Meaningful Increase Goals. Examples of a SMIG might be "to improve relationships with a particular customer," "to modify a part of a work process to reduce costs," or "to help group members communicate more openly."

Unlike bold maneuvers, actions at this level typically do not make headlines. Yet the leadership mechanics are the same, and such actions still represent boldness at the local level. A SMIG requires you to confront an issue that has festered, been overlooked, or not been addressed for a while. Perhaps others didn't clearly recognize it because they did not completely map the territory. Or maybe no one else was willing to step up with a leadership direction. I frequently hear people make comments in response to SMIG leadership directions. "It really made a big difference" or "That idea wasn't much in itself, but it had a big impact." Such feedback clearly demonstrates the bold direction you can provide at the local leadership level.

Bold leaders chart a course that challenges the "we've never done it that way before" mind-set. Such thinking represents a ubiquitous pattern of nonleader thinking. I propose that many instances occur in organizational life where you can chart a leader course in response to such thinking. You demonstrate the essence of this skill every time you offer initiatives that overcome such thinking.

Accept that boldness means you will deliberately destabilize the established order. A meaningful or bold course of action cannot be achieved by tweaking the system. Lead with the terribly obvious intent that you are not trying to sneak up on people. Recognize, too, that the established culture creates a strong immune system that fights off anything different. Bold direction confronts the cultural defense mechanisms, or antibodies of resistance, that counter your leadership effort.

48. Take the Highest First Action

Master leaders chart a course that counts. They effectively review alternatives and select the direction to meet the most important need first.

Take your highest first action with a focus on rooting out the unnecessary, the redundant, and that which does not contribute to desired results. Chart a course in response to the pressing change forces that must be met and will have the most significant impact. Define the critical path, the course of action that takes the essential steps to meet the need to lead. Remove obstacles along the way to maximize the capacity to continue on the critical path.

Ask yourself, "What action would resolve the problem's root cause?" This approach invokes a form of the well-known 80-20 rule: That is, 80 percent of the problems come from 20 percent of the issues. Chart a course that addresses the 20 percent root causes first. Other, less significant problems can sometimes almost automatically be alleviated with this approach.

Chart the highest first action for an opportunity by asking yourself, "What course of action would maximize the greatest possible outcome?" Apply "strategic eyesight" (skill 41, Chapter 6) to chart the course that maximizes leverage: an internal strength matched with an external opportunity. For example,

Empire BlueCross BlueShield is the largest health insurer in New York State. Empire recognized the need to boost productivity, minimize errors, stay in touch with the organization's ten sites located throughout the state, and foster trust between senior management and employees. Empire saw a way to take advantage of Internet broadcast technology to meet this possibility. The company delivers live webcasts to employee desktops. The move offers Empire unprecedented access to unfiltered discussions between senior management and employees. The broadcasts allow greater connection between individual roles and Empire's broader goals and vision.

Chart your highest first action to make the difficult decisions that make a difference. Empire BlueCross BlueShield recognized the risky nature of live Internet broadcasts. The company had to open the door to full disclosure. David B. Snow, Jr., executive vice president and COO, understood the power of information when used properly. The company decided to make the tough choice to open the communication lines. In addition, the use of Internet broadcast technology itself demanded operating with an experimental approach. Kenny Klepper, Empire's senior vice president of Systems, Technology, and Infrastructure, clarified that the company was not sure where the conversation in the broadcasts would go. He also acknowledged that any substantial level of censorship would defeat the purpose of the process. Initial results suggest this highest first action has worked. Snow reports a drop in error rates in key activities such as claims processing. The Empire story illustrates how this course of action meets the critical, high priority need for fast organizational action in a rapidly changing industry such as healthcare.[4]

49. Create a Vision, Mission, and Values

The need for a vision, mission, and values set is well documented in leadership theory and practice. These concepts are deeply entwined with leadership action. Vision defines the attractive and credible organizational future. Mission spells out the organization's business arena. Values refer to the principles that guide action. Exceptional leaders set the vision, mission, and values to establish a "big picture" course of action. They do not simply create these concepts to become fancy posters on the walls, news for annual reports, information for advertising copy, or other points to make in public pronouncements. Leaders define the vision, mission, and values in order to focus everyone throughout the entire organization.

Master leaders create vision, mission, and values as a coherent portrait that others can recognize and use to guide their action. Those who fail to carefully craft their vision, mission, and values limit the directional potential of these concepts. Consider Eastman Kodak Company's 140-word mission statement. The stated mission is to increase both the use of images in general and the relevance of images in people's daily lives. Yet the word *image* does not appear until more than one-third of the way into the statement. A more effective statement would emphasize the importance of image in the first sentence.

Review your company's vision, mission, and value statements. Consider the statements as a whole package. Assess how well they create a complete picture that provides a clear direction in response to your mapping insights. Look next at each element separately. Evaluate the vision. Is it a concrete, inspiring, and achievable future that directs people to action? Do people identify with it? Consider the mission statement. Does it clearly define the business in which the company operates? Do the words offer clear direction? Does the mission help people make decisions about where and how to spend their time and focus their energy to meet a need? Review the values. Are they relevant and meaningful behavior guides or simply platitudes? Are the values reinforced by corporate actions? For example, "belief in people" sounds like a meaningful value. Yet organizations send a mixed signal about their commitment to belief in people when they do not match authority with responsibility. In one organization that touts the value "belief in people," people get a serious mixed message because they have to get permission to use the copy machine.

Concerns about vision, mission, and values typically center

in top management corridors. If you live in the lower ranks, you must take initiative to "lead up," which means influence upper management to follow your direction and improve the organization's vision, mission, and values. Recognize that the creation of vision, mission, and values takes time. You will have to involve many organizational levels to make these concepts meaningful. Make the time. An environment that sustains effective action for the long haul begins by fleshing out these concepts.

50. Develop Scenarios

Scenarios are hypothetical courses of action. They represent a form of what-if thinking. For example, "What if the new manufacturing process increases production capacity 30 percent?" or "What if the new manufacturing process takes six months longer to implement than is expected?"

Scenarios provide the opportunity to consider multiple futures and chart courses of action to meet those multiple realities. The best leaders identify alternate scenarios to help them prevent surprises and broaden the potential for successful leadership action. They use their multiple scenarios to chart their course into the uncertain leadership arena. They know that the value in scenario building comes in the analysis behind the action paths. The creation of multiple futures helps leaders synthesize a diverse set of information. It helps leaders select a path they believe will "most likely" address issues raised during their mapping-the-territory activities.

Identify three key scenarios: best, worst, and most likely. Each scenario crystallizes the information gathered from all your mapping efforts. Best or most optimistic case scenarios assume all indicators will be positive and all hoped-for behaviors will be successful. For example, a best case scenario may include continued availability of key raw materials and no unforeseen equipment problems. Worst or most pessimistic case scenarios assume that the most adverse and realistic events will occur. For example, inflation will increase 2 percent, labor costs will double, and key raw materials will not be available for six months. Most likely or most probable case scenarios define the meaningful balance course of action.

Begin your scenario development by defining what you consider to be the "definites" for a particular time frame. Definites are high-level certainties you project for an action path. For example, an Internet business can appropriately consider it a definite that faster and more convenient Internet access will be available to customers over time. Then identify the fairly certain make-or-break points along the path that represent crucial turns, stop signs, or caution flags. For example, companies that seek to provide hyperfast, "always on" Internet access recognize how the move to fixed wireless Internet services creates an important turn away from cable TV lines. Similarly, any form of government intervention into Internet access may raise a red flag with consumers. List additional factors that may occur along your path. Evaluate all these factors on a probability continuum of low, medium, or high.

Armed with these assessments, generate your best, worst, and most likely case scenarios. Use the rule of thumb that best and worst case courses of action each have a 20 percent probability and most likely case courses of action have a 50–70 percent probability. Include other people in your scenario-building activities, too. Key players you addressed in your "work like Walton" (skill 37) activities could be useful participants. Anyone else who can offer you insights into the validity of your scenario assumptions should be part of the scenario-building process.

Of course, scenario building requires judgment. Assigning probabilities is a form of guesswork. Invoke the "use your whole brain" skills (skill 10, Chapter 3) to maximize your capacity when charting scenarios. And recognize that the value in the scenario-building process comes from the synthesis it creates among a complex set of information. Travel along your path with your headlights shining brightly as you pursue your most likely case. Be ready to reconfigure the path as new and unexpected information comes across the road.

51. Chart Local Action to Support the Big Picture

Those who lead at the global level create the organizational vision, mission, strategy, and long-range goals. However, these are not formulated on a daily basis. They represent the more special case, less frequent forms of leader direction. More frequently, leaders direct small groups, organizational units, and individuals.

Master leaders know that their course of local action must be congruent with organizational vision, mission, strategy, and long-range goals. They make the daily decisions with global goals in mind. They chart a singular-focus course that supports the larger strategic framework. Local action actually represents the more general case of leadership direction. The natural born leader label goes to those who set a direction that takes the group where it needs to go now and one that helps the group make it over the long haul.

Apply bifocal vision (skill 38) and adjust your sights to keep an eye on the big picture as you lay out any course of local action. Ask yourself how your day-to-day action path affects key stakeholders in your immediate vicinity and in wider spheres of influence. Consider how a move to support one customer group affects the entire range of customers you serve.

52. Focus on Customers First

In today's competitive environment, the primacy of customers should be etched deeply in every person's brain. Thomas M. Siebel, CEO of Siebel Systems Inc., gets this point. His company walls contain pictures of customers who have purchased Siebel's sales-management and customer service software. He engages a twenty-four-hour engineering SWAT team to solve problems when customers call. Company commissions and bonuses are tied to how clients feel about the service they get. Because his company sells customer service software, Siebel believes he must model service to his customers with laserlike intensity. Sales at Siebel Systems rose 80 percent in 1999.

Master leaders know they must focus on two categories of customers, external and internal. External customers are the people who purchase an organization's products or use its service. External customers represent the reason for the organization's existence. Internal customers are equally essential and often overlooked when people discuss customer service. Internal customers are people who work for a company and support each other. For example, both the bellhop and hotel desk registration clerk serve hotel guests, their external customers. The desk clerk represents one of the bellhop's internal customers because the clerk needs the bellhop's support to effectively serve guests. Meeting internal customer needs determines the organization's overall success in meeting external customer needs. All of the mapping-the-territory skills (Chapter 6) uncover external and internal customer issues and concerns. The best leaders chart a course that focuses on both types of customers.

Chart each step of your course with this simple but most important thought: "How will this action meet the needs of my internal and external customers?" Consider the trade-off if you do not meet a particular customer group's needs. As Michael LeBoeuf explains in *How to Win Customers and Keep Them for Life*, 96 percent of customers who have a complaint say nothing to the offending organization.[5] They simply do not come back. It takes six times more resources (e.g., marketing dollars) to attract a new customer than it does to keep an existing customer. A dissatisfied customer tells eight to ten people about the problem. It takes twelve positive service interactions to make up for one negative interaction. Businesses rated as having low service quality average only a 1 percent return on sales and lose market share at a rate of 2 percent per year. Businesses with high-rated service average a 12 percent return on sales and gain market share at a rate of 6 percent a year while charging higher prices. Remind yourself of these simple statistics as you decide on your course of leadership action.

53. Chart a Course in Response to Change

Exceptional leaders chart a course that offers a meaningful response to the demanded and desired forces they uncovered while mapping the territory. They lay out a realistic path through the wilderness of uncertainty created by change.

Chart your course with a matched response to demanded and desired change forces. For example, Blockbuster Inc. Chairman John F. Antioco recognized the demanded or required change forces hitting his industry. Video rental stores face challenges from multiple other sources that offer in-home entertainment. Satellite, cable, and broadband Internet loom as big players to bring movies and other couch-comfortable media into homes. Antioco signed a twenty-year deal with Enron Corp. to deliver video-on-demand services using Enron's high-speed fiber-optic network. He linked Blockbuster with DirectTV to create a satellite distribution source. Blockbuster. com announces movies on video and company promotions. The company has an alliance with America Online (AOL) to promote the Internet provider's products and services in Blockbuster stores. You can even make an online purchase of food and have it delivered to your home along with your movie through the hookup of Blockbuster, Food.com, and Takeout Taxi. Antioco's course of action has readied Blockbuster to respond to whatever change force wins in the drive toward more in-home entertainment.

Antioco is also inspired to expand Blockbuster's existing retail distribution. As of September 2000, a Blockbuster store existed within a ten-minute drive of 70 percent of America's households. The company has 45 million homes signed up for its video rental program. Antioco offers his inspired-desired course of change when he notes that America has 88 million households, which means 43 million more homes are available to become potential Blockbuster customers. Antioco notes that home video did not kill the movies and pay-per-view services have not pushed out rentals. He believes the $20 billion plus growth over the past twenty years in this industry could grow to $30 billion in the next five. Antioco describes his inspired course of action by saying, "People who believe it is a zero-sum game really don't understand the nature of consumer appetite for entertainment if they can easily access it."[6]

Adopt Antioco's approach. Define action choices that match the impact of the demanded and desired change forces identified by applying your skills for monitoring the forces of change (skill 40). Chart a course that meets both current, local change as well as future, global change based on needs identified with your bifocal consciousness (skill 38) and your ability to recognize trends (skill 39). Integrate information from your "work like Walton" skills (skill 37) to address issues and concerns raised by others.

Chart a realistic course to create a real possibility in response to the change reality. Ask yourself, "What can really be changed, in what time frame, and by whom?"

Chart your action course to provide people with the necessary job skills to support your change course. Ensure that the path juggles the multiple realities complex action always involves. A large government agency failed to do this and suffered from it. The agency recognized it had to change in response to increased demands from its customers, who are other government agencies, for faster and more accurate response times. A course of action was defined. One piece of the plan was the introduction of a new computer software program. Everyone received training on the software as soon as the overall course of action was announced. The software was not installed for six months for a variety of reasons. By then, no one remembered very much from the training. This stalled the success of the overall course of action.

Include action steps that alter the systems necessary to support your course of action. Leaders at the government agency recognized they had to adjust their mistaken course of action. They retrained all their people to use the new software. Leaders also stepped up to change the agency's performance management system so that it rewarded those who most effectively used the full range of the software's capabilities. This effort had a very positive effect on achieving the overall plan.

Always ask, "What resources are necessary?" to respond to the change forces your action path intends to address.

Stay in touch with customers as you chart your course in response to change. Typically customers play an important role in creating the need for change. Consequently, chart your course with continued involvement of customers, both external and internal, to ensure it meets their needs.

Accept the need for tolerance of ambiguity. Charting a course through change typically involves speculation about what might be and could be, rather than a certainty about what will be. Set sail into the sea of change with the understanding that you can never fully know if your course will take you where you need or want to go. Put the keel in the water and take the rudder. Work on your self-awareness skills (Chapter 3) to reinforce these capabilities. Review your ability to achieve success over stress (skill 3) and to remain flexible in the face of difficulty (skill 6) to support your efforts while charting a course through change.

54. Demonstrate Political Savvy

Political savvy refers to getting things done when others desire different outcomes. It means taking action when multiple paths exist to accomplish a result. It involves charting a course when resources are scarce. Political savvy does not mean being "political," which is a delicate way of labeling someone as untrustworthy or lacking substance. Political savvy represents a prudent, conscientious choice in the face of challenging circumstances. It enables leaders to chart a course that successfully works through the realities of resource limits and the maze of individual egos and empire building that exists in all organizations.

Get clear about the political realities in your organization. Who wants what? What resources exist? How will others respond to your course of action?

How does your leadership direction affect different stakeholder groups? Outline the key issues of major stakeholders.

Apply the test of immediacy. Determine which stakeholder needs are most important now and which will emerge at later stages of your action path. Balance those things that are doable and fulfill the immediacy test with the long-term impact such a course of action will have.

For example, how would you rate the political savvy of United Airlines (UAL) during its battle with pilots during the summer 2000 travel season? The carrier and its 10,000 aviators were in dispute over wages. In 1994, pilots took a pay cut in exchange for UAL stock. In April 2000, pay was still only at 1993 levels. The pilots, believing they deserved better salaries, decided to refuse overtime work. Massive flight delays occurred that stranded thousands of customers. The friendly skies started losing droves of customers to other airlines. United made peace with its pilots in September 2000 by giving them an immediate wage hike of 21.5 percent to 28.5 percent. With that course of action in place, United either must raise fares or accept lower profitability. Higher ticket prices could send passengers to other airline ticket counters. Lower profitability may send stockholders to the emergency exits. Other unions, such as the International Association of Machinists and Aerospace Workers, which represents nearly 50,000 mechanics, baggage handlers, and ticket agents, may also want a pay hike soon.

United felt it had to give in to get pilots back in the cockpits. The company also wanted to move ahead with its hoped-for acquisition of US Airways Group, Inc. United may make out okay if other big carriers, such as American and Delta, get hit with higher pay demands from their pilots, too.[7] Fare hikes may occur across the board. The full-fare business travelers may have to remain belted in to large carriers because they control key routes. Do you think United made a politically savvy move? Why? What would you have done to lead United through this politically charged situation?

Consider your similar realities. First, identify what is possible. What course of action can you take given the political realities of different goals, alternate paths, and limited resources? Determine how you can comfortably challenge those limits. Reinforce your relationship-building skills to help in this area. If rapport is high with all, it will be easier to chart a course that limits some while it aids others.

Ultimately, political savvy requires that you master your "get quiet and listen" skill (skill 1). It may be easy for some to simply become devious and try to deceive. True political savvy maximizes the intelligent use of all information based on priorities that serve the greater good.

55. Shape and Mirror

Charting a course creates a unique demand on leaders. The leader's direction must guide followers forward through uncertainty. However, followers must commit to the leader's direction to make it meaningful. Leaders face a paradox: They need to shape the future through their action and also mirror what followers will accept. Master leaders push people to the next level while they simultaneously calibrate their direction in line with the speed at which people can move. Skillful leaders remain in the driver's seat steering people with a sure and steady hand, and they respond to and reflect the many elements followers experience as they consider getting on board and moving along the road.

Consider the words uttered by Andrea Jung, who became Avon Products' CEO in November 1999. Speaking to 13,000 Avon representatives, Jung declared, "Avon is first and foremost about you. I stand here before you and promise that will never change." Yet Jung has cast a leader course to challenge the traditional direct-sales, door-to-door model that has been the company standard since 1886. Jung has little choice but to shape a new course. Direct selling accounted for only 6.8 percent of the $27 billion cosmetic and toiletry market in 1999, which was down from 8 percent in 1995. Avon's sales growth has slowed to a minuscule 1.5 percent in 1999. Despite the overall strong economy, Avon has struggled.

In response, Jung wants to put Avon into retail arenas. In a clear move to shape the future and mirror the sales force's (i.e., the followers') needs, Avon will sell from mall kiosks that are franchised to the "Avon calling" representative. Jung has also charted a "shape and mirror" course for using the Web. A Web-based sales site supports existing Avon representatives and the Avon catalog. Anyone from the backbone sales force can become an "eRepresentative" who sells online and earns commissions for orders shipped direct or for orders they deliver. The Web makes it easier and quicker for reps to make money. Jung shapes the future course while mirroring the needs of her sales reps. The Web also saves money for sales-weak Avon. It only costs 30 cents to process a Web order compared to the 90 cent cost of the traditional door-to-door sales order. Jung continues to monitor how well her course of action mirrors the needs of sales representatives. She polls them about the website and inquires about the kind of technology they think can help them.[8]

Failure to either effectively shape or mirror chases followers away. Senior executives whose path no longer suits their corporate board get no support. Steve Jobs was fired from Apple, the company he started, when the corporate board no longer felt his direction met the company and competitive needs. Jobs was later hired back because the board felt he could shape a meaningful course that mirrored the board's desires.

Chart your course to represent a meaningful balance between what the future could bring and what the followers' interests are. Test your choices. Float a trial balloon with select individuals and groups whose general support you already have. Get their feedback on how well the course of action mirrors what they would follow. Consider their input and if necessary modify the path a few steps further in one direction or by pulling it back some.

56. Demonstrate Good Citizenship

Exceptional leaders gain support from a wide range of followers when their path models good citizenship. On the global level, their action demonstrates a path with "the world is my family" as an underlying theme. Think of high-profile leaders such as Gandhi and Mother Teresa. At more local levels, leaders chart a course that demonstrates "the group is my family."

Test the citizenship of your path. Ask yourself how your direction serves the struggles of those who experience the toughest time and greatest difficulty. Ponder how your course of action affects those who operate with the fewest resources or least support. Chart a course that includes improvement on the most important social issue faced by your group, organization, community, or nation.

Good citizenship represents a value issue. You have to decide your value set based on self-awareness skills. Continually challenge yourself to upgrade your citizenship. Consider the question, "What more can I do for my people?" on every leadership action you take.

57. Know When to Hold 'Em and Know When to Fold 'Em

The best leaders know they need flexibility when charting a course. They know that planning is paramount and that plans can become meaningless if something unexpected occurs. They know that it is impossible to consider all contingencies. Something can always pop up to destroy the best-laid course of action. Skillful leaders live with a willing acceptance that unpredictability always exists. They know they cannot control the outcomes. They can only focus on taking action. They commit to a course and hold to it as long as it seems like the best hand to play.

Chart your course with the full intent that it will meet the need for which you are leading. Define standards of evaluation up-front regarding when you might want to "fold 'em." Set time limits on how long you are willing to "hold 'em." Then take off and move with full speed. Be ready to change course if necessary. Monitor your movement in terms of the predefined standards. Sometimes a small course correction early on can eliminate big problems later. Keep in mind the saying, "If you can catch a snake when it is still a small snake you can avoid being poisoned."

Willingness to fold does not mean loss of focus or lack of intensity in your action. Stick to your course as long as the cards look good. Know that charting a course always involves probabilities, just like in the game of poker. Accept and embrace the risk that always accompanies taking leader initiative. Your action will be either a great adventure or a serious threat to you and others. Your choice may result in a loss or a way to make a great contribution. You cannot eliminate the element of risk. You can focus on playing your best hand to achieve success.

Continually work on the skills you need to map the territory (Chapter 6) as you work through your course of action. Sometimes a course of action seems as if it cannot fail. The best leaders know that just because the dog wags its tail and licks your hand, that doesn't mean it isn't going to bite you later. Continue to go into the GAP (skill 36) to update your view of situations and work like Walton (skill 37) to gather information from multiple sources. Review how well root causes are being addressed (skill 42). Constantly keep your senses tuned to new possibilities (skill 43). Test again and again how the oncoming forces of change impact your action (skill 40).

Recall Forrest Gump's famous phrase, "Life is like a box of chocolates, you never know what you're going to get." Be willing to move on when your box of chocolates gives you something you never expected and do not want. Take reasonable risks. Do not be fearlessly foolish. You can bluff in poker and sometimes win. Avoid betting the farm if you are bluffing. Throw in your cards if you must. Then learn from the experience. Remember, there are no real failures, only learning events.

58. Step Up and Act: Be Decisive

When all is said and done, charting a course means taking action. At a certain point, you have to swallow hard and jump off the cliff. Master leaders step up and act decisively. Most people will be decisive when a building burns in raging flames. Master leaders are action-ready and decisive at all times. They operate with a "make something happen" mind-set. They think with "get a result" logic. They demonstrate the willingness to march forward with a bold, positive, and resolute step.

Consider Peter I. Bijur, CEO of Texaco Inc. Three months after he took the helm, the company was rocked by a racial discrimination lawsuit. An audiotape surfaced in which senior executives were heard making derogatory racial remarks. Bijur did not hesitate. He acknowledged the problem openly. He settled the suit at a cost to Texaco of $140 million. He fired one executive and stripped away the benefits from two others who had already retired. He worked for the next two months to root out and change a negative culture that reinforced discrimination within the workplace. He hired prominent African-Americans into the company's senior ranks. Today, civil rights leaders point to Texaco as a model for eliminating discrimination. Contrast Bijur's handling of a bad situation with Russian President Vladimir V. Putin's response to the *Kursk* submarine disaster. Putin acted slowly to seek foreign assistance. He delayed his trip to the scene. He allowed the military to play down the news.

Come to work every day with the readiness to take initiative. Procrastination and waffling do not attract followers. Look for situations that require initiative. Decisive action can help a meeting get back on track. A direct suggestion can aid an individual trying to complete a report. A key comment can help resolve a conflict among team members. Step up when you find yourself in these situations. Be willing to make a suggestion to improve a production process, meet a new customer's need, or modify a product. When you take such action in a consistent, frequent, and spontaneous manner, you earn the natural born leader label.

This skill begins with will. It requires that you skillfully focus on the highest first, shape and mirror, and know that you may have to fold your hand. Then step up. Chart a course! Slip on your leadership Nikes and just do it!

Recognize the value in analyzing, considering, and weighing options. Such thinking helps us act. Also understand that action helps us think. Action creates a result. Results help us learn to take better action. Leader action represents an experiment, as it were, that helps us figure out how things will turn out. Use all the time you have to consider your choices. Do not decide until you have to decide. Then act swiftly when the time comes.

Review your self-awareness skills—your ability to get quiet and listen (skill 1) and live with passion and direct it with precision (skill 2). These skills will reinforce your ability to take the decisive step of leadership initiative.

Endnotes

1. Charles Fishman, "Whole Foods Is All Teams," *Fast Company* (April–May 1996), pp. 103–109.
2. Joseph Nocera, "I Remember Microsoft," *Fortune* (July 10, 2000), pp. 123–131.
3. James C. Collins and Jerry I. Porras, *Built to Last* (New York: Harper-Business, 1994).
4. Gail Meredith, "Breaking Down Barriers," *iQ,* pp. 510–514.
5. Michael LeBoeuf, *How to Win Customers and Keep Them for Life* (New York: Berkley Publishing Group, March 1989), pp. 13–14.
6. Martha McNeil Hamilton, "Blockbuster Branches Out," *Washington Post* (September 19, 2000), pp. E1, E7.
7. Michael Arndt, "The Industry Will Pay for United's Deal with Pilots," *BusinessWeek* (September 18, 2000), p. 52.
8. Nanette Byrnes, "The New Calling," *BusinessWeek* (September 18, 2000), pp. 137–148.

8

Develop Others as Leaders

One immutable fact defines the leadership reality. You cannot lead alone. First of all, leaders *and* followers create the power of leadership. Both contribute to the process. Leaders offer direction and followers commit to it. In addition, multiple leaders can and do emerge at all organizational levels. In fact, success demands that leaders live throughout an organization. No one person can possibly guide even a modest-size company through all the twists and turns it takes to succeed. Master leaders must multiply themselves. They develop others to master the 108 skills of natural born leaders.

All truly great performers have a coach. Michael Jordan, Rudolf Nureyev, Joe DiMaggio, and Luciano Pavarotti all had someone help them develop and continually refine their skills. Ronald Reagan, the "great communicator," used Roger Ailes as a speaking coach. Anyone who became a "world's greatest" in their field got coaching every day and quite often several times a day.

Leaders develop others on an individual basis. John Nerger, head of the Army Chief of Staff for Instillation Management, regularly meets with each of his sixty staff members to discuss ways each can improve. Jack Welch, *Fortune* magazine's "Manager of the Decade" for the 1990s, spends 50 percent of his time hiring, coaching, and developing others to be more effective leaders.

Leaders also develop others on a group basis. Nikki Tinsley, Inspector General (IG) for the United States Environmental Protection Agency, provided leadership training for every single person in her 350-member organization: managers, supervisors, administrative staff, and support staff. Her logic was simple. Tinsley saw the need to transform the IG office into an organization that more effectively met customer needs, more successfully fulfilled key tasks, and, in the final analysis, helped the EPA fulfill its role in protecting the environment for the American people.

The EPA IG office had been a traditional command-and-control, top-down, superiors-over-subordinates culture. Tinsley recognized how this limited the IG mission. She realized that leaders had to emerge every day at every level. She realized that all organizational members could and should consciously apply their efforts to contribute to the overall success of the organization. Many organizations desire to empower their members. Some simply pay lip service to the ideal. Nikki Tinsley put the rubber to the road with leadership training for the entire organization. Tinsley also provided total quality management and team development programs to help members improve work processes and enhance how they interacted. Tinsley took an additional rare step by providing formal and informal follow-up to the leadership training. She provided IG members with reinforcement tools and self-assessments to continuously upgrade their performance. She engaged members in group discussions about how to maximize their application of the training.

Master leaders know that people in key positions around them are like the DNA in their organization. Their skill level directly affects overall leadership effectiveness. Developing others becomes a form of gene therapy. The best leaders offer nutrients to help the already existing genes emerge into practical skills. They also splice in new genes to develop new skills. Natural born leader status goes to those who skillfully develop others to become master leaders.

Mastery of the skills in this chapter will enable you to:

- Attract high potential people to develop as leaders.
- Enhance others' leadership skills through formal and informal methods.
- Improve all aspects of others' potential.
- Institutionalize leadership development in your organization.

59. Attract Rising Stars

Ultimately, the best leaders focus on developing everyone's leadership skills. However, they also recognize the limits to their time and energy resources. They begin their efforts to multiply themselves by attracting the rising stars—those with raw talent and the desire to turn it into real results. Exceptional leaders expend their energy on those who have the greatest capacity and willingness to grow. Skillful leaders apply their developmental effort where it can do the most good in the fastest manner possible.

Conduct an audit of those within your immediate workgroup, unit, or organizational division who are potential rising stars. You already have a relationship with these people, which makes it easier to attract them to your developmental efforts. Rate them on a "rising star scale" by asking questions such as:

- Who has already demonstrated a desire to grow?
- Who typically steps up and tries to lead?
- Who has directly indicated an aspiration to improve their leadership capacity?

Identify those who rate at the highest end of this scale. Focus your first efforts on them, then expand your rising star search into other areas within your organization. Use the same questions to decide where to put your attention. Consider the value in bringing such people into your work area. Could you influence people to move to your group or division to make it easier to develop them? Job switching invigorates some people. Of course, you have to clarify expectations with others before using this strategy. You do not want to get a reputation for "stealing people." Focus on individuals who would benefit from the switch and whose move to your area would not negatively impact where they are now.

When you do look for rising stars outside the organization, offer realistic job previews. Let new candidates know what it's really like to take the lead in your organization or area. Give them a no-holds-barred account of the challenges involved in developing their skills. This will scare some people off. The realistic job preview serves as a cut-off mechanism for those who will not or cannot truly rise as stars. You want raw talent that wants to grow within the realities they will confront. Some organizations try to keep the skeletons in the closet during recruitment. This becomes a long-term error. Eventually, new people find out what's what. The disillusionment causes some to quit and others to simply sit and stew. Avoid either result with a realistic up-front account.

Focus on attracting those with potential as opposed to only focusing on experienced players. Typically we look to those with established experience and a track record of results. We believe such background makes it easier to move them forward more quickly. However, experienced people can be hard to redirect, improve, or change. The fact that they have a lot of experience may limit their willingness to change. They may not believe they need any significant improvement. They may think you cannot offer them any real development because their "experience" tells them they already know what to do.

Attract rising stars with the personal touch. This approach brought Nancy Kelleher to work for the U.S. Department of the Treasury. Kelleher was a highly successful member of the McKinsey & Company consulting group. When she was approached about a position with Treasury, Kelleher had only modest interest in the job. She agreed to interview for the position as a courtesy. She had a one-on-one meeting with then Treasury Secretary Robert Rubin to discuss the post. Kelleher told me that this personal contact with Rubin sold her. She left

her very important position at McKinsey to give her energy to
public service.

"Lead up" to influence senior managers regarding the formal organizational recruitment process. Convince them of the
need to make it easier to attract and retain high-quality potential talent. Many organizations I consult with stumble over
repressive selection policies. Managers want to attract high-
potential players, but find it difficult to do so because of the
recruitment procedures. Confront this systemic limit and work
to change it. Apply the influence skills in Chapter 9 to help you
with this difficult challenge.

60. Use "World Class" as the Standard

Consider this simple reality. The average leader is, by
definition, average. Average leaders are not really terrible and
they are not really that great. Leader development efforts that
focus on average ways to think and act result in average outcomes. Exceptional leaders do not direct others to be in "the
average middle." They ratchet up their efforts to create world-
class winners.

Consider your leader development task as a challenge to
get people to play at a world-class level. Remind people how
winners work and make that your standard every day. Consider
the example set by Clark Graham, president of Litton Marine
Systems (LMS), an international marine navigational equipment manufacturer. Graham took over LMS when the firm was
struggling to meet its financial goals. Its parent organization put
the company under the gun: Make the necessary numbers or
suffer the consequences. Graham could have focused on simply
raising people to meet the bar set by corporate headquarters.
Instead, he challenged his senior managers to compare themselves to world-class players like General Electric. During a
two-day off-site meeting, I engaged Graham and his managers
in a simulation to assess the group's capacity to work together.
The simulation involved four rounds of action. After each
round, I raised the goal for the group. In the fourth round, the

group did better than any group I had ever engaged with this simulation. I told them they had set the "world's record" for the activity. The group admitted that, in the first round, they would have thought it impossible to do so well.

Graham seized on this "world record" result as the standard for the group. He referred to the simulation often as a reminder of his desire to develop world-class standards for every manager. Graham told me that he set world class as the standard to identify those who were truly committed and to flesh out those who wanted to live in the less meaningful middle. Eight months after I started to work with LMS on a consulting assignment, Graham described the positive signs of world-class thinking. He showed me a particular performance graph that clearly demonstrated dramatic upward movement. What was even more telling was the response from one of his senior managers regarding the graph. "The numbers are actually better than that," the manager exclaimed with a deep sense of pride.

Continually compare current levels of action with world-class levels. Provide hard, tangible feedback when making these comparisons. This action speaks volumes to others about what you believe it means to be a leader and the level of success you believe people can achieve.

61. Coach and Train

Coaching refers primarily to one-on-one, face-to-face, day-to-day developmental activities. Coaching improves, extends, refines, or redirects behavior where a person already has some knowledge and skill. Training refers primarily to individual or group learning activities to teach or instruct people in knowledge and skills they do not already have. Obviously, coaching and training can overlap. Exceptional leaders use a combination of the two approaches to develop others as leaders.

Begin your coaching efforts with clarification of your coaching beliefs. Effective coaches have success and possibility beliefs. They believe people can learn and want to improve their performance. They believe people will improve if given the proper direction and support. Take a moment to reinforce these beliefs within yourself before you begin your coaching effort.

Conduct a "coaching analysis" to determine the exact coaching direction you want to provide. The analysis begins with an assessment of the person's current performance level. What specific skills do you feel need improvement? For example, a person may not put any time into building common ground with key others. Or a person may lack bifocal consciousness (skill 38) and focus solely on local issues without giving attention to global concerns. Pinpoint the specific behaviors you want to change. What, precisely, do you want the person to do differently? For example, to build common ground, you may want the person to set up one-on-one discussions with key others. To enhance bifocal consciousness, you may want the person to study long-term marketing reports or review industry documents. Think in terms of world-class standards when you select specific behavioral changes. Outline the results of current performance and the consequences to the person. Explain the benefits for individuals when they do improve and define the impact on them if they do not change. Armed with this information, you can begin the coaching interaction.

Discuss your coaching analysis with each individual you coach. Ask each person whether he or she recognizes the need for change in the areas you believe need improvement. The discussion itself may be a catalyst for change. In my experience, the discussion results in one of three outcomes. The person may know he needs improvement and may have been working on changes. Or the person may not know he needs improvement, and the fact that you have mentioned it motivates the person to make his own suggestions for improvement. In other words, your feedback alone was an effective coaching tool. Third, the discussion may reveal that this person wants and needs your help to make a change.

The discussion of the coaching analysis also creates a meta-effect. As you review the skill you feel needs improvement, the specific behaviors that need to change, the world-class standard you seek, and the consequences of performance, you create "buy in" with the individuals you are coaching. They feel a part of the improvement process because you involved them in a discussion.

When people indicate they need your help, apply the coaching behaviors that I believe all successful coaches use. The behaviors can be used in any order and combination. Consider what works best for you. Apply these behaviors based on what you believe will produce the best results with the person you want to coach.

Five Successful Coaching Behaviors

1. *Tell people what they need to do to improve.* Some individuals respond with complete success simply when given a verbal directive to change. For example, "I suggest you set up one-on-one meetings with each person in your area to build more rapport. Talk with them about common interests, background, and goals to establish a sense of shared experience with them." You can also use the "tell" approach to clarify what the person should *not* do (e.g., "Don't talk only about business issues when you are trying to establish rapport").

2. *Show people how to improve.* Model the specific behavior. Some people need a clear demonstration of what needs to be done. For example, conduct a discussion with the person about the need to build a common ground and use the experience to demonstrate how to build common ground. It may also be useful to show people what *not* to do. That is, demonstrate what not to say or which nonverbal behaviors will not support rapport building. For example, show the person how sitting across a desk does not communicate as much common ground as sitting next to someone.

3. *Clarify the consequences of behavior.* Some people do not clearly recognize the relationship between an action and an outcome. For example, some people may not understand the powerful effect that being accessible and approachable (skill 16) has on building rapport. Good coaching sometimes requires explaining the consequence links. Skillful leaders define both

positive and negative consequences. For example, effective coaching would clarify how being accessible and approachable makes it easier for leaders to gather information when using "work like Walton" skills (skill 37). Effective coaches also explain how poor listening limits the degree to which others perceive them as accessible and approachable.

4. *Provide the big picture.* Give people a glimpse through your bifocal consciousness lens (skill 38). That is, explain how specific behaviors affect the global situation. For example, you can explain how leaders who work the grapevine (skill 29) create a more accurate flow of information, which creates a more open organizational culture (skill 97).

5. *Use a confidence builder.* Sometimes coaching does not involve a direct change of a person's behavior. People may know what to do and how to do it. Rather, coaches may need to build confidence to help people improve. Confidence builders can include a simple, "I know you can do this" statement of encouragement. A good story, especially one about your own experience, can also serve as a confidence builder. Think of a time when your confidence was low and something pumped you up to perform. Relate your experience to instill the same "can do" confidence in others.

One-on-one coaching takes time and effort. Make time for coaching, especially for your rising stars. Develop leaders through training with the following steps.

Tips for Using Formal Training

1. *Identify the training need.* Determine the precise knowledge or skills that people need. You may need to consult with a training specialist who can augment your own diagnostic efforts with standardized assessment instruments for a large group.

2. *Review the content and process of training programs designed to meet the need.* Evaluate the specific links between the training needs and the course content, methodology, and application. For example, your needs analysis may suggest training to de-

velop stress management skills. The training program should include the meaning of stress, its effect on performance, and how to manage stress more effectively. The program should cover a variety of stress management techniques and explain the expected results of each. The program should also provide participants with ample time to discuss the application of the training. Assessments would be useful to help people evaluate their own levels of stress. The assessments could also be administered after the training to measure improvement. Consider the use of a training specialist to support your efforts to review training programs if you don't feel confident you can effectively evaluate training content and process.

3. *Request that the training be customized for specific people and their needs and for the organizational culture.* Require that the trainers learn enough about the organization so they can use examples that relate to your trainee's work experience. Explain any unique jargon that trainers should incorporate into the training. Demand that the trainers demonstrate how to apply the program to the trainee's job situations.

4. *Demand a follow-up process that can be used internally to reinforce the training.* It would be nice if you could simply have the training organization you are working with come back every week to do follow-up work. That would be nice for the training company, anyway, since its training specialists would get rich! However, you can maximize your training dollar and ultimately create a more useful program with an internally generated follow-up process. Demand specific tools from the training organization to help remind people of key training points. Require a method to assess training application. Indicate that you must have a structured set of activities or discussion sessions to keep the training content alive in the organization after the formal program is ended.

5. *Conduct a pre-course discussion with trainees.* Explain your expectations before people attend the training. Agree to a specific set of behavioral changes that you and trainees expect to be provided as a result of the training.

6. *Conduct a post-course discussion with trainees.* Review the program evaluations and talk about key aspects of the program.

Did the content meet the desired needs? Was the program delivery conducive to knowledge and skill learning? Did the training provide an understandable and systematic method to apply the program? Answers to these questions will ensure trainees got "take home value." The answers will also guide your selection decision for future training programs. If the training did not meet your expectations, discuss the failings with the training organization. Ask for a follow-up, at the training organization's expense, to get your money's worth.

62. Polish the Whole Diamond

Whether you focus on coaching or training, your ultimate success in developing others as leaders demands that you cultivate the full range of a person's potential. People are whole beings. People take action (handiwork), experience the pressure of action (bodily stress), and have ideas and information about how to do their work (their intellectual capital). Developing leadership demands a holistic approach. Those we label natural born leaders invest in improving not only a person's industry knowledge, technical expertise, or political savvy; skillful leaders focus on more than simply the current task or job or company conditions. They polish all facets of people's potential to prepare them for any leadership possibility. Such action enables the best leaders to leave a legacy.

Polish the whole diamond by having others assess themselves in terms of the 108 skills of natural born leaders. Direct them to work on improvements in the same ways you have approached this book.

Suggest that people plot a long-term career and life development path. Discuss where would they like to be in five, ten, and twenty years. Take an expansive view during this process. Too often career planning plots a course toward a specific position (e.g., to become a senior vice president in five years) or a specific outcome (e.g., to own my own company in ten years). Go beyond this approach. Think about long-term development and view people's potential with a wider angle lens.

Ask people to identify the kinds of experiences and challenges they want to have in their career. Perhaps being a senior vice president doesn't meet those needs. Help people think through how they would like to use their time. Owning your own company demands a major investment of a person's time, which some people may not actually want to make. Ask people to describe a fulfilling day in the future. This exercise will clarify the types of developmental activities they need. For example, consider someone who explained that a fulfilling day would involve working closely with many different people. Clarify the need to work on relationship-building skills and to seek experiences that involve working with others.

63. Appraise Continuously

General Electric (GE) and McKinsey & Company have a reputation as "CEO machines" because so many people from their organizations go on to become CEOs of top corporations. GE and McKinsey use constant appraisal to improve their personnel. Both companies provide feedback that is deep, honest, frequent, and comes from all sources. The companies constantly evaluate their people and use appraisal to weed out those who do not measure up.[1]

Appraisal contains the root word *praise*. Appraisal includes positive recognition and rewards for the full range of performance. Too often praise focuses only on the outcome or result of a project. The winner gets rewarded and everyone else earns the label "loser." The best leaders recognize that the full range of performance includes the outcomes achieved *and* the process involved in getting results. It also includes any behavioral improvements and refinements made along the way. Tennis great Martina Navratilova once said, "The moment of victory is much too short to live for that and nothing else."

Appraise people along the full performance range. Naturally this means recognizing results. Send a personal note about a positive outcome. Acknowledge a person's achievement in a meeting. Offer a congratulation about work outcomes in a one-on-one discussion. In addition, praise people for improvement. Perhaps someone did a substantially better job in the application of the "work like Walton" skill (skill 37). The person gathered more information and used ideas from many more sources than in the past. Acknowledge this improvement. Reward movement in the proper direction. For example, someone may not have outlined the most effective course of action to meet a leadership need. However, the person may have demonstrated an improved use of political savvy (skill 54) in her choices. Praise any movement made to incorporate this important issue in the person's choice of direction.

Appraisal also focuses on corrective measures to improve performance. Assess where people do not perform up to their potential or your world-class standards. Clearly indicate what they need to do better. It is easy to praise others because people like to be told they are doing well. Corrective feedback is tougher since people can get defensive.

Apply specific methods to offer effective feedback when appraisal demands rooting out unacceptable behaviors or results. Be descriptive before evaluating performance. Be specific as opposed to general. For example, if you say, "The report does not include any consideration of how the field organizations feel about the project," you are describing a specific weakness in a report. "The report is terrible" is not a useful comment since it is general and evaluative. Such feedback simply makes a person feel bad. It gives no indication of why expectations were not met.

Focus on the problem, not the person. Provide a corrective action that is doable. For example, you might say, "You need to use your bifocal consciousness and understand how both the field and headquarters perceive this issue. I suggest you set up some interviews to talk with the field supervisors this week and redo the report to include their input." This feedback focuses on the problem, which was a failure to include the field. It offers doable action for improvement. In contrast, consider this statement: "You have no clue about how to map the territory! Come on, get this report done right and do it quickly!" This feedback merely blames the person and gives no meaningful direction on what needs to be done differently.

Appraise continuously by making assessment and evaluation ongoing. Silence is not golden when it comes to developing people as leaders. No news is not good news. The value of continuous appraisal is so obvious in other fields. For example, consider any sport. The players always know the score, which helps them adjust and direct their performance. Players also know where they are in the game. They know how much time is left in a basketball and football game. They know the inning in baseball, the set in tennis, and the hole being played in golf. Be the scoreboard and time clock in your development efforts. For example, offer constructive and meaningful assessment every time you interact with those you want to develop. Effective appraisal blends into daily activities rather than stands out as distinct. Keep a continuous watchful, but not oppressive, eye on action. Comment on useful actions and those that need improvement.

Offer updates on outcomes whenever possible. Once again think about the methods used in sports. Football teams call huddles after every play. Other sports have frequent, short time-outs to direct and improve player action. My experience suggests those who appraise continuously create a positive desire in others to get feedback. Ongoing assessment and evaluation motivates people to readily accept positive praise. It also helps people be more open to corrective feedback since such feedback is part of the effortless and spontaneous (that is, "natural") part of the leader's actions to develop them.

Include others in your appraisal efforts. Gather feedback from all sources. Take the lead to institute a 360-degree feedback process in your organization. Such instruments provide a person with feedback from the boss, key coworkers, and subordinates. Many established instruments exist. Contact the American Management Association for choices.[2]

Take your development efforts full course. Lead up to ensure that the praise you offer for positive development gets recognized within the formal organizational evaluation system.

64. Empower for Results

Developing others ultimately demands they be empowered. Empowerment involves three elements:

1. People are empowered when they have the opportunity to identify problems, issues, or concerns.
2. Empowered people have the freedom to define solutions or courses of action in response to problems, issues, or concerns.
3. Empowered people have the authority to implement their solutions or courses of action.

Empowerment is not a license to do whatever someone wants. A sixteen-year-old with $500, a fifth of scotch, and the keys to your car is empowered. The teenager is also dangerous. Empowerment means a person is given freedom to act and the person has the ability to act responsibly.

Empower people by giving them the opportunity to demonstrate they have the ability to identify, define, and implement solutions to solve problems. Give people the chance. They can surprise you. They can achieve levels of excellence. People can learn from their experience, which means they need to have experiences that teach them something.

Review the competence of those you are developing as leaders. Empower them in accordance with where they are now. Offer only small degrees of empowerment when competence is very low. Focus on coaching such people to develop their skills. Allow some degree of empowerment when skills are still formative. Let the empowerment roll out slowly.

When you provide a higher degree of empowerment to some people, include the provision that they let you know their progress after each stage in the process. Ask for a review after a person has identified a problem. Offer your input where appropriate. Get feedback after a person has determined solutions and provide your input again. Review the suggested implementation plan as it unfolds. Fully empower those who demonstrate enough competence to take on the entire process. Enjoy the result of their success. Praise and coach them to the next level of their leadership development. Offer refinements when necessary.

Consider the person's level of confidence also. A person may have the competence to be fully empowered but may lack the confidence to take on the entire process. You can serve in a support role to build confidence when needed.

Empower people with an understanding about the value of "failure" in development. For most people, the experiences that really teach are the "failures." Failure simply means action that does not lead to the results people want. Keep an eye on failures as you provide people with greater degrees of empowerment. Seize these moments as positive instances for learning.

65. Teach Situational Wisdom in the Action Continuum

We label some natural born leaders because they have the wisdom to know when and how to take leadership action. Developing others as leaders includes helping them develop this situational awareness. Exceptional leaders develop others to recognize the action continuum. It includes proactive, reactive, inactive, and coactive responses.

♦ *Proactive responses.* The proactive response is most commonly associated with leading. Many situations require assertive, forward-focused action. Develop the wisdom to recognize such action with examples that call for a proactive response. Explain the variables and cues you use to identify the need to be proactive. Use your recognize trends skill (skill 39).

♦ *Reactive responses.* Leaders also operate in situations that call for a reactive response. Consider a situation that requires a "wait and be ready to act" response. A government regulation may be passed in a few months or a new technology may be approved for use in the near future. Some situations also simply come as a surprise. No matter how much planning and analysis the leader does, something unexpected can come up. The reactive response represents the only possible choice. Develop the wisdom to recognize the value and need for a reactive response with examples from your experience. Differentiate between procrastination and reaction. Those who procrastinate should act but simply delay. Clarify the differences between appropriate reaction and procrastination.

♦ *Inactive responses.* An inactive response—when you do nothing—may be appropriate also. Consider a situation where resources are limited and no viable action choice exists. Use of scarce resources might simply waste them. Or think about operating in a short-term chaotic change environment. With the landscape constantly being altered, any choice may prove wrong. Any response may be useless until more information can be known. Holding back makes sense when action can only be taken as a blind shot. Offer examples that demonstrate when not doing anything served you and the organization.

♦ *Coactive responses.* Leaders also live in situations that require coaction. Such circumstances involve a combined effort or partnership with others. Consider the AOL–Time Warner merger. America Online head Steve Case realized he needed a source of "content," such as movies and publications, to take AOL to the next level as an information-entertainment provider. Time Warner chief Gerald Levin knew he did not have access to the Internet, which he realized would only continue to grow as a distribution method for information and entertainment.

The decision to be proactive, reactive, inactive, or coactive cannot be prescribed in a formula or model. That is why it requires wisdom. Help others develop this skill with stories and examples. Engage them in discussions about the ups and downs of each choice. Review positive and negative results of key business decisions to help "season" others. Use examples when a wrong choice was made to develop situational wisdom. The well-known story of how Bill Gates offered to sell the MS-DOS operating system to IBM Corp. for $75,000 demonstrates the liability of an inactive choice. IBM refused Gates's offer; instead, he ended up accepting a small licensing fee for every IBM computer that used his system. Gates got rich, Microsoft took over as the PC software standard, and IBM was left in the dust.

66. Push Constant Preparation

The will to win is important, but the will to prepare is vital.
—Joe Paterno, Penn State football coach

People may fail in their efforts to lead. No one is immune to missteps or flubs. However, exceptional leaders know that there is no excuse for someone to underestimate the leadership challenge. There is no excuse not to prepare effectively. The best leaders develop others by focusing them on constant preparation.

Direct people to continually prepare by helping them develop their skills in mapping the territory and identifying the need to lead (see Chapter 6). Coach them on how to go into the GAP and "gain another perspective" (skill 36) so they can recognize leadership issues. Encourage them to work like Walton (skill 37) so they make gathering information from multiple sources a part of their normal routine. Remind people that preparation requires the use of bifocal consciousness (skill 38) so they continuously appraise both the local/immediate and the global/long-term issues. Test their capacity to recognize trends (skill 39) so they enhance their awareness of important patterns that affect leadership action. Consider where each person stands on all these skills and push them to constantly prepare their skills in these areas.

Push for constant preparation regarding the foundational skills. Help people understand where they may be one skill away from success. Focus their efforts for ongoing preparation on that skill until they master it.

When preaching constant preparation you must move the mind and spirit. Coach people to think about preparation by making it exciting, important, and urgent. Great athletes love to play and they love to prepare to play. Some people think about preparation only when a challenge falls upon them. Often that means it is too late. Direct people to consider how they could specifically be better prepared to improve their opportunity to succeed. Ask people to think about how preparation helps them achieve what the organization expects, what customers value, and what it really means to lead effectively. A clear mental connection must exist between the value in preparing and the enjoyment of playing and achieving success.

67. Use Diversity as a Strength

Master leaders know that differences make a difference. They recognize the variety of factors that define diversity. Race, age, gender, lifestyle, and religion represent the obvious forms of people's differences. People also have different biases, motivations, knowledge, abilities, and performance capacities. Diversity demands that people be treated differently. People are not in effect "equal" in the sense that they are duplicates or uniform. Skillful leaders provide equitable treatment versus equal treatment. They respond to others in reasonable and just ways. They treat people as they deserve to be treated: fairly and in an equitable manner as opposed to the same or identical.

Review the rapport building (Chapter 4) and expectation clarification (Chapter 5) skills. Equitable treatment requires genuine relationships and clear and agreed-on expectations about differences that make a difference at work. If necessary, increase your focus on these skills where diversity is an issue. Realize that in a society of multiple cultures, multiple motives are acceptable. Find out what people want and expect and find a way to give it to them or clarify why they cannot have it.

Seek out the assets in each person. Focus on how and where each person adds value instead of focusing on differences in that person. Jesse Jackson once said, "Our flag is red, white, and blue, but our nation is rainbow. Red, yellow, brown, black, and white. We are all precious in God's sight." Find that precious place in everyone.

Ask others how they perceive their differences as adding value. Part of our difficulty working with people who are different is that we do not know how to respond to them. We are unaware of what strengths they bring because they are not like us. Discuss the range of challenges you recognize from applying your mapping the territory skills. Ask diverse others to define their map of issues and concerns. Identify how their map improves yours. Ask them how they can make a unique contribution to meeting leadership challenges.

Lead up to convince senior management to address diversity. Clarify to senior management that diversity is a business issue. The ever-increasing numbers of diverse people in the workforce demand that organizations find ways to attract, embrace, and retain them. Influence upper management to conduct a "diversity audit." This process explores when and how people are disadvantaged or advantaged on nonwork or non-performance-related standards such as age or tenure. Point out instances where the organization fails to consider or value points of view from diverse others. Create open forums to discuss the results of the audit with others. Use the results to chart a correction course for the organization. Include diverse people in your development of these action choices. Focus on eliminating the nonwork, non-performance-related factors that advantage and disadvantage people. Identify ways to create more equitable treatment for all. Reward those who use and value diversity as a strength in their performance appraisals so that these skills are reinforced.

Recognize also that at some deep level people are unified. A "diverse" group may have needs quite similar to those in the dominant majority. Minorities want inclusion, encouragement, and opportunity. These needs exist in most people.[3]

Focus on your own ability to transcend potential prejudices. Educate yourself about different cultures, lifestyles, and preferences. Partner with a person different from yourself. Learn from that person and teach each other about your differences. When you recognize a difference with another, explore that individual's point of view to fully understand it. Avoid the tendency to force diverse others to justify their point of view. Making the effort to understand someone else's point of view helps build rapport and enables you to guide their improvement in a more constructive way.

Remind yourself that equitable treatment transcends perceiving differences as wrong. Confront your own biases when you fall below this standard. Use your ability to sense possibilities (skill 43). Ask yourself, "If this difference was a strength, how could it be used?" or, "In what ways is this difference actually an advantage now?"

68. Differentiate between Can't and Don't

Exceptional leaders recognize that people can doubt themselves, get discouraged, or lose their desire. People may not believe that they can achieve certain results or that specific outcomes are possible. These beliefs limit people's ability to develop their leadership capacity.

Confront the "can't" mentality. Clarify where "can't" actually refers to a skill, resource, or belief deficiency. Apply the "tell" and "show" coaching behaviors, listed earlier in this chapter, to improve skills. Uncover where "can't" exists in resource constraints. For example, a sales group that believes it can't move into a new market may be using data or operating on assumptions that are no longer valid. Apply your skills for mapping the territory (Chapter 6) to help the salespeople recognize that what they can do is being obscured by their "can't" thinking. Demonstrate how and when they have the necessary resources. If necessary, lead up to acquire those resources that actually are unavailable to them.

Expose the belief-based source of the "can't" response. Apply the fact-based thinking skill (skill 27) to help overcome fear-based beliefs. Apply the action-results connection skill (skill 32) to provide clear images of behavior and results that demonstrate possibilities. Display unsinkable optimism (skill 33) to move people beyond their specific belief-based responses that tell them they can't do something. Your optimism models a "can do" attitude. Use the "confidence builder" coaching behavior to overcome limiting "can't" beliefs.

Similarly, you want to address head-on the "don't" response. The fact that people do or don't reflects will. They may be able, but they simply do not take action. Clarify expectations to understand their lack of will. Ask people to explain why they don't take action; ask for specifics. Revitalize people's awareness of core identity, vision, mission, and values to determine if their "don't" response reflects a lack of clarity about overall purpose. Use the name the game skill (skill 28) and make it clear that the "don't" response is no longer an acceptable expectation.

Move people past their can't and don't beliefs by using real-world models. Recall how Winston Churchill convinced the citizens of Great Britain that they could still win the war over Germany despite the darkest days the British people had experienced. Tell the story about how Franklin Roosevelt gave America the sense it could climb out of the Depression and had "nothing to fear but fear itself." Remind people how Lee Iacocca drove Chrysler back on the road to success with his "can do" approach.

69. Be an M&M: Model and Motivate Excellence

The best leaders develop others by modeling mastery. People always look to the leaders to set the example. People gauge their own actions in comparison to the leader's action. Exceptional leaders live the ideals they espouse to develop others. They motivate others through their example.

Model and motivate people every day. Model the behaviors you want people to develop. Let people see you applying the skills to build rapport. Visibly demonstrate your commitment to establish clear expectations. Make mapping the territory skills so obvious that people cannot help but notice. Illustrate how you can chart the course (Chapter 7) in ways that signify how such skills define what it means to be labeled a natural born leader. Your overt model will motivate many to step up. Enhance the motivational impact of your model with direct, face-to-face encouragement and reinforcement when others demonstrate their motivation to develop the 108 skills of natural born leaders.

70. Pace the Marathon Race

Developing others as leaders compares to running a marathon race. The best runners set up at the starting line. The many other runners line up in rows each further and further behind the line. In some races with thousands of runners, the last row of runners can be as far as a mile behind the starting line. When the gun sounds to begin the race, the first rows of runners race past the starting line. Those at the back of the pack may not even cross the starting line for up to ten minutes. Exceptional leaders pace the marathon race to develop others as leaders. They recognize that some may take longer than others to even begin effective mastery of their skills.

Consider where people stand in relation to specific skills based on your appraisal efforts. Set winning as the standard to motivate others toward achieving their best. Apply your expectation clarification skills to set agreed-on standards that people need to meet to stay in the race. Coach and train people on how to move ahead. Clarify the need for preparation for each mile in the race. Accept that some people will not finish the race because of lack of will or an inability to master certain skill excellence.

Commit to the entire race. Work with others to bring them to the starting line and keep them moving across. Encourage those who can quickly sprint across the line. Take the time with those who move with a more measured pace. Remind people that leader development ultimately occurs as a marathon run over a lifetime. An old saying states, "Go the extra mile. It is never crowded."

71. Be First Follower Ready

The traditional view of leadership causes many development efforts to overlook a key method to enhance leader capacity. In *The Nine Natural Laws of Leadership,* I clarify that to be a leader requires gaining willing followers. Followers represent the leader's allies; their willing support actually "makes" the leader. This insight offers another critical method to develop leaders: Be a willing follower for those you want to develop.[4]

Exceptional leaders multiply themselves with their willing support for others who provide appropriate leadership direction. I will guess this is part of your experience. Think of the best boss you ever had. Did he or she frequently and willingly follow your lead? Did that action motivate, reinforce, and inspire you to want to develop your leader skills?

Practice first follower readiness by looking for opportunities when you can visibly support another's direction. Consider a meeting in which a rising star you have been coaching charts a course in response to a challenge facing the group. Seize this moment to say something like, "I think it's a great idea. I'm behind it!" This simple statement verifies the person's direction as credible. It offers the person concrete evidence of forward movement toward becoming a more effective leader. Lee Iacocca demonstrated first follower readiness during his tenure at Ford Motor Company. A manager who worked a few levels below him in the Ford hierarchy once told me how Iacocca always tried to surround himself with people smarter than he was. Iacocca was always ready to willingly follow those with good ideas. In fact, both the Chrysler Minivan and Ford Mustang, vehicles that made Iacocca famous and successful, were actually the brainchild of Hal Sperlich. Iacocca was Sperlich's first follower.

72. Lead Up to Formalize Leader Development

Your efforts to develop others as leaders will be greatly enhanced if you can get organizational support for the effort. The best leaders influence their organization to make ongoing leadership development a formal performance standard for the organization.

Nikki Tinsley of the U.S. Environmental Protection Agency Office of the Inspector General took the lead to make this happen. As part of the larger transformation of her organization, she instituted continuous learning as a key performance standard. The GE and McKinsey "CEO machines" have institutionalized ongoing formal leadership training as fundamental roots to their cultures.

Consider who in upper management you need to influence to make your leader development effort a required aspect of work. Use the skills in the next chapters to gain their commitment to this leader direction.

Endnotes

1. Geoffrey Colvin, "CEO Super Bowl," *Fortune* (August 2, 1999), p. 238.
2. American Management Association, 1601 Broadway, New York, NY 10019, www.amanet.org.
3. Stephanie N. Mehta, "What Minority Employees Really Want," *Fortune* (July 10, 2000), pp. 181–200.
4. Warren Blank, *The Nine Natural Laws of Leadership* (New York: AMACOM, 1995).

III

LEADERSHIP INFLUENCE SKILLS

9

Build the Base to Gain Commitment

The capacity to gain willing followers at any moment in time often depends on what has occurred up to that moment. Followers attach to those who have an established base of credibility and power. In 2000, Jeffrey Immlet landed the CEO position at General Electric because of his success as head of GE Medical Systems. In contrast, Jill Barad, the feisty former CEO of Mattel Inc., lost the support of many by making ambitious promises for growth and then failing to deliver.

Followers commit to those already close to them and with whom they have an established alliance. Recall the comment by Rudy, one of the summer 2000 participants in the television show *Survivor,* during the final vote. He supported Richard "because we had an alliance, and I am going to honor it." Followers also offer their support to those who have supported them. Groups of voters, such as a union, commit in blocks to candidates who have demonstrated concern for their particular needs.

Exceptional leaders build their commitment base with every action they take. Followers observe the leader's model and use it to gauge their return commitment of support. The head of a large hospital spent several hours each week walking through the hallways, talking to staff, and meeting patients. He learned each of the 1,400 staff members' names and would give them a personal hello when he saw them. He would take the time to sit with nurses and support service personnel to encourage them to work together more effectively. The hospital president did not have to ask twice when he called on hospital personnel to dedicate themselves to improve customer relations or improve processes that affected patient care. Those who skillfully establish a firm base of commitment are perceived as natural born leaders.

Mastery of the skills in this section will enable you to:

♦ Create the conditions necessary to gain commitment.
♦ Enhance your credibility as a leader.
♦ Position yourself to have more influence.
♦ Maximize your flexibility and responsiveness to followers.

73. Build Credibility

Credibility means believability. Leaders become credible when followers believe in the leader and the leader's course of action. Credibility creates commitment to the leader and the leader's direction.

Some people develop instant credibility. Consider a meeting in which a new team member offers an insight or idea that rings true to all members of the group. Credibility comes immediately because the group instantly believes the idea makes sense. Imagine a group discussion about how to approach a new client. One participant suggests calling a particular person to join the meeting because that individual used to work for the client, knows all the client's top managers, and has years of successful experience attracting new clients. The person called in has immediate credibility based on his or her background and experience.

Typically credibility comes more slowly. People build their base of believability over time. They repeatedly demonstrate they can be counted on to follow through. They provide leadership direction that supports important concerns such that others say, "She's a person we can depend on."

Credibility can also erode slowly or be lost quickly. Consider the gradual undoing of Lyndon Johnson over the Vietnam War. Recall Richard Nixon's decline from his impressive victory in the 1972 presidential election to his resignation over Watergate. Recall the almost instant fall from grace of Gary Hart over his marital infidelities in the 1988 presidential campaign. Think about Jeff Bezos, who catapulted to *Time* magazine's "1999 Man of the Year" because he took Amazon.com to amazing heights. By October 2000, the stock value of Amazon.com had tumbled 75 percent, raising questions about Bezos's effectiveness.

To build credibility requires knowing its secret. Credibility is subjective. Credibility comes from how *others* perceive you. To illustrate, think of the following people: Mohandas (Mahatma) Gandhi, Jim Jones (the preacher and cult leader in Guyana), Abraham Lincoln, Eleanor Roosevelt, David Koresh, Michael Milken, Alan Greenspan, Donna Karan, and Carl Icahn. Which of these individuals would you willingly follow? Your answer indicates your subjective perception of each person's credibility. Think about the list again. Every one of these people had a core of completely committed followers. In other words, each of them was perceived as credible by their followers.

You turn the key to build your credibility by first identifying the credibility markers that others use. That means you have to determine what followers believe makes a person or a course of action believable. Make a list of those you need to willingly follow your lead. Your list probably includes your boss, some key coworkers, a few important subordinates, a couple of essential customers, and other critical stakeholders. Find out what each person thinks are key credibility indicators. You can ask some people the direct question, "What makes someone credible?" With others, you may have to be somewhat indirect. Ask, "Who do you think is really reliable and can be believed? Why?" You may have to be even more indirect with some people. Ask, "Who do think is a great leader? Why?" The responses you get to these questions indicate each person's key credibility markers.

Once you know the important markers, assess yourself. How well do you measure up to the standards mentioned by each person? For example, assume your boss indicates credibility comes from an established track record of success. Review your track record. As another example, assume an important coworker feels that follow-through on tasks counts as an important credibility marker. Assess your level of follow-through on assignments.

In some cases you will not have to do much to build your credibility because you already stand out in areas important to others. Your boss may already know you have a strong track record. With other people, you may have to reinforce your credibility. For example, you may need to demonstrate task follow-through with the key coworker.

Develop your capabilities in areas where you may not be as strong. For example, assume field experience is important to a key customer and that you lack such experience. Find a way to get some meaningful time working in the field. Take on an assignment that provides you that exposure. Assume an advanced degree represents an important credibility marker for some. You may have to go back to school to gain credibility.

When I conduct leadership training sessions, I always ask the group to discuss the key credibility markers in their organization. Several factors come up frequently. They can serve as a general guide to build your credibility. People often perceive technical expertise as an important indicator of credibility. You can build this form of credibility by studying to become more expert in an area. You can also use the language associated with a technology area. Simply being able to use the correct terminology enhances credibility. Consistency also comes up as a typical credibility marker because credible people are perceived as reliable. Seek out tasks and do whatever it takes to demonstrate consistent action. Other typical credibility markers include extra effort, honesty, and a willingness to stand up for your ideals. Put forth the extra energy, be absolutely honest, and fight for your beliefs to demonstrate your credibility in each of these areas. In fact, the 108 skills in this book represent different forms of credibility typically associated with master leaders. Developing or strengthening any of these skills contributes to your overall credibility.

Ask what I call the "put up or shut up" questions. For example, ask yourself, Would others come work for me if I went to a new organization? Would others recommend that I be hired to work in their group or company? Would others want me to be on a critical project team with them? These fierce questions get right at the nub of credibility. They create the credibility crossroad sign because a yes or a no answer signals your degree of believability.

The subjective nature of credibility can create unfair standards. Think about a person with a nonmilitary background who works in a military organization. Imagine a young person just out of school assigned to a project team where everyone else has more than twenty years' experience. Both the nonmilitary and younger person may be highly motivated and competent. Yet others may rate their credibility as low, which limits their capacity to gain commitment. Obviously, such credibility standards are unfair. When you land in such situations, you do have some choices. One alternative is to build credibility in areas that offset what may be an unfair standard. For example, in one organization, a nonmilitary person identified two key markers that the military personnel felt defined credibility: the ability to analyze complex issues and the capacity to be decisive. The nonmilitary person knew she had achieved an important level of credibility when she overhead the comment, "Well, she's not military, but she can really cut through the tough problems and make a decision."

74. Establish a Core Cadre of the Committed

A core cadre of committed followers perceive their leader as credible. They have high rapport and a set of mutually agreed-on expectations. They back the leader's efforts based on established commitment. Their backing provides a strong indicator to others about the leader's worthiness. People commit more willingly to those who have an established base of loyal followers.

The core cadre of followers also serve as exponents of the leader's direction. Consider Christ's twelve disciples. They carried his message much farther and gained more converts than Christ could have alone. The core cadre preaches the leader's gospel. They will carry out the leader's direction without constant direct oversight.

Reinforce your relationships with those who already support you. Provide them with additional access and approachability. Work on building greater common ground with these individuals. Invest extra time and effort in them by developing their leader skills (Chapter 8) to demonstrate their importance of you. These efforts will solidify their commitment to you.

In some ways this skill can simply end up producing a bandwagon effect. That is, some people may jump on board merely because everyone else does, which may mean you do not really have their strong commitment. In another sense, a core cadre of the committed enhances credibility. A person must be believable if many others stand strongly in support of the person. Keep a clear head about who has truly joined your core cadre and who may be along for the ride. Work to solidify everyone's commitment and pay attention to those you know you can depend on the most.

75. Position for Power

Power positioning derives from how one operates within an organizational structure. It doesn't refer to getting a formal place in an organizational hierarchy, and it isn't dictated by the organizational chart. Although organizational appointments do provide power, formal position power represents managerial influence conferred by an organization. Leader power does not come from formal authority.

Power positioning means being central in a communication network and/or operating from a critical place in a workflow. Power positioning also includes taking on tasks that are visible, relevant, and allow flexibility. Power positioning gives you power because it increases the extent to which others depend on you.

Create power positioning by placing yourself in positions central to the flow of communication. This allows you to direct the flow of information. Volunteer to be the flipchart or whiteboard scribe in a meeting. You then decide what gets written on the board and with what words. Take on the job as "central processing unit" for information gathered for a project or discussion. You then formulate the thoughts of the entire group. Agree to answer inquiries related to important tasks. You become the person who resolves issues for others or serves as the link to others. Take the job of public representative for key issues. That allows you to become the group's spokesperson. All of these capacities give you an expanded form of power. You get to shape opinions. You decide what information goes where. You speak for the group.

Establish power positioning by taking on tasks that are critical to the workflow. Volunteer to organize the final budget numbers into a coherent package. Agree to go to a client to ensure the installation of a specific product. Your power increases with these assignments because you are directly connected to the completion of important work requirements. Develop expertise for tasks that no one else can perform very well. For example, many people find it difficult to handle angry customers. You will gain power if you are the only one who can calm upset customers. Many people are frustrated by poorly run meetings. You increase your power by being an effective meeting manager. Others will seek you out when they experience difficulties in these areas. That means you have a broader base of power.

Take on tasks that are visible, relevant, and have more flexibility to increase your position power. Visible tasks are those that allow you direct access to others in important roles in the organization. Take on tasks that provide face-time with important people in your organization. You become the subject of attention, which gives you a form of power. Relevant tasks are those essential to accomplish key organizational objectives. Relevant tasks are the high-priority strategic jobs that allow the organization to achieve competitive advantage in dominant areas. Such tasks include a project to enter a new, critically important market or a new process that everyone in the company feels is essential to success. Working on such tasks provides power because of the task's distinctive importance to company or unit success. Flexible tasks have few rules or established procedures. Such tasks give you power because you determine how you want to operate and the actions to be taken.

Power positioning must be balanced against the possibility of burnout. Power positioning demands high levels of physical, mental, and emotional energy. Watch for early-warning signs of burnout: irritability, a lack of clear thinking, an inability to sleep or even relax, poor digestion, or remarks from others that you seem "off." Work on achieving success over stress (skill 3) to maintain the necessary balance.

76. Share the Power

Power has a paradoxical property. It increases to the extent that leaders share it with others. The best leaders know they build their commitment base by allowing others to have power. The more a leader allows participation, the more the leader's power gets magnified. The mechanics of this process are quite simple. When a leader allows others to have power, that means people are dependent on the leader for it. Power sharing also increases the leader's base because it creates a sense of equity. People recognize the leader as fair. They see that the leader doesn't need to take all the glory. Equity translates into a form of credibility. Equity builds rapport. Both are formative forces of power. By sharing power, leaders also have more time for other things, which gives them more flexibility.

Share power by peeling off aspects of already-acquired power positions. For example, allow a key person to take a central communication task or a part of a relevant task after you have built your power base with that task. Involve, inform, and include specific people as much as possible. Knowledge is a key form of power, and sharing it enhances your power with others. People recognize you as an important source of information. Offer an after-hours class on how to apply any of the 108 natural born leader skills that you have already mastered. Offer a similar class on how to do your job. Let those who become your shared power students take the lead and pick up aspects of your work.

Demonstrate that you are first follower ready (skill 71). Your willingness to follow others demonstrates a willingness on your part to share power.

Of course, power sharing can be risky. Some people will deceive, connive, and abuse your willingness to share power. Calculate the gain you get from sharing power with the return you get. Consider your choices carefully. Recognize that in the long run you cannot have all the power unless you operate in a very small circle of influence. Think big to avoid the trap of hoarding power and select your power-sharing partners carefully.

77. Champion and Shield

Master leaders champion others and their work. They also shield others from the inevitable challenges and unfair criticisms that occur within organizations. Being a champion and shield builds the leader's commitment base because it reinforces rapport, fulfills followers' expectations of the leader, and creates credibility.

Take overt actions to champion others. Talk up your followers' successes to key people in your organization. Point out your followers' movement toward success. Sponsor others for assignments on key projects. Advocate others' proposals. Promote the work of others within your established sphere of influence. Broadcast examples of how others have responded to your efforts to develop them as leaders. Acknowledge others in meetings when they demonstrate the use of any of the 108 natural born leader skills.

Shield others with conspicuous support. Defend their work when unfairly mocked. Buffer them from tasks or intrusions that are inappropriate or that they will not enjoy. Protect their interests when resources are scarce. Confront those who criticize or otherwise run down those you want to shield.

Of course, use discrimination when you champion and shield others. Promoting those who do not deserve it will not reflect well upon you. Protecting others to cover up mistakes translates into a poor use of shielding skill. Apply the "appraise continuously" skill (skill 63) to give people feedback about how you perceive them and their actions. You can then honestly champion those who are committed to making progress. You can also honestly shield those who make a sincere effort to overcome a weakness.

78. Adapt to the Follower Continuum

Consider potential followers as arrayed along a continuum that includes four anchors:

- Totally committed followers
- Middle-of-the-road followers
- Convenience followers
- Herd members

Totally committed followers support a leader with unyielding determination. They go to the mat for the leader at every turn. Middle-of-the-road followers support a leader only as long as it does not demand too much for them. Convenience followers only support a leader when it is totally convenient for them. We often recognize such followers on political issues. A person running for office may support a cause not so much for its merits, but because it stands as politically popular. The polls say it matters, so the politician proclaims support for it. Convenience followers turn away quickly if some other direction better suits their cause. If a new poll suggests the voters no longer care about one issue in favor of another, a politician may flip-flop.

Convenience followers bounce like a football, this way or that, depending on the situation, issue, or mood of the time.

At the lowest end of the continuum fall the least reliable followers: the herd members. Such people simply go along with the pack. They are often not even aware of why they support a leader. You may have noticed herd members at a rally you watched on television. Sets of people wave at the cameras, jump up and down, and mouth the words, "Hi, Mom!" They attend the rally to have a good time rather than because they care about the issues. The herd can create a swell of support for a leader's direction. The herd can also rush off in a different direction without any real sense of what drives them. Herd members do not create reliable followers.

Understand and adapt to the reality of the follower continuum. Rely on your rapport building and expectation clarification skills to identify where people stand along the continuum. Focus your first and most intense efforts on those who could become totally committed. Seek to build your commitment base with middle-of-the-road followers. Do not count on them too much if you perceive tough times down a particular path. Remain very cautious toward convenience followers since they can turn quickly. Avoid investing your base-building skills in them for critical issues. Accept them into your fold with the same sense they bring to you. That is, when it is convenient, build on their support. Understand the herd psychology. Use the fact that a large herd can create a stampede for your cause, but maintain a safe distance so that the herd does not turn and trample you.

79. Wear Multiple Hats

Exceptional leaders build commitment through multiple roles. They take on the teacher role to help followers understand the realities, issues, and complexities behind a course of action. Recall the impact Ross Perot had in the early part of the 1992 presidential election when he displayed simple but powerful charts regarding the national debt. Perot captured the voting public's attention by educating them. Thomas Jefferson believed an educated public is the key to true democracy and that education was "the resource most to be relied on for ameliorating the conditions, promoting the virtue, and advancing the happiness of man."

The best leaders also wear the inspiration hat. They know how to boost people and get them to accomplish great things. Ronald Reagan was a master of this role. In the late 1970s and early 1980s, America suffered in the doldrums of a poor economy. Reagan inspired Americans with the notion that we could be great again because America was a "shining city on a hill." His optimism and unabashed patriotism reinvigorated many Americans. Skillful leaders also wear the cheerleader hat to keep followers moving along a path. Lee Iacocca used to walk through Chrysler's plants exhorting the workers to keep the production lines moving.

Master leaders also know how to demonstrate strong emotions. They know how to show anger and frustration as a way to get people's attention. Pat Riley calls this the "temporary insanity" role in his book *The Winner Within*.[1] Consider again the example of Ronald Reagan during one of the 1980 Republican primary presidential debates. At one point he angrily shouted, "I paid for this microphone!" His show of force positively impacted voters in that election.

Bob Zincke, president of the Houston-based Southwest marketing area for The Kroger Company, offers a good model for building a base for commitment because he wears different hats. Zincke regularly sits in on parts of the company's manager training programs. He often puts on his teacher hat and speaks to the managers about an issue or concern. Zincke frequently visits Kroger stores. He will step up to sack groceries during a busy period. His action inspires the young checkers and sackers to work hard at providing good customer service. Zincke also lets people know when he is not satisfied with their actions and performance. He snapped a district manager to attention with strong words about the manager's need to improve or consider employment elsewhere.

Zincke has established one of the most successful Kroger

marketing areas in the country. Senior managers from corporate headquarters have asked to "look his operation over" to figure out how he does it. His skill in donning multiple hats is not lost on his customers, either. While visiting a store, Zincke noticed a physically challenged shopper who needed help getting to her car. Zincke worked with the shopper for several minutes to get her on her way. When he returned to the store, another customer approached him. "I saw what you did," the customer remarked, "and I know who you are. You are the reason I shop at Kroger."

Work on the different roles you need to play to build your commitment base. Develop the teacher role by organizing the information from your mapping the territory skills (Chapter 6) into a coherent "lesson plan." Use the information to help others understand the need to lead that you have already discovered. Assess the energy and commitment level of potential followers to determine when and how the inspirational and cheerleader hats may be useful. Use these roles when energy levels are low and people seem to need a boost.

Use your strong show of emotion selectively and keep it brief. Bobby Knight, former Indiana University basketball coach, stands as one of the game's most successful coaches. He influenced many individual players and had a positive impact on the game as a whole. By spring 2000, however, Knight's bursts of anger and rage had caught up with him, resulting in his dismissal. Keep your shows of "temporary insanity" in check.

80. Model Commitment

Master leaders build a base of commitment by the example they set. Potential followers closely watch leaders to determine whether they should get on board.

Consider Clark Graham, president of Litton Marine Systems (LMS), an international marine navigational equipment manufacturer. Graham felt that his company's success depended on whether LMS personnel would "live the company values" and "produce results." He displayed these parameters in a four quadrant box. People who lived the values and produced results were "in the green," represented by the upper right hand quadrant. People who did not live the values and did not produce results were "in the red," the lower left hand quadrant. Those who either lived the values and did not produce results or who did not live the values and did produce results were "in the yellow," defined as the other two quadrants. Graham exhorted his people to be "in the green" in every way possible. As part of a team development program, the twenty-five top managers rated each other in terms of the four quadrants. Graham was ranked "in the green" by every manager in the group. His actions clearly demonstrated he was the arrowhead for action regarding LMS values and results.

Exceptional leaders, like Graham, model commitment. They do not dabble, sip, or taste-test. True commitment by the leader fosters commitment from followers.

Build your base of commitment by being the model you want others to be. Prove what you stand for with your every thought, word, and deed. Recognize that every action you take tells a story about your determination. Wear commitment on your sleeve. Some people may scoff at a strong display of concern or passion. Consider the source if you receive such criticism. Doubters and cynics rarely build a base of commitment or effectively lead people.

Remind yourself of this simple standard: Do you believe in your direction enough to live it completely every day no matter what the cost?

When trouble hits, as it always does, redouble your commitment. In challenging times, people test the leader's resolve to determine if they really should commit. Use the tough times to demonstrate your resolve. Consider the poor example set by one company president during a financial downturn. The firm had invested heavily in management training. The training yielded positive results in terms of financial indicators, morale, and other measurable factors. The company president had frequently stated how committed he was to the training effort. During a budget meeting, the numbers for the next quarter suggested a shortfall. A few of the managers proposed canceling the training programs to cushion the financial setback. The president agreed without much debate. The company chief's mixed message confused people regarding the importance of training.

81. Form Alliances

You broaden your base to gain commitment by forging alliances. You expand your capacity to influence others by creating a pact with key people. Allies can be called upon as advocates to directly support you. Their allegiance reinforces your efforts when you need to attract others as willing followers.

The best leaders have always relied on alliances, or coalition formation, to shore up their base. Recall the days when European heads of state married to reinforce their power. William the Conqueror married Matilda of Flanders in 1053 to forge an alliance between England and France. Presidential candidates frequently choose a running mate whose allegiance garners support from a portion of the population. John Kennedy's choice of Lyndon Johnson is perhaps the most notable example. The two men did not really like each other. Yet they recognized that together they could win the White House. The Japanese business alliance known as *keiretsu* describes an affiliation of multiple businesses that can reinforce and support each other in their quest for market success.

In 2000, the U.S. Army created a unique program called Partnership for Youth Success that aligns them with key corporations such as The Pepsi Bottling Group Inc. and General Dynamics Corp. The program offers recruits a two- to six-year military stint in which they learn traditional soldiering tasks. The Army also trains them in one of nearly 100 different fields. Soldiers are also guaranteed a job with one of the partner companies upon completion of their tour of duty. The promised pay ranges from $25 to $30 per hour plus benefits. According to *Business Week,* 130 companies are eager to align with the Army in this program. The Army benefits because it can attract more and better recruits. The companies benefit because, as Kevin

Cox, Pepsi's senior vice president for human resources, states, "There aren't many sources that can provide the volume, the quality, the level of maturity, and disciplined worker that the Army can."[2] Alliances create loyalty to you and your cause.

Think about whose support will enable you to influence others more effectively. Plot out the key alliances that will help you attract a larger group of followers. Assess how and in what ways you can form a mutually satisfactory alliance with these people. Realize that the alliance must offer both partners something of value. Furthermore, you must be able to offer people something they cannot get from some other source. A true alliance will stand despite possible challenges both parties may face.

Recognize the possible pitfalls to alliances. Alliances demand loyalty, which exists as a two-way street. People who are loyal to you expect loyalty in return. You have to uphold your end of an alliance if you form one. That requires extra effort on your part. You may also end up with no support if a supposed ally turns against you. The turncoat behavior displayed by the castaways on the TV show *Survivor* stands as a vivid illustration. Several participants agreed to support each other, then a few turned against the alliance to support only themselves. Accept that some people will create an alliance with manipulative or deceitful intent. You can only take responsibility for your own intentions when creating an alliance. Work on your rapport building skills in order to demonstrate rock-solid integrity (skill 22) and build trust (skill 23) to reinforce your own worth as an alliance partner.

Endnotes

1. Pat Riley, *The Winner Within* (New York: Berkley Publishing Group, 1994), p. 175.
2. Jennifer Merritt, "Uncle Sam Wants You—And So Does Pepsi," *BusinessWeek* (September 4, 2000), p. 52.

10

Influence Others to Willingly Follow

Master leaders influence others to commit to a particular course of action. They know followers will support their direction if the followers perceive a benefit to themselves. For example, the subject of military spending cuts arose while I worked with a group of military and civilian personnel at an Air Force base. They sincerely believed America's defense capacities had been spread too thin to meet the unique challenges created by the many small-scale conflicts that popped up throughout the globe. The participants almost unanimously agreed that their votes in the 2000 elections would go to those candidates who favored increased military funding.

The best leaders also influence others by effectively communicating their message. In one sense, leadership influence is the highest form of selling. It involves saying to followers, "This specific direction will serve you, take it." Master leaders use influence methods that create a sense of shared comprehension about their direction. Jay Sidhu, CEO of Sovereign Bancorp, Inc., has been quoted as saying, "Communication is in the mind of the recipient: You're just making noise if the other person doesn't hear you."[1] Master leaders get their message across with the language of agreement, cooperation, and true communion.

Exceptional leaders also recognize that no influence methods can guarantee followership. They know how to respond when they get resistance. They bounce back when others simply refuse to commit. They "lead up" to gain the willing support of top management so that, when necessary, they can rely on others with formal authority to direct people.

Skillful leaders influence others with their spoken words, their written words, and their actions. We label those who demonstrate the capacity to influence others to follow as natural born leaders.

Mastery of this skill will enable you to:

♦ Convince followers that your direction has merit.
♦ Present the content of your message in a compelling manner.
♦ Ensure followers understand your direction.
♦ Upgrade your influence efforts when others do not follow.
♦ Write with more impact.

82. Show Others What's in It for Them: WII-FM

Master leaders understand that followers support their direction because it meets the followers' needs. They know that effective influence depends on "tuning in" to the follower's frequency of WII-FM—What's in it for Me? The best leaders continually assess follower needs. They then look for ways to meet people at their level and lead them in the direction the leader wants them to go.

Several needs have already been identified as important to people. For example, the needs for those in the new economy culture:

1. Desire for freedom and self-direction in work
2. Purpose and contribution through work
3. Wealth creation through work

People today want to follow something that they are passionate about and that offers material benefits.[2] These needs are not new. In the 1970s, J. Richard Hackman described the needs people seek to fulfill in their work. His research indicated the importance of five key needs:[3]

1. Variety (i.e., the chance to do many different types of work)
2. Identity (i.e., a sense of personal connection to the task)
3. Significance (i.e., work that made an important contribution or difference to people and society)
4. Autonomy (i.e., the freedom to make decisions)
5. Feedback (i.e., tasks that provided information about the results of the work)

Test whether the needs above are important for your potential followers.

Tune in to your particular followers' frequency of WII-FM by talking about needs as part of your rapport building and expectation clarification skills. Ask people to describe key factors that matter to them in their jobs, their careers, and their development.

Ask people directly, "How can I meet your needs?" While I consulted with a manufacturing plant, a senior manager told me how surprised he was that some people would be more supportive if he simply spent more time on the production floor. They admired and respected the manager and wanted his personal attention. Once he understood this need, he made more frequent trips through the shop.

Provide a clear, direct connection between how following your lead helps others meet their needs. Focus on benefits, not features. For example, Robert Stevens holds the staff development-training coordinator position at The Kroger Company's Houston marketing area. Stevens saw the need for a long-term management development effort to upgrade the store and department manager skills for the 187 locations in the area. Some of the district managers (DMs) were reluctant to free up the budget for the training. Stevens clarified the extent to which

DM success was directly tied to store and department manager expertise. Using the results of a needs analysis, he showed the DMs the limitations current managers experienced. He explained how the training would overcome those limits. Stevens's comments struck the right note for the DMs and they gave him their support. Three years after starting the project, several of the DMs applauded Stevens for the positive improvements in manager performance as a result of the training.

Demonstrate how the multiple benefits of your direction meet multiple needs. Robert Stevens talked about bottom-line profits to the DMs because that was a key need. He also emphasized how the training would improve customer service, which represents a key grocery industry competitive advantage in the tough fight for shopper loyalty. Stevens also clarified that the training would impact employee turnover, which can be as high as 150 percent in the grocery industry. Turnover in the Houston Kroger area dropped more than 42 percent after the first two years of the training, which was one of the lowest turnover rates for Kroger stores throughout the United States.

Remember that WII-FM is essential because nobody has to willingly follow another. Some people will support your lead because they believe it is the right thing to do. That means they share the same values and beliefs you hold regarding a specific direction. Others must be attracted with different incentives because they can just as easily reject a leader's call for support by saying, "It's not my job." Continually ask yourself how your leadership direction can offer a meaningful incentive to attract others.

Lead up the organization and establish formal methods to determine people's needs and how well they are being met. Get senior management to conduct a yearly needs assessment. Identify the extent to which these needs are being met. Influence the top brass to create ongoing focus groups to get regular input about needs. Convince the organization heads to establish an electronic mail feedback system to identify needs.

Accept that you may not be able to meet certain follower needs. Focus on those whose needs you can meet. Some people may desire greater pay, better working conditions, or other hard resources from work. Every organization faces limits to meet such needs. Lead up the organization and try to garner whatever hard resources you can acquire to fulfill such needs. Clarify when you will not be able to meet such needs. Ask, "What else matters to you?"

83. Stay on Message

The best leaders determine the key point they want to make when trying to influence others. They stay on message and do not get distracted by alternate issues. Consider Bill Clinton. Despite the controversy surrounding Clinton, even his harshest critics agree he is a very persuasive, influential communicator. Yet his skills had to be developed. In the early days of the 1992 presidential campaign, Clinton's comments failed to connect with the voters. His penchant for long-winded answers and long-winding policy analyses obscured his message. Campaign adviser James Carville set the candidate straight. He coined the phrase "It's the economy, stupid" to clearly and succinctly communicate Clinton's key message. The statement created a key decision parameter Carville felt would distinguish Clinton from President Bush and help win the election.

Stay on message by first determining the precise, key issue behind your leadership direction. Stick to that message. Of course, the message must reflect key followers' WII-FM. Stay on that message to maximize your influence. During the first 2000 presidential debate, Al Gore consistently hammered away at how George W. Bush would provide a tax cut only for the richest 5 percent of taxpayers. Bush pounded away at his theme that he could bring Democrats and Republicans together to get things done. Recognize that staying on message also reinforces your resolve. It reveals your intense focus, which keeps followers aimed at your direction.

84. Use Precise Speech

Master leaders use language that moves people. They speak with precision and clarity. They demonstrate flawless use of vocabulary fashioned for their particular followers. They know how language shapes people and cultures. They rely on terms that have a transformational effect on listeners. They know that the right word serves as a powerful agent to prompt people at every level. They know that their choice of words reflects who they are, what they believe, and how they view the world. The best leaders influence others more effectively through accurate speech.

Pick up a thesaurus to beef up your knowledge of more precise terminology. Most people have between 2,000 and 10,000 words in their working vocabulary. The English dictionary contains more than 500,000 words. That means people only use one-half to 2 percent of the entire language available to them. Building your word base does not mean you have to become more loquacious or effusive. Precision means accurate, correct, and exact words. "We're going to make a big difference in the market this year" is a grand statement, but to say, "Sales will increase at least 20 percent this year" is a much clearer statement of the goal.

Use vivid words and phrases to more precisely convey your meaning. The word *snake* creates a less precise image than a cobra. A Corvette represents a more precise picture than a car. Marketers know that "selling fried dead chicken" won't have customers flocking to the door, but "offering crispy, delicious, twenty-one herbs and spices chicken that is finger-licking good" will.

Use transformational words and phrases to communicate the full meaning of your message. Compare these simple examples of how transformational words increase the intensity and impact of language:

Low impact	High impact
"A move into a new sales area"	"A laserlike entry into a new sales area"
"Getting customers interested"	"Captivating customers"
"Paying attention to the market"	"An intense focus on the market"

Offer your direction in the most specific terms possible. Avoid vague references such as "you know what I mean" or "some such things." Define action steps and results that can be measured. Say what you mean and give your direction a meaningful name. Get the "um," "you know," and "ah, like" utterances out of your speech. Ferret out repeated and empty word choices such as, "Well, if you ask me . . ."

Practice persuasive speech with a tape recorder. Tape a talk or conversation and notice when and how you make empty word choices or imprecise references and utterances. Practice with a speech coach if necessary to root out the ambiguous elements in your speech.

Work on grammar and syntax. "When you ain't got nothing, you got nothing to lose" makes a great line for a protest song. It can grate on potential followers and suggest you lack the ability to communicate. Use active verbs. Suppose you say, "This approach will have the effect of joining the work we do in our existing stores and our online business." Compare that statement with this one: "This approach links our instore and online business." The second statement provides a more active and precise picture. Use words such as "drives" instead of "has a driving effect" or "creates" instead of "will cause to be created."

Use of precise speech does not mean you must eliminate all slang or popular speech. In fact, precise speech often means you adopt language that defines current realities. Consider that the following words and phrases did not even exist as part of our common vocabulary in 1980: *net ready, downsizing, web-based, reengineering,* and *e-commerce.*

Precision does not mean volume, however. Shouting and yelling may help people hear you, but it rarely makes the message clearer.

85. Use Statistics, Stories, Symbols, and Metaphors

Master leaders infuse their message with statistics, stories, symbols, and metaphors. These tools ramp up the leader's message and communicate with compelling clarity a direction that influences others to follow.

Pick up any business magazine and skim through the cover story. Numbers, graphs, and other data fly off the page. Exceptional leaders know statistics allow meaningful and precise comparisons. Statistics reinforce the leader's message and verify the leader's course of action.

For example, if you were trying to influence your human resources group's willingness to hire a leadership trainer, you could cite many different statistics: U.S. employers will spend $54 billion on formal training in 2000, according to *Training* magazine's website. While 95 percent of surveyed organizations measure trainee reaction to courses, according to the 1999 American Society for Training and Development "State of the Industry" report, only 3 percent make a real effort to measure the business results of training programs.[4] Furthermore, 90 percent of trainees do not use the skills they learn in nontechnical training after six months, according to *The Learning Alliance* by Robert Brinkerhoff and Stephen Gill.[5]

Statistics satisfy the logical reasons people need to willingly follow a leader. Would you be able to influence the training group to select a particular training organization that did offer cost-effective follow-up methods to measure and reinforce training? Managers need to hear things expressed in measurable terms. For example, continuing our HR example, consider an approach to increase training application from 10 percent to 70 percent. The process includes self-directed study follow-up tools to reinforce key learning points. It includes a structured, small group, self-managed coaching system to provide analysis and practice procedures for continual skill development. A multistage trainee evaluation provided for three months beyond the training continually monitors skill application. These evaluations come from external and internal customers. The overall process costs little since documents are delivered via the company's internal e-mail. The process improves staff interaction by establishing a formal coaching structure. Customer service also improves by increased attention to customer feedback. A company that spends $500,000 on nontechnical training could enhance the application of its investment by $300,000 with this method. Do these statistics persuade you as a manager?

Statistics influence the rational left brain. Stories, however, speak to people's "soft side," or the right brain, which responds less to figures or facts and is more intuitive and creative. Stories impact the right brain and represent an age-old communication method. Their power stems from how they represent a complex idea or capture an important idea in a vivid example. In their book, *A Passion for Excellence*, Tom Peters and Nancy Austin relate how Domino's Pizza distribution never wants any of its stores to run out of pizza dough. However, the unthinkable and unacceptable did occur at one Domino's location. To demonstrate their remorse over not being able to serve their customers, the distribution manager, Jeff Smith, purchased black armbands for the distribution staff to wear. The story spread through Domino's to make Smith's action memorable.[6]

Statistics and stories combine to create a potent message. In a 1984 speech, Jesse Jackson used the David and Goliath story to describe how African-Americans and other minorities could and should play a more important role in the political process. Jackson explained how the wrathful Goliath dominated the people in his community. No one felt the behemoth could be beaten. David, armed only with a slingshot, found a rock on the ground and used it to fell the mighty giant. Jackson proclaimed that each voter represents a rock. He cited the statistic that Ronald Reagan won Massachusetts in 1980 by 20,000 votes, but 180,000 college students did not even register. "Rocks on the ground," Jackson said. He offered similar statistics about Reagan's margin of victory and how many people did not vote in one state, then another, then another. He demonstrated that Reagan's win could have been halted by the thousands of unregistered voters in each state. "Rocks," he continually repeated to revive the David image and bring the potent storyline to life.

Master leaders also influence others with the power that is packed into a symbol. Symbols serve as reminder messages of something that matters and that people instantly understand. For example, the Lincoln Memorial is a temple to the Union. It conveys Lincoln's anguish and our own. The Washington Monument symbolically defines the axis around which Washington, D.C., revolves. It evokes the singularly important role George Washington played in America's formation as a nation. The Vietnam Memorial, a wall of names cutting into the earth, acknowledges both the pain of war and nobility of sacrifice. Symbols clarify with simplicity and depth a complex message such as heroism, sacrifice, or freedom.

Whenever the president of the United States speaks to a group, the podium is adorned with the Presidential Seal. When the head of a corporation addresses key personnel, the company logo is clearly evident. These symbols are visibly displayed to communicate the speaker's importance and to tell us that we should pay attention to what the speaker says.

Simple symbols can also convey critical points. Louis Katopodis, the president of Texas-based grocery chain Fiesta Mart, Inc., placed a can of Del Monte peas on the conference table in a meeting with senior managers. Katopodis explained that every grocer could stock and sell Del Monte peas for the same price. The product offered no distinct advantage to attract customers. He explained that Fiesta's only choice was to surround the sale of peas with an enhanced customer service approach. The peas became a symbolic method to compel store and department managers to provide that higher level of service for customers.

A meaningful metaphor can also have a powerful impact. Jack Brooks, vice president of human resources at Efficient Networks, Inc., a Dallas-based communications equipment manufacturer, charted a course for a systematic leadership development process for the organization. He saw a weakness in the firm's existing approach, which he labeled as "wishin' and hopin' " based on the Dusty Springfield song title. Brooks used this metaphor to remind managers they could not develop leaders without a well-thought-out, carefully constructed training and development effort.

Consider also the compelling impact of the metaphors that *Fast Company* author Regina Fazio Maruca compiled that reflect the promise and peril of the new economy. Paul Saffo, director at the Institute for the Future, compared his role as a technology forecaster to a seismologist standing at the epicenter of the 1906 earthquake in San Francisco. Pehong Chen, founder, chairman, and CEO of Broadvision, Inc., cautions that not all companies that "leap out of the starting gate will make it to the finish line." Earthquakes and races create convincing comparisons to influence followers.[7]

Add choice statistics to make your core message more compelling. Quantify your direction with accurate data. Select valid, qualified evidence to support your view. The Web offers enormous volumes of such data. Rely on your own experience bank of key events and meaningful moments for anecdotes. Read business magazines for additional stories. Consider how you can symbolically represent your message. Can you find a can of peas or some other simple symbol that captures your idea and persuades followers? Think about your leadership direction as a metaphor for some experience or event everyone has to deal with in life. A corporate VP told me a story about vacationing in the more remote regions of Kauai. "We found some of the greatest spots to swim, but we had to drive to the end of the road to find them," she explained. Can you use this as a metaphor that explains the need to go as far as possible to achieve a specific outcome?

86. Build the Message

Exceptional leaders build the content of their message to present it in a more compelling manner. They recognize that follower comprehension of their direction develops in stages.

Build your message with information that moves from the simple and familiar to the more complex and less familiar. For example, saying "We need to improve our website to make it more user-friendly" defines a leader's direction in simple and familiar terms. The leader would then go into a more complex description of how and why this improvement is possible and necessary and would identify less familiar components, such as a new software package and how to use it, that are vital for achieving the end result the leader wants.

Think through the content of your leadership direction. Identify the most simple and familiar words and phrases that describe the purpose or bottom-line outcome of your course of action. Present evidence and examples to flesh out the more complex and less familiar territory you want people to accept.

Build from simple and familiar to establish points of agreement. Recall that willing followers must be committed, not simply convinced. Agreement points give followers time to warm up to your viewpoint. Simple-familiar to complex-unfamiliar also works because it explains how people learn. That is, comprehension comes by building on what people already know and accept.

Build your message by repeating key refrains. Recall how the repetition of "I have a dream," in Martin Luther King's famous March on Washington speech, catalyzed the crowd. Remember Ronald Reagan's effective use of "There you go again" when debating Jimmy Carter in the 1980 presidential race. Jesse Jackson used the word "rocks" each time he offered another statistic about how many people did not vote in the 1980 election. Develop a number of phrases and sentences to use as answers to questions such as: What is special about my direction? What do people get as a result of following my lead? Repeat the phrases you develop to reinforce your message.

Use contrasting phrases to build your message. John F. Kennedy brilliantly applied this method with statements such as, "We shall never negotiate out of fear, and we shall never fear to negotiate." Franklin Roosevelt's "We have nothing to fear but fear itself" also demonstrates this skill. Consider the enhanced impact of the statement, "We need to improve our website to make it more user-friendly," when it becomes "Web-friendly sites make friendly web customers."

Use a timeline to build your message. Consider John F. Kennedy's speech at the Berlin Wall in 1963. He drew a timeline from the past to the present and into the future. He told the crowd that in the days of the Roman Empire, the "proudest boast" one could make was to be from Rome. He then told them how they, the citizens of Berlin, could proudly today stand as the pioneers in the fight against communism. In the future, he argued, history would look back on those in the audience as the defenders of freedom who outlasted Communist oppression.

Create a bridge of personal connection between yourself and followers. Kennedy used this technique in Berlin also. He said, "All free men, wherever they may live, are citizens of Berlin. So as a free man, I take pride in the words, 'Ich bin ein Berliner.' " Kennedy conveyed that he was a man of Berlin, just like them.

Recognize that the order in which people are given information determines how they think. Frank Luntz, a Republican pollster, first uncovered this fact while working for Ross Perot's 1992 presidential campaign. Luntz conducted a Detroit focus group test of three Perot television ads. Perot was unstoppably popular at that time; however, the focus group members indicated they did not like him. Luntz learned this by accident. He intended to show ads of a Perot biography, a Perot speech, and testimonials from other people about Perot. He inadvertently ran the ads in the reverse order: testimonials, speech, biography. The focus group saw Perot's opinions as extreme when his ideas were not presented with the biography first, which outlined his impressive rags-to-riches life story. Luntz's findings[8] indicate that if your message produces a strong opinion, no subsequent information will get people to change their minds. Build your message to ensure you first stake out the key factor you want to resonate in the followers' minds.

You can also build your message by using the fact that people remember the beginning and the end of a message. The middle gets muddled for most people. Build your message with several beginnings and endings. Chunk your message into parts. Start and end each part in a definitive manner. Phrases such as "Let me make another important point" signal to the listener that something new is coming. Conclude by saying, "This is an important issue."

The best leaders also build their message with emotion. They pull emotional levers that influence followers. They know people need more than the simple logic. Your course of action may meet important business needs such as increased profits, improved service, or reduced turnover, but you need to add the emotional hook to influence others. Instead of only putting more profits in front of followers, present your idea by adding, "We will be the company Wall Street cries to own." In addition to stating that your direction improves customer service, add, "We are going to serve people in ways that cause them to love us!"

Present the "feeling" your direction provides. Add the element of intense passion. Demonstrate a level of oratory excellence and inspired rhetoric to take your message far above the nonspecific, bland, and sometimes unintelligible comments given by many about their vision or where they stand on certain issues.

Address key emotional forces that speak to how people want to be treated at work. People want to feel that they are in on things and fully appreciated for their work participation and results, and they like sympathy for personal problems. These factors represent "soft" incentives that influence action. Demonstrate how following your lead will meet these needs. Translate your direction into an emotional appeal that strikes that inner chord followers frequently seek.

Vary your message between feelings and the cold facts. "This course of action will reduce 99.99 percent of accidents" makes a solid case. Consider the additional genuine emotion reflected in the statement, "We will all sleep much better at night knowing we work in a safe environment." Facts provide information that people logically analyze before they follow. Emotion provides the internal interpretation people use to get comfortable with a course of action.

87. Communicate Confidence, Conviction, and Enthusiasm

Followers believe leaders who believe in themselves and their direction. Exceptional leaders communicate with confidence, conviction, and enthusiasm to inspire others. People sense when someone seems committed. Some people can fake this commitment, but most of us are not very good actors. The best leaders believe their leadership direction will create the results they say it will. Their heart tells them that their course of action will benefit followers. They uplift others to recognize and accept those benefits.

Recognize that faking it is not the answer to mastery of this skill. Review the skills for gaining self-awareness in Chapter 3 to reaffirm your own sense of self. Realize that you may not be as bubbly or gregarious as some other people. Recall Al Gore's statement, "I may not be the most exciting politician," at his Democratic convention acceptance speech. He acknowledged his style and he expressed his confidence, conviction, and enthusiasm within his comfort range. His standings in the polls changed from 19 points behind Bush to 9 points ahead after that speech.

Realize that followers will not be more excited about your direction than you are. Ambivalence creates ambivalence. Ratchet up the level of passion and concern in your message. Always consider the specific audience. Remember the adage, "Don't whisper to the deaf or wink at the blind."

I have worked with many law enforcement organizations. Their members work in tough situations and face criticism and even physical danger every day. When I've conducted training for such groups, they typically begin in a very cautious mode. They need to look me over. They must make sure I am safe. Communicating in an overly animated or exuberant way does not win over such groups. However, I have great success when I start them from a comfortable place that is just a notch above their existing energy level. I increase my intensity slowly and move them up one level at a time. Their overt response at the end of a seminar rarely turns into the wild cheering that occurs when I'm talking to a sales group. Yet many of these very serious people who do very difficult work shake my hand at the end of the day and make comments such as, "This was the best program I ever attended. You really inspired me." Everyone enjoys being moved into that place. You set this tone with your confidence, conviction, and enthusiasm.

Realize that this aspect of influence should show you at your best and help followers know how they can become their best. According to media expert Roger Ailes, television has changed the rules and impact of communication. In his book, *You Are the Message*, Ailes argues that people expect to be made comfortable in every communication situation.[9] Leaders have to communicate in ways that allow people to relax and listen just like they do when watching TV professionals who entertain people while they sit in their living room. Leaders have to appear just as comfortable, knowledgeable, and to the point as our nightly news anchors. Recall the easy manner of Dan Rather or Peter Jennings. Leaders need to create the same feeling created by a good talk show host. Picture Jay Leno or Johnny Carson comfortably chatting with a guest. The relaxed, informal, crisp, and entertaining personalities we continually watch on television are the modern standard for effective, persuasive communicators.

Use the communication techniques that work on television. Be brief. Pay attention to pacing. Use visual reinforcements and colorful language. Ailes labels such language as the "headline society" phenomenon. Long-winded will not work. Punchy and graphic does.

88. Speak the Follower's Language

Master leaders ensure that followers understand their direction by presenting it in the followers' particular language or the way followers process information. Skillful leaders know they cannot influence everyone with the same message. They adjust their message in terms of how followers make sense of information. This skill does not address the content of your direction. It involves your flexibility to alter your message while maintaining its meaning. It focuses on how you present the message to followers.

Speak the follower's language in terms of three key components:

+ The technical language of the follower's discipline (also known as jargon)
+ The follower's preferred method for processing information
+ The values followers hold as important

Speak the follower's technical language. For example, describe the financial aspects of your direction when trying to influence finance people. Discuss the impact on production efficiency when trying to influence manufacturing types. Present the legal implications when trying to influence attorneys to follow your lead. Recall the need to build credibility (skill 73), which involves using the unique terminology associated with particular fields. You also speak the follower's language when you use jargon familiar to followers.

Speak to followers bearing in mind that people have modes or codes for understanding and interpreting information based on their specific information-processing method or code, just as a computer code defines the rules to process information. For example, some people focus on details while others care only about the generalities or bottom-line implications. Offer lots of details to those who like the nitty-gritty. Give a broad overview to those who only want the bottom-line essentials.

Some people prefer visual information, so it is useful to literally use a graphic illustration or draw a picture with your words. For example, "I don't see it as useful right now. Your idea is a bit hazy to me." The comment clearly reveals a visual person because of the use of the words *see* and *hazy*. Restate your direction using more visual details. Draw the person a picture to show what you want the person to see. Similarly, some people respond to action-feeling information, so use words and phrases such as "get a handle on it" or "drive this point home." Speak to followers who need to "hear" your direction by using words or phrases such as "ring a bell" or "say and listen."

Carefully craft your message to match the follower's pre-

ferred method of processing information when you get an ob-
jection to your direction. If some people object on the basis of
details, say, "Let me fill in all the specifics for you." If they seem
to reject the overall direction, their preferences probably tend
toward generalities, in which case you might suggest, "Maybe I
have not really explained the bottom line." Use a variety of
words to appeal to people's visual, action-feeling, or auditory
responses.

If you have traveled abroad you have probably noticed that
you quickly pick up the need to use the home country language. People's information-processing preferences represent a
subtler form of language that is just as important. Using this
subtle language increases your capacity to influence others to
follow just as much as your ability to say, "Wo xiang yao bei
shui," when you want someone to give you a glass of water in
China.

Speak the follower's language in terms of the values followers hold as important. Values define the follower's decision
rules regarding what they believe is good or bad, right or wrong,
important or unimportant. Present your direction so it directly
demonstrates a match with the follower's value dimensions. Reinforce key values you know followers hold dear. For example,
consider the values of stability and personal responsibility. State
how your direction matches these values. Al Gore used this approach when talking about Social Security reform in the 2000
presidential election. Gore presented his plan as one that would
give Americans a choice that would ensure the safety of their
money. He labeled his opponent's ideas as "risky."

Of course, you have to know your audience to speak the
follower's language. Rely on your rapport building and expectation clarification skills (Chapters 4 and 5) to gather this information. Ask people to give you a general sense of their preferred
information-processing methods and values in various fields. I
find engineers prefer details and visual information. Pay close
attention to cues people give in response to your direction, then
adjust your message accordingly to speak their language. For
example, when trying to influence a person who works in the
R&D function, use the technical language and jargon of R&D.

Talk about the "hypothesis" behind your direction. Mention how your direction offers a better quality approach. Suggest to R&D types that your direction is an "experiment" that needs to be tested.

89. Communicate with Congruence

Exceptional leaders have more influence because every aspect of their message resonates as a coherent, unified complement to every other part of the message. They know they have about eight seconds to connect with their listeners because people only take that long to decide whether a particular speaker is worth their time. They also understand they have about thirty seconds to maintain their listeners' attention. Congruent communication enhances the leader's ability to meet those difficult demands.

Match your choice of words, tone, and nonverbal signals to demonstrate congruence. For example, consider the statement, "We must take a serious step to meet the difficult challenge we now face." This statement demands a somewhat solemn tone. The congruent speaker would have a concerned look on his or her face.

Nonverbal signals communicate important messages as well. Dacher Keltner, psychology professor at the University of California–Berkeley, analyzed the facial expressions of Al Gore and George Bush during the 2000 presidential race. According to Keltner, Bush communicates mockery, contempt, and disdain with the upside-down smile in which he raises his lips while tightening the corners. Gore communicates concentration, focus on problems, and dominance by turning his eyebrows down. Bush suggests playfulness by funneling his lips. Gore expresses inhibition and constraint by pressing and pursing his lips. Keltner concludes that both men communicate mixed messages rather than a congruence with such nonverbal signals.[10]

Develop your congruent communication skills by asking trusted allies to assess your effort to influence them on a particular issue. Ask the allies to assess the extent to which your words, tone, and nonverbal signals form a coherent message.

Videotape yourself and watch your facial expressions and gestures. Observe whether you frown when the meaning of the words actually calls for a more open face. Recognize that a closed-face expression often communicates a lack of belief on the speaker's part. An open-faced expression communicates enthusiasm and optimism.

Smile sincerely and smile more. A smile begins in the brain, then comes out on the face. A sincere smile communicates openness, honesty, and a relaxed, inviting pose. Think of a smile as an identity creator. The word *smile* looks like "simile," which is a comparison, analogy, or metaphor. Use your smile to create that identity between yourself and your followers. Your smile and other nonverbal expressions link with followers by communicating the message that "We are compatible. My idea is just like yours. You and I are alike." This creates acceptance of you and your idea. Consider ways you can show more genuine and appropriate emotion on your face when you speak about something that really matters.

Pantomime gestures in front of the mirror to get comfortable with moving your hands and arms. Watch television newscasters with the sound off to observe the very effective ways they use a variety of nonverbal tactics to communicate with congruence. Eliminate gestures such as shaking your finger because they push people away by communicating a condescending message.

Listen to your tone to enrich your vocal variety. Assess the level of "music" in your voice. That is, listen for whether your tone moves up and down or stays flat. You can improve tonal quality by humming your words a few times to get a sense of when and where to add inflection.

Practice making your first eight seconds memorable. Punch up your presentation with something meaningful in the first eight seconds. Use a short anecdote. Provide a relevant statistic. Make an emotionally charged statement.

Improve your eye contact to let people know you are speaking to them. Avoid a nonblinking stare when talking one-on-one. Pan the audience when talking to a group and let your eyes connect for a few seconds with individuals. Give a few more seconds to those who give a visible sign of recognition such as a head nod or positive facial gesture. Your extra focus communicates, "I am with you, too," in response to their acknowledgment of you.

Your posture is also important and can support the message. Everyone knows it is important to stand up straight. Go to the next level and position your body to match the message. Push your chest out, move your shoulders back, and lift your head up when describing a positive future possibility. Lean forward toward your audience when you want to express concern and that you can relate to them. Recall how stiffly George Bush sat on his chair during the town meeting debate in the 1992 presidential campaign. Remember how easily Bill Clinton walked up to the audience to draw the crowd toward him. Both Al Gore and George W. Bush learned from Clinton and used this technique during their 2000 town meeting debate.

Let care, interest, and attention mark your message to make it congruent. Accept that leaders in today's media-intensive world are broadcaster masters. They offer their message, use a method, and reflect themselves in a congruent manner. What they say, how they adapt to the audience and situation, and who they are come across as a "natural package." Everything fits together, reinforces, and corroborates everything else.

Some complain that attempts to develop this skill mean they have to be actors. Roger Ailes, the very effective speaking coach, offers an important perspective in response. He believes the most effective communicators play themselves. They communicate with total congruence by saying words with a tone and nonverbals that really represent who they are. Ailes argues that Ronald Reagan's true greatness as a communicator was that Reagan simply presented information as Reagan.[11] Ailes believes acting isn't necessary if you are communicating your own ideas, beliefs, values, and passionate concern. Congruent communication depicts you at your best. Play yourself, not some part.

90. Reframe to Motivate

Master leaders know that the meaning of any message depends on the frame or context within which it is interpreted. For example, the statement that "60 percent of retail shoppers surveyed prefer to purchase nonperishable food items on the Internet" could create thrills for an online grocer. The same statement signals a death knell for a bricks-and-mortar grocery chain with no online strategy. Skillful leaders "reframe" their direction when it is necessary to offer an alternate way for followers to interpret their direction.

Consider the direction you want others to accept. Does it create a hardship, present an important obstacle, or otherwise represent a significant challenge followers must overcome if they commit to it? Have you tried to tune in to WII-FM, use statistics, stories, and metaphors, and build your message, and in the end people still withhold their commitment? Perhaps you need to reframe your direction.

Change the meaning by focusing on the positives. For example, if 60 percent of retail shoppers prefer online shopping for nonperishable food items, a reframe for a bricks-and-mortar grocer could be that "40 percent will still drive to our stores." Reframe by clarifying possibilities—"We have the distribution capacities. In one year we can easily move into online sales." Reframe by countering an implied downside with the hidden upside—"Our brand name recognition will attract more shoppers once we get online. We have the capital to stay competitive while most startup e-companies are flying on shoestrings."

Reframing does not work without trust. In politics, reframing becomes a four-letter word: "spin." Spin describes a deceitful attempt to manipulate followers. However, the mechanics of reframing and spin are the same. Both attempt to change the meaning to motivate others in a particular direction. The difference lies in the leader's intention. Each of us knows our real motives. When we get quiet and listen (skill 1), we know why we say and do something. Those who spin must accept responsibility for their intent. Those perceived to spin crack rapport and violate expectations. They ultimately limit their own ability to effectively influence followers because they violate trust.

Speech analysts Christopher Peterson and Fiona Lee analyzed the impact on companies that spun bad events in their annual reports. Stock prices went down in the following year. These authors indicate that the general public can detect spin and they find the process suspect.[12] Avoid spin. Reframe with the sincere intent to show followers that your direction will be valuable to them.

91. Work through the Resistance

Master leaders realize that their course of action creates change and that change challenges followers. They take into account the discomfort their direction may create. They know followers may have to give up or let go of what they do now if they follow. Followers may experience a sense of loss, and people do not like to experience loss. Skillful leaders influence others by working through the resistance to change.

People can handle change that they totally understand and that does not create a problem. People rarely even view it as "change." For example, the weather can change every day from sunny to rainy or windy. No one really gets bothered by these forms of change. A hurricane or blizzard creates a different impact.

The case for the leader's direction creates a tension between what is and what the leader wants to be. The leader charts a course for an improvement, a reduction, a new approach, or a different emphasis. People will support the change if they immediately recognize the benefit for themselves (WII-FM) or some aspect of the organization they care about (another form of WII-FM). Even unskilled leaders can influence others in this case. This means it is not the change that actually creates the problem. People resist following a course for change when it takes them in a direction they do not want to go.

Think about it. To what extent would you get resistance if

you charted a new course that people believed would create more productive and interesting work and a chance to ensure their and the company's success? However, consider trying to lead others to change work processes and improve customer service. Have you observed people resist such initiatives? Skillful leaders understand that their direction may create resistance. They extend their WII-FM influence method by working through the reasons for resistance.

Identify the specific reasons the change inherent in your leader direction creates resistance. Use your expectation clarification skills (Chapter 5) to root out the reasons for resistance. Ask people directly, "What makes this course of action problematic for you?" or, "Why does this direction cause you to resist it?" Identify these reasons in both one-on-one discussions and with small groups.

Typically, I find people resist a leader's course of action because of two issues already addressed in this book: lack of rapport and no perceived benefits. If necessary, reread Chapter 4 on rapport building to bolster your skills in this area. Review the WII-FM skill (skill 82) discussed at the beginning of this chapter and use it to overcome lack of commitment based on no perceived benefit. I also find people resist change because of three additional reasons: fear, powerlessness, and inertia.

Work through fear by understanding its roots. People fear a new course because it represents the unknown. Fear generates the very human "fight or flight" response. Resistance in this state is a form of protection from harm. Everyone wants to protect themselves from harm. People overtly oppose or run away when danger approaches. The opposite of these responses can be foolhardy behavior.

Provide information to help people overcome the fear of change. Knowledge dispels fear. Consider that no one actually fears the dark. We fear what we think is in the dark. We fear the unknown that the darkness may hold. Your course of action may create an unknown. Shed light on it with as much information as possible. Ask people what more they need to know about your course of action. Do not rely on simply "announcing" information or putting your course of action in an e-mail.

Get into face-to-face discussions with key followers to provide them with the information they want to know. Clarify the logic, the rationale for your course of action. Make your argument as airtight as possible with hard facts. Facts create friendliness in the face of fear.

Identify the factors you anticipate along your path and how they will affect each individual on a personal level. Admit it if new methods of work or action will be needed. Remind people of the purpose of your direction.

Test the clarity of your signals to make sure people understand. Ask them to restate what they think you have told them. Locate the communication "vacuums"—that is, find the places where bad news festers, where rumors run amok, and worst case thinking dominates. Confront these black holes with clear information to overcome fear-based resistance. All this work requires time and effort. Focus on key first followers first.

Work through powerlessness by acknowledging that people need to feel a sense of power to be effective. Power is associated with competence and confidence, and no one likes to lose either of these abilities.

Your leadership direction may require a massive change initiative that creates powerlessness. Break the big job into smaller, more manageable pieces for those who experience that loss of power. Clarify the meaningful part people can and will play to accomplish your course of action. Preach the possibilities for a greater sense of power that will come by following your lead. Translate your direction into a story that engages people as a way to recognize you understand their feelings and you also believe they can make the change. A great story builds tension. Events occur, characters have experiences, forces align themselves. Use your story to get people to anticipate "What will happen next?" "How will the characters work through this or that situation?" The story can invoke their imagination about how they could and will take action, which reinforces their sense of power.

Work through inertia by identifying its source. For some people, inertia-based resistance originates from the sense of comfort and certainty they enjoy with the way things are. Disrupting that state can create resistance. Work through inertia by comparing the costs of not changing with the cost of following your direction. Illustrate the new levels of comfort and certainty your course of action will create.

For others, inertia simply means people are RIP: retired in place. They do not want to change simply because they do not want to do anything differently. You have a more difficult road with those whose inertia stems from RIP. You can use the expectation clarification skill, name the game (skill 28), and confront those who demonstrate RIP behavior. Ask them, "What specific concerns do you have about the course of action I have charted?" Put the burden back on their shoulders. Restate why you feel a need to lead exists based on your mapping the territory efforts. Challenge others with the question, "What do you think will resolve the problem?" Demand that they support their comments with well-founded information from their map of the territory. Respond with your own data from your mapping efforts. If necessary, challenge RIP action by reminding people that they are still on the payroll. You may also have to lead up and get management support to move such people. That means you will have to gain a willing follower up the chain of command who uses his or her authority to demand that RIP personnel comply.

Keep the dialogue going to monitor reasons people resist. A person may first feel fear and then experience powerlessness. A person may commit to change for a while and then hold back. Frequent communication and continual attention are necessary in the face of change resistance.

Working through resistance can be exhausting. Reinforce your ability to achieve success over stress (skill 3). Recognize that resistance also means others experience stress. Their resistance may mean they are confused or overwhelmed with the change created by your direction. People can fail to hear things clearly the first or even second time when boggled by stress. Some may warp or deny the message. Direct others on ways to manage their stress to help them through the change.

92. Bounce Back When People Won't Follow

The best leaders accept an important and often overlooked law of leadership: Not everyone will follow. Some will dissent, criticize, or otherwise put down the leader's direction. Exceptional leaders recognize dissension can reflect resistance to change. They use their ability to work through the resistance (skill 91) to address it. They know that dissension occurs because others have a different map of the territory regarding the need to lead. Skillful leaders review their own mapping skills to verify their map's accuracy or change their map in response to new information. The best leaders also know that some people simply have a different set of values and beliefs. They turn inward; that is, they get quiet and listen (skill 1) to what they believe is important. Leaders also know some people dissent with deceitful or manipulative intent. Leaders know they cannot control anyone else's intentions.

Therefore, despite their best efforts, master leaders may still fail to gain willing followers. They bounce back when they hit a barrier of nonsupport. They do not run down their internal battery in a futile attempt to attract certain followers. They push off in another direction and continue their march.

Think of the leaders of great social movements in American history. In civil rights: Martin Luther King, Jr., Andrew Young, James Farmer, and Jesse Jackson. In the women's movement: Gloria Steinem, Elizabeth Cady Stanton, and Susan B. Anthony. Recall those who pressed for freedom from British rule in India: Gandhi, Nehru, and Patel. These individuals were repeatedly rebuffed by people in powerful posts. They did not, however, stop moving. They refocused their energy on those they could attract to their causes.

Accept the leadership limit; you cannot influence everyone to follow. Redirect your attention to those who might follow. Move past the "impossible condition people," those who will always find some point that causes them to say "your idea cannot work." Such individuals seem to thrive by creating conditions that make your direction seem impossible. Avoid spending too much time on them if they continue to create conditions where your lead cannot be possible. Do not waste your time on people who appear ignorant, crazy, or downright evil. Imagine if the American civil rights marchers had spent all their energy trying to win over Bull Connor, the racist police commissioner in Birmingham, Alabama. They confronted Connor, and they kept going once they realized he was not going to follow.

Jesse Jackson, during his 1988 Democratic National Convention speech, summed up the essence of this skill: "Leaders must be tough enough to fight, tender enough to cry, human enough to make mistakes, humble enough to admit them, strong enough to absorb the pain, and resilient enough to bounce back and keep on moving."

93. Work the Web

Leader influence does not come from formal authority or a position in the hierarchy. However, leaders do live within the formal organizational structure. The linear, up-down organizational influence framework can create a barrier for leader influence. Leaders may not be able to gain access to needed followers up the ladder. A leader's organizational position does not provide the right to press a peer to support a position. You cannot demand that your boss do anything because your boss has authority over you!

Skillful leaders work the web of organizational connections in response to hierarchical authority limits. They move in multiple directions, like a spider's web, to influence others in different parts of the up-down ladder. For example, they can enlist the support of a peer in another division. The peer can then influence his or her boss, who can then win over those in the leader's area.

Working the organizational web overcomes the typical constraint—"I'm not in charge"—that people always face when working in large bureaucracies. The best leaders know they do not need to be in charge to lead. They rely on connections based on relationships, not hierarchy. They use established networks to create a web of influence that transcends the limits of formal authority.

Work the web by first considering the people you need the most to follow your lead. Have you tried to gain their support and not been effective? Are you limited because you cannot even meet with them face-to-face? You need to work the web. Which individuals in the organization could be potential links to help you gain the most important people as willing followers? Focus on the web link individuals. Apply all the natural born leader influence methods at your disposal, then direct your web links to apply those same skills to those you need in other parts of the web. Coach web-linked people on how to present your direction so they reinforce your influence in each subsequent part of the web.

Follow up to test the progress through the web. Recharge the web if your efforts get stalled at a particular place. If necessary, attack the effort from a different entry point in the web. For example, assume you influenced Mike, a peer, to speak with his boss, Jacquie. She then gained some support with Bryan, one of her peers. But the process stalled with Bryan. Review the links you have to Bryan. Consider whom else you can try to influence that is connected with Bryan and begin your web work again.

Recognize that working the web creates constraints for you. It takes longer to work through several links. Your leader direction may be modified as it moves along the web. You may not ultimately get the credit for the leader direction, especially if it has to go through several layers. People may take ownership for your ideas because, to some extent, they truly do become owners of the initiative. You need to reinforce your self-awareness skills to successfully work through these very real constraints. Keep in mind your passion (skill 2). Work on handling the stress (skill 3). Remember that you may have no other alternative but to use the web. Get quiet and listen (skill 1) to reaffirm your real intentions about taking the lead on this issue. If the issue matters to you, if it creates a gut impulse that demands action, everything else will be less important.

94. Focus on First Followers First

The best leaders know they may not have time to use all these influence skills. Even if they did, it would take a lot of effort unless only a very small number of followers were needed. Skillful leaders focus on first followers first. They make a conscious choice where to begin their influence efforts. They put their attention on the key players whose early support is essential for a specific leadership direction. They single out those whose first followership will generate a groundswell so others come along to support that direction.

Identify key first followers by answering these questions:

+ Whose support is essential to get this effort off the ground?
+ Who has key resources that can make or break accomplishing the result?
+ Who might be easy to win over and can be counted on to generate support with many other people?

Work on building your credibility first with the people you identify from these questions. Form alliances with them and position yourself in ways that impact them first. Share power with them first. Champion and shield them first. Work on this group of key first followers and then expand your commitment efforts to the next ring of key followers.

95. Write for the Front Page

Exceptional leaders rely on the written word to attract willing followers. They apply many of the aforementioned skills to enhance their writing. Their writing clarifies the WII-FM need that people have. They stay on and build their message in their text. They use statistics, stories, symbols, and metaphors in their writing. They also apply several newspaper writing techniques to improve the impact of their writing.

Put your key point first. Avoid the novice news reporter

mistake called "burying the lead." Put the most important idea you want the reader to remember in the first sentence. Cluster supporting evidence in consistent categories following your main idea.

One basic writer's rule is, write to write better. Writing is like exercise. Continuity is important. Write, write, and write. Get your ideas on paper. You can easily edit later. Skip a line or two when you write in longhand. That makes it easier to revise the text later. Do your research after you have fleshed out your main ideas. Fit the research in to support those ideas. Avoid the tendency to find the perfect place for a new fact in what you already have prepared. The place for added ideas will surface as you edit your text.

Use personal pronouns (I, we, you, me, and us) and the active versus passive voice in your writing. And use short sentences to avoid excessive verbiage. A statement such as, "Improving sales and service will only become more vital as European and U.S. markets begin operating as one globally based economy," can be expressed better by saying, "Sales and service must improve as Europe and the U.S. become one global economy."

Revise your text several times until you have it right or you have reached your deadline. Revise it first with your "skim" finger. Scan the overall document to ensure the general content and flow makes sense. Revise it next with your "block" finger. Read through each section to test its simplicity, clarity, and conciseness. Focus on what you can shorten or eliminate or what you may have left out. Make your final revision with your "microscope" finger. Focus on the details of grammar, punctuation, word choice, and spelling. Let your word processor help you by doing a final spell check on the document.

Good writing pushes language to the limits. Review your writing with the standards that it should be concise, direct, and clear to test the resourcefulness of your written words.

Endnotes

1. Pamela Kruger, "A Leader's Journey," *Fast Company* (June 1999), p. 116.

2. James Collins, "Built to Flip," *Fast Company* (March 2000), pp. 131–143.
3. J. Richard Hackman, "Work Design," in J. Richard Hackman and J. Lloyd Suttle, *Improving Life at Work* (Santa Monica, CA: Goodyear Publishing, 1977), p. 129.
4. American Society for Training and Development, "State of the Industry," *Training* (October 1999), pp. 37–38.
5. Robert O. Brinkerhoff and Stephen Gill, *The Learning Alliance: Systems Thinking in Human Resource Development* (New York: Jossey-Bass, 1994).
6. Tom Peters and Nancy Austin, *A Passion for Excellence* (New York: Warner Books, Inc., 1989), p. 276.
7. Regina Fazio Maruca, "Voices," *Fast Company* (September 2000), pp. 105–144.
8. As reported by Nicholas Lemann in "The Word Lab," *The New Yorker* (October 16 & 23, 2000), pp. 100–112.
9. Roger Ailes, *You Are the Message: Getting What You Want by Being Who You Are* (New York: Doubleday Books, 1989), p. 16.
10. Dacher Keltner, "Reading Their Lips," *Psychology Today* (September–October 2000), pp. 52–53.
11. Ailes, op. cit.
12. Christopher Peterson and Fiona Lee, "Reading between the Lines," *Psychology Today* (September–October 2000), pp. 50–51.

11

Create a Motivating Environment

Be to each other like water. It brings nourishment to all it touches.

—Lao-tzu

Master leaders gain willing followers within a larger context. Factors such as the organizational direction, goals, culture, and roles affect motivation. The quality of communication, decision making, feedback, and degree of conflict impact people's willingness to support the leader. Ever-increasing levels of diversity demand that leaders direct their efforts to consider context when trying to influence others. The best leaders create an overall environment that will support their effort to gain followers. They ask, "What systems and structures affect the people I want to influence to follow my direction?"

Many of the skills in this area demand that leaders focus their attention "up" the organizational ladder. Senior managers can use their authority to implement new initiatives, and subordinates have to comply with what the "boss" tells them. Leaders do not have that luxury because they have to gain willing followers, not compliant subordinates. Leaders often have to convince senior managers to follow them to create a motivating environment. To shape a motivating environment takes time and effort. Those who step up to influence the hierarchy and make the commitment of their time and energy earn the label natural born leaders.

Mastery of this skill will enable you to:

♦ Establish an environment that supports your efforts to gain willing followers.
♦ Apply the motivational aspects of many of the other 108 skills.

96. Establish a Core Identity

The best leaders define the core identity, the deepest intention that drives action, for their group or organization. They view their group or organization as an expression of energy, creativity, and intelligence. They motivate others by describing that expression, or core identity, in a clear, complete, and cogent manner.

Core identity precedes vision, which defines the attractive and credible future, and mission, which defines the business the organization is in. Core identity reveals what the unit or company really does in the marketplace. Louis Katopodis, president of Fiesta Mart, Inc., the Texas-based grocery chain, described his company's core identity as "serving the underserved." Fiesta specializes in quality products at affordable prices in largely Hispanic and African-American communities. Katopodis continually reminds people of this most fundamental force to motivate their focus about what is important in Fiesta's business.

Investigate if your group or organization has defined its core identity. Many organizations are unclear about this concept. For example, TRW used to be a company that did credit checks for people who wanted bank loans. It sold that business in 1991, but was often perceived as a credit report company. TRW wanted a clearer sense of identity. A business consultant investigated the question and found TRW was in two businesses. It made a variety of unique automobile parts and made all the electronics that were in the F-15 fighter jet cockpit. These disparate businesses did not seem to lend themselves to a core identity until the consultant suggested that TRW's core identity was to make "discoveries that count." TRW managers loved the idea. It captured the firm's essence and it expressed the fundamental feeling that motivated people.[1]

Analyze the identity you feel should be the banner to lead your group or organization. Think about the deepest motive for action that drives the operation. For example, leading people to solve information-processing problems defines a more fundamental motive than leading people to service computers.

Lead up to institutionalize the core identity. Typically concepts such as core identity fall within the work of senior management. Step up and propose your core identity concept to the top group. Clarify the need for a core identity as a motivational tool and use your influence skills to gain their commitment.

97. Mold a Strong and Adaptive Culture

An organization's culture represents the basic pattern of assumptions and shared beliefs that drive its members. Culture defines the deep internal fabric of unwritten but powerful rules, norms, beliefs, and patterns that impact people in organizations. Culture is analogous to the roots of a tree. While hidden beneath the surface, the roots nourish all aspects of the tree and determine its ultimate health. Organizational culture roots explain how members cope with and respond to their environment.

Skillful leaders mold a strong culture so that its impact pervades all parts of an organization. For example, leaders who form a strong, consistent entrepreneurial culture foster innovative thinking at all levels. Those who sculpt solid and integrated customer service culture roots motivate their people to make superior service a top priority in all actions.

The best leaders know that a strong culture creates the glue that holds people together. They also know that "culture glue" can harden and restrict the organization's adaptive capacity. Culture can cause people to stick with an approach that no longer works. Culture can become a boundary marker that people do not cross. People become accustomed to acting within a framework and find it difficult to break out.

Consider the limiting culture root within U.S. car companies in the 1970s. Their initial unwillingness to recognize the value of Japanese manufacture and customer service standards nearly drove them out of business. Similarly, IBM Corp. over-relied on its culture root of slow, methodical decision making. By the early 1990s, this once useful approach created a drag on action that almost crushed Big Blue because fast-paced decision making became essential in the rapidly changing technology industry. Master leaders mold an adaptive culture to maximize a group or organization's capacity to respond to any need or opportunity.

Evaluate the current culture. Start with a review of the vision, mission, and values statements. Do they represent an integrated, coherent profile that suggests motivated action? That is, do these fundamental statements define a strong culture? Moreover, do they have adaptability built into their conceptual framework? It may be necessary to reform the vision, mission, and values to reform the culture.

Evaluate the current culture with your mapping the territory skills (see Chapter 6). Uncover the roots that drive individual and organizational action. Note any restrictive or limiting roots. Listen for the frequently made comments that define the general group mind-set. Statements such as "Take it slow," "Don't volunteer for anything," and "Don't trust corporate" do not suggest the most positive, responsive culture. Uncover how and why these comments are part of the current culture.

Seek input from customers, both external and internal, to determine the need for culture change. External customers represent those who buy your product or use your service. Internal customers are the company employees who support each other. Discontent in any form from these groups can signal a nonresponsive culture.

Expose culture roots that specifically limit adaptability. Any shared assumption or belief that hinders individual capacity to take action crushes the organization's responsiveness. A high level of command-and-control management inhibits employee initiative. A pervasive perception that certain customers are problems suggests an overly rule-minded culture. Challenge the existence of such roots. Apply your expectation clarification skills (see Chapter 5) and create a dialogue about how and when certain culture roots no longer serve the group or organization.

Identify alternate, more proactive culture roots that promote adaptability. Refer to the vision, mission, and values and build on the most adaptive aspects of those statements. Assess companies that represent an adaptive, cutting-edge culture in your particular industry or with customers and employees in general. For example, Levi Strauss & Co. emphasizes participation, diversity, accountability, teamwork, and two-way communication up and down the organizational ladder. Sound pretty good? Find out how Levi makes these terms a reality in the organization at the most fundamental levels. Explore how Levi's people behave in meetings. Find out how employees speak with their boss in the hallway. Examine what is said and done when Levi employees interact with customers. Find ways to adapt positive aspects of the Levi culture to your group.

Rely heavily on your ability to influence others to willingly follow (Chapter 10) when you present your insights. Established culture roots represent deeply embedded beliefs. It takes a lot of WII-FM—what's in it for me?—discussion (skill 82) and the ability to speak the follower's language (skill 88) well to help others recognize the limits of those beliefs.

Recognize the paradox of culture formation. Only a strong culture guides consistent action. Yet that strength must bend like a willow in the face of change. Accept the long road you must travel to significantly change a culture. Organizationwide culture change typically takes three to seven years. Begin now and start where you are. Mold even one more adaptive culture root in a small group to get the process moving. For example, make listening and responding to customers a primary goal in all your group's activities. By definition this simple act will infuse more adaptable action into the way your people do business.

98. Create Action Scorecards

Most leadership action takes place in the trenches in localized situations. Leaders must respond to a particular customer need or overcome a production problem. They tackle a software integration issue or redirect a dysfunctional group. They implement a method to cut costs on a specific project or heal the wounds of mistrust between two departments in conflict. While core identity, vision, mission, and values define the larger performance context, skillful leaders create action scorecards between themselves and others to guide local action and measure results.

Recall again that leading means gaining willing followers. Leaders can't rely on traditional organizational control mechanisms such as rules or policies or employment contracts. Such tools require managerial authority to implement. The leader's action scorecard offers structure and standards; however, it relies on follower commitment, not compliance. Skillful leaders create performance scorecards to establish a motivational environment.

Chris Hornung, currently an area manager for Enterprise Rent-A-Car, models the action scorecard skill. When he was a location manager, Hornung sat with all new staff members on their first day. He showed them the performance standards the company expected them to achieve in their first thirty days. He clarified the importance of these standards and the implications if they were not met. He also outlined his standards and the results he expected. Hornung was clear and direct about what it would take for an employee to excel in his location. His former location employees speak of him in glowing terms. They express their deep appreciation for his effort to clarify the action scorecard they needed to achieve success in the company.

The action scorecard has a motivational power similar to the impact of most recreational activities. People can be completely burned out from a hard week of work. Yet, tell them you have a tee time reserved at a local golf course or a court reserved at a tennis club and they perk up, energized to play. Part of the power in recreational activities comes from the fact that we keep score when we play games. People know how many points they have. They can compare their score with others. Score keeping motivates and creates winners because winning means knowing the score and how to achieve the best score. The Notre Dame locker-room wall has a sign: "Winners keep track of results. Losers keep track of reasons."

The motivational impact of score keeping is not unique to sports. Part of the driving force behind a musical composition lies in the measurable aspects of music. A violinist knows the difference when she bows the right chord instead of producing a scratching, grating sound. A drummer can tell when he maintains the right beat. In a jam session, each player in a band can hear when and how their sound supports the entire group. Think about it. We call a musical composition a "score."

Create an action scorecard by clarifying the meaning of success as it relates to your leadership direction. Identify clear goals, desired results, important milestones, and key behaviors that represent success markers. Use the scorecard to help followers gauge movement along the way to a successful result. Identify high performance norms as part of the scorecard. Discuss the standards of behavior (i.e., the norms) that represent success. For example, typical high performance group norms include speaking up when you have an idea, respecting others' opinions, exploring all options presented, and helping others meet deadlines. Reinforce goal and norm performance standards from day one to solidify the importance of the scorecard and reinforce the motivational environment you want to create.

Accept the challenges you create when using an action scorecard. If you do not create a performance scorecard, you cannot fail. An old saying counters this logic: "If you have no way to measure, you cannot win, either." To create a substantive scorecard takes time. Meaningful measures may be difficult to determine. Another old saying states, "If you are too busy to measure, you are too busy to succeed." You also face the challenge set by a scorecard. You may not reach the standards. That truth can be painful. A third adage reveals, "The truth will set you free, if you are willing to see the truth."

Focus on simple and objective standards as much as possible. Include the opportunity for self-assessment. Allow for a comparison between past and current individual performance and between individual and organizational "best" standards. Keep the scorecard continuously available if possible. Everyone reviews the scoreboard at a sporting event. Telling someone at the end of April about how they did in early March has less motivational impact than getting the score every day.

Define the end point beyond which you will not work with a person. You cannot move everyone to achieve results no matter how much motivational effort you devote. While leaders without managerial authority cannot fire anyone, they also do not have to invest in those who won't respect the scorecard. Lead up so that management uses its position power to hold people accountable. Realize at some level you are doing people a favor when you do not allow them to fall below scorecard standards. They will either improve from their experience with you, or they will continue to fail at work. Letting people off the hook for performance failures ultimately does not help them, and it certainly does not motivate them to improve.

99. Position the Players

People need to know the part they must play to achieve results. A lack of role clarity (e.g., "What am I supposed to do here?") is a key reason people experience stress and conflict at work. Master leaders position the players so they know their role in the leader's course of action.

Positioning players differs from the management role of hiring and assigning the best people to the job best for them. Leaders gain followers who carry out responsibilities that move the leader's agenda. Managers assign subordinate roles. Managers can always default to their authority and say, "Do what I tell you," or "That's the job I hired you to do," or "You will have to stay in this job until we can find another one for you." Leaders do not always have this luxury. Leading is not based on a formal job requirement. Followers support leaders because they want to follow. They can stop at any time or transfer their allegiance to others.

Match followers to tasks that motivate them and allow them to succeed. Rely on your rapport building and expectation clarification skills (see Chapters 4 and 5) to determine how to create such matches. Analyze the individual and the task's demands. It will be difficult for people who thrive on human contact to succeed where the task does not allow them to leave their cubicle. It will severely challenge people who need structure if they are given a task with no clearly defined parameters. The work that followers do to support the leader has to resonate with the followers' abilities, preferences, and real potential.

Don't try to read people's minds. Ask them directly what they think about taking on different tasks to fulfill your leadership direction. Offer to coach and train people (skill 61) as they take on new or different tasks. When the role involves a big job, make it manageable by breaking it up into smaller, more easily doable tasks.

100. Put Everybody in Charge

Exceptional leaders recognize everyone has the capacity to lead. They reinforce how everyone can be part of the leadership power in an organization. They encourage self-directed, individual action and group-directed action. They put everyone in charge to build on the power of autonomy and sense of personal accomplishment that motivates most people.

Create the self-directed action necessary to put everyone in charge with a detailed and intense expectation clarification session. Lay out the intent behind your willingness to put everyone in charge. Clarify the action you want people to take. Get input to ensure your motives are clearly understood. Define the boundaries that must be maintained when you put people "in charge." You do not have to give people the combination to the safe.

Identify the specific area you want people to take charge of and any specific parameters they must keep in mind. Be realistic on two counts. First, put them in charge where they have the power to identify what must be done, find ways to take action, and can implement their action without having to rely on someone else in charge. Second, you do not really put people in charge when the task is trivial. I observed a failed attempt to give people a real sense of being in charge while consulting with a hospital. A group was tasked with making the patient reception room more "customer friendly." The group recognized that the room lacked the feeling they wanted patients to experience. They also saw the effort as a meaningless gesture since it was not a major issue facing the organization.

Let people know you will serve as a resource to support them. Set up a mutually agreed-on feedback mechanism to reinforce this role. Avoid the impulse to use this mechanism to overcontrol. Coming by to "just see how things are going" without being asked may send the message, "I'm checking up on you." When you do offer feedback, make suggestions that you believe will help people win. Allow them the discretion to counter your suggestions.

Applaud every step of the process that you truly believe meets high standards. When people take a step you do not believe will accomplish the task, ask them for information or an explanation as opposed to simply discounting the action. Conduct a "lessons learned" discussion at the completion of the project, at any time the group may be stuck, or when you feel they need some coaching.

Help the group identify its own leadership power. Ask the group to clarify when and how specific individuals provided direction and gained willing followers. Point out the value in even the "little" leadership events. Show people how each event contributes to the overall group success. Take the next step to put everyone in charge by asking, "What do you want to work on now?"

101. Foster Open Communication

Open communication indicates everyone's input is important and respected. Open communication energizes people with the power of ideas. Skillful leaders know that feeling important, being respected, and creating energy motivate people.

Assess the current lines of communication. Find out when and how people feel that they are "out of the loop" or that communication is blocked. Ask people what kind of information they would like to receive that they currently do not get. Find out where too much nonessential information creates overload. Determine who needs to talk to whom. Chart the conversation flow in meetings. Recognize when some people dominate the discussions while others seem to be left out and cannot get a word in edgewise.

Foster open communication with an expectation clarification session. Define your open communication goals. Ask for input on how to resolve problems you found or that others bring up. Model open communication with key phrases to facilitate information flow. Ask, "What does that mean?" to gather more information and verify understanding. Ask, "What do you think?" to engage others, especially those who have been silent for a while. Help others build on information with statements such as, "We have heard three ideas about this topic. What else do we want to add?" or "Are there any underlying themes that need to be defined?" Note when several people speak at once. Intervene with a suggested sequence of response such as, "Let's hear from you first, then you, and you next." Test clarity about discussion topics with a summary and question: "So it seems we have said . . . Is that what you have understood to be the key ideas?" Point out minority perspectives: "It seems that everyone wants to do X except David, who has suggested Z. Let's talk about that for a few minutes."

Accept negative news. Do not kill the messenger. Use bad news as a signal to get more information. Ask, "What else do we need to know about this issue?"

Use open-ended questions to generate discussion. Such

questions require a description versus a single-word answer. "What are your thoughts about the new product?" engages the other person to give a substantive response. "Do you like the new product?" requires only a yes or no reply. Use close-ended questions when brief replies are appropriate.

Have a meeting about meetings. Ask people how meetings could be conducted to foster more open communication. Get input on how and when the meetings are not conducted in the most efficient manner. Meetings typically make people crazy. Use the "experiment" technique to try out new meeting methods. Decide to implement a meeting improvement suggestion for a set period, say, three meetings. Agree that the suggestion will be reviewed after the experimental period.

Record the key points made in meetings on a flipchart or using a computer projector. The visible display of information keeps everyone focused. Send out meeting minutes within twenty-four hours that summarize key discussions and action items.

Use the telephone, e-mail, and fax to speed up and improve communication, but don't use them as a total replacement for face-to-face dialogue. Fifty-five percent of communication is nonverbal, which means a great deal of information is lost without visual contact.

Accept the time demand required to truly open up communication. Perceive open communication as a journey, not a destination.

102. Maximize Decision Participation

Exceptional leaders maximize decision participation because it typically yields better decisions. It also creates a motivating force because it means people have a say in decisions, which gives them ownership for the actions and outcomes.

Conduct an expectation clarification session about the decision-making process. Ask people when and how they would like greater participation. Identify problems when previous decisions did not allow participation. Gather ideas on participation specifics that would have alleviated those problems. The very act of having this discussion will spark motivation because the discussion itself models participative decision making.

Involve anyone who will have responsibility to implement a decision. Invite each person to participate during discussions. Say, "We have not heard from you yet. What do you think?" Apply the aforementioned open communication skills to maximize discussion.

Verify decisions with the "eyeball technique." Restate the decision: "We are going to conduct customer service training." Then look each person directly in the eye and ask, "Do you agree with the decision?" The eyeball technique yields some interesting responses. You may notice a flicker or glaze of uncertainty in some people. They probably were not paying attention or are unsure about the decision. Do not react to their uncertainty. Simply restate the decision and ask again, "Do you agree?" Your tone should invite them to respond so that you can clarify their understanding and acceptance of the decision. Don't accept a shrug or a "sure" if you still do not think the person sounds committed. Say, "Tell us why," or "I want to be sure you agree. What are your thoughts about the decision?" If you continue this probing a few times people will know you are serious about wanting their true participation in the decision.

Review key decisions that were useful and those that did not turn out well. Reconsider how and when participation could have enhanced the decision. Recognize that more participation typically increases the time to make decisions. Identify when and how the group gets bogged down and takes too long to make a choice. Establish group norms regarding time limits for decision making. Revisit these norms periodically to ensure they maximize decision effectiveness.

103. Forge Feedback Loops

The best leaders rely on feedback to motivate because it reinforces the positive and helps people recognize when, where, and how improvement must be made. Skillful leaders forge effective feedback loops to maximize the motivational qualities of the environment. They know that the biggest mistake many people make is believing they are infallible. Feedback helps overcome that fallacy.

Establish a format for feedback. The same guidelines used to appraise continuously (skill 63) apply here. Motivating feedback provides specific, not general, information. Energizing feedback describes rather than simply evaluates. Motivating feedback focuses on behavior or the problem rather than the person. Effective feedback is given when people are ready to hear it.

Conduct a "feedback round" in a meeting to give people practice applying these guidelines. Have each person give feedback about an item in the room such as a picture, the meeting chairs, or the ceiling tile. Then ask people to give the group feedback about its last meeting. Request that they give only positive feedback. Suggest a way the last meeting could have been improved, then ask for volunteers to provide feedback about that same issue. Have the group analyze the feedback in terms of the guidelines.

Encourage people to talk back. Ask people to challenge you and each other to create meaningful feedback loops. Make dissent and playing the devil's advocate acceptable roles to foster more feedback.

104. Melt Conflict Icebergs

Conflict means people have an important difference. Skillful leaders recognize that little or no conflict can signal that people do not care, feel uninvolved, or do not believe their ideas matter. Too much conflict creates destructive tension and bickering and locks people up. Master leaders also know that conflict is inevitable. It exists in every work setting. Conflict can be a creative, motivating force when it is resolved effectively. Master leaders use conflict to move and motivate. They resolve it by melting the conflict iceberg.

Consider the reality of an iceberg. About 90 percent of it is under water. Conflict resembles an iceberg. The conflict issue, say a difference over software compatibility, represents the tip of the iceberg. People clearly see an iceberg's tip just as they readily recognize the conflict issue. The conflict lines then get drawn quickly. For example, two parties that differ over ways to address the software compatibility issue become entrenched in their view of the issue. One group wants to purchase a totally new package. The other group wants to change computer hardware. No easy resolution presents itself because the conflict issue creates mutually exclusive options. Both parties have a long list of reasons their solution is best. Neither party wants to budge. The conflict issue stands out as a stark indicator of the stalemate.

To resolve the conflict requires going beneath the surface to address the interests behind both parties' issue. Like the bulk of the iceberg, the bulk of the conflict and potential resolution lies hidden beneath the surface issue. Exploring each group's real interests represents melting the bulk of the iceberg. As interests become apparent, areas for mutual agreement emerge. In the software compatibility issue, both groups may share concerns about reducing the need for training on new hardware or software. Both parties want to keep costs down. They both want to improve overall systems integration. Putting shared interests on the table draws the conflicting groups together. When you direct them to find ways to meet those shared interests, you translate the energy consumed by conflict into a positive focus on ways to work toward common goals.

Apply the iceberg melting approach. Ask conflicting parties to state their issue. Then move beneath the surface with a series of "why" questions. "Why is that important?" "Why does that matter?" "Why do you say that?" Direct the conflicting parties to present facts and measurable information. Steer them away from emotive comments or accusatory statements.

Set aside enough time to melt the bulk of the iceberg. That means you need enough time to get all the interests on the table and discuss them fully. You also need time to seek resolution. Ask, "Where do you both share a common interest?" Inquire further, "How can both of your real interests be met?" Do not respond to unhelpful comments such as, "They should just give in!" Confront such comments if they get out of hand by saying, "We know you want your issue. You're not making it easy to get what you want with such comments."

Seek consensus, not mere consent, to resolve important differences. Consensus means all parties agree. It signals that everyone is on board and accepts the resolution. Consent means majority rule. Consent implies that people have to go along and swallow the differences that created the conflict. Consensus motivates because it signals, "Well, it wasn't my first choice, but I can see some value in it." Such resolution aligns people to work together as opposed to having to comply with the majority.

Use a third-party facilitator when the conflict involves deep-rooted issues that may be beyond your skill level. A neutral third party can also be useful when you identify strongly with one side of the conflict.

Not all conflicts have a win-win hidden somewhere within them. It may be necessary to get a 60-40 or even 70-30 resolution where one party has more of its interests met than another. Clarify this reality up-front. Meet with the party that gave up the most. Reinforce your commitment to their participation. Ask what you can do beyond the conflict issue to maintain their motivation.

105. Begin with a Win

A motivational environment enables people to feel like winners. Exceptional leaders find a way to begin with a win to form a motivating feeling. They create small and quick wins early and then continually reinforce success and celebrate results.

George Allen, the professional football coach, took over the Washington Redskins in the early 1970s. He focused on making his first season with the Redskins a winning season. His goal was to be in the Super Bowl, and he knew that an initial winning season was necessary to motivate his team for the long term. Allen's team did have a winning season its first year and got into the Super Bowl the next year. He also established a longer-term success tradition within the Redskins, which resulted in consistent winning seasons, four Super Bowl visits, and two Super Bowl victories.

Create the conditions to begin with a win. Establish a difficult but achievable task for your followers. Do whatever it takes to make it happen. Review the event to reinforce the follower's capacity for success. Choose a second task with an equal concern for challenge and "doability." A few well-crafted early wins foster the tradition of victory necessary for a motivating environment. Hard, tangible results that show followers they can succeed speak volumes.

Catch people in the act of victory. For example, consider making winners out of those who successfully work customers through a difficult problem. Recognize the power behind lauding those who get a small group meeting back on track.

106. Use the Entire Arsenal of Incentives

Master leaders know that people are different. They rely on the complete range of incentives to motivate others and create the environment they seek.

Understand the incentives people value by applying your rapport building and expectation clarification skills (Chapters 4 and 5). Consider the specific incentives people want and how well the environment provides them. Ask people, "What incentives in this job, group, organization, or career will motivate you to excellence?" Demonstrate how the environment already provides those incentives when it does. Take action to provide unmet incentives. For example, a group of European managers in one international firm did not believe their ideas were given full consideration in meetings with their American counterparts. The VP of human resources instituted a set of specific communication techniques for the meetings. The methods ensured that everyone had a chance to speak and each idea was discussed and that members understood each other. These managers were motivated by recognition and consideration. The VP found a way to provide these important incentives.

Use appropriate "hard" and "soft" incentives to motivate people. Hard incentives include pay, benefits, promotion, job security, and working conditions. Hard incentives are powerful motivators. Lead up to ensure people receive adequate levels of these incentives. Recognize also that hard incentives always have two important limits as motivators. First, no matter how much money people have, they can find a way to spend it. This means they typically want more money. Second, most people do not totally control the application of hard incentives. Think about it. Can you give someone a salary increase any time you want? Can you guarantee job security? Accept the boundaries hard incentives create. Clarify the limits you face in terms of offering hard incentives.

Soft incentives include involving people in decisions, showing sincere appreciation for their work and results, and sympathetically responding to individual concerns. These incentives often matter more than hard rewards in circumstances where people are paid a reasonable wage and work in acceptable job conditions. Furthermore, few factors limit the application of these incentives.

Apply soft incentives whenever you can. Provide more participation in meetings and discussions. Overtly acknowledge people who do their jobs. Keep in mind the old adage, "Little things don't mean a lot. Little things mean everything." Work on the tune in to MMFG-AM—make me feel good about myself—skill (skill 20) to improve your capacity to provide soft incentives. Discuss with others ways to make work more fun so it exhilarates people. Find ways to engage people in their work so they feel more connected to their jobs. Take action to make work more exciting so people see their jobs as more meaningful.

Recognize how equity affects the incentive to work. People often make a conscious calculation about the amount of work they do and the reward they get for their work. They compare their calculation with a "significant other," someone they believe is a meaningful comparison. The resultant level of equity impacts motivation. If a person gets $100 a day for doing a specific kind of work, but a comparison "other" gets $200 for the same day's work, the person feels an inequity. A lack of equity thwarts motivation. An individual may work less hard, complain about the need for a raise, or sabotage the work of the comparison person.

Use your rapport building and expectation clarification skills to root out equity problems. Speak with individuals about their equity comparison. Redirect them to change their comparison if necessary. For example, let's assume a software engineer compares herself with a salesperson. Both have important roles. The salesperson makes more money because she works on commission. Clarify expectations with the software engineer to help the person realize the inappropriate comparison being made.

Clarify any valid reasons for an inequity. For example, it may be appropriate for those with longer tenure to get paid more for the same work new people do. Realize, too, how that logic does not wash when new people actually work harder and produce more. In such cases, lead up to balance the work-rewards calculation. Help senior management recognize the limiting motivational aspects of an inequitable environment.

Set clear, specific, measurable performance targets. Goals create incentives for people because they provide a standard for achievement. Include people in the goal-setting process to establish ownership for the outcomes. "Buy in" creates a powerful incentive for purposeful action.

Overcome your own potentially limiting biases regarding incentives. Some people believe, "No one did it for me, and I made it." Others regard soft incentives as too touchy-feely or use reasoning that says, "We have important work to do here and there is no place for such patter." Self-refer (i.e., listen to your inner voice) to consider if such beliefs create the most motivating environment.

107. Set the Ethical Edge

The best leaders create a motivating environment that reflects just, fair, honorable guidelines of conduct. A corrupt work environment demotivates.

Review the core identity, vision, mission, and values to determine how clearly they define understandable ethical standards. Lead up to influence management to establish a code of ethics for the company if one does not exist. Create a personal code of ethics and commit to living it. Display the code in writing as a formal statement of your commitment to the ethical edge.

Create discussion groups around ethical concerns. Most people want to do the right things, but they may not be sure where the ethical edge lies on particular issues. Lead up to establish formal ethics training programs. Ensure the content addresses examples of what constitutes ethical versus unethical behavior. Lead up to make ethics considerations a part of the selection and recruitment function. Influence senior management on the importance of laying out the company's ethical edge to people during the recruitment process. Confront potential ethics violations immediately.

Recognize that lofty statements on paper or a once-a-year meeting with solemn speeches does not define the ethical edge. Actions tell the story. Set the ethical edge with consistent behavior that illustrates high ethical standards.

108. Be the Thermostat

A thermostat sets the temperature. Master leaders create a motivating environment by setting the range within which they want individuals and groups to operate. They set the tone to move events the way they want them to go. They keep things cool when people and situations heat up. They also instill the necessary fire to get people moving when necessary.

Consider John Wooden, perhaps the most successful basketball coach in history. His UCLA Bruins teams won seven NCAA championships in a row and ten in eleven years. Wooden was famous for never getting riled. He never showed strong emotions and never let the pace of the game overshadow his thinking and action. He also never complained to the referees. The only tension Wooden ever showed was to tightly roll up his game program. In the final game of his career, Wooden sought championship number ten. His team was down and did not seem as if it would rally. After a close officiating call that went against the Bruins, Wooden exploded at a referee. The uncharacteristic action ignited his players and they went on to win. Some analysts also argue Wooden's action shook up the referees. Some suggested it caused the refs to give Wooden's players the benefit of close calls for the rest of the game. Whatever Wooden's real intent, he set the temperature for the game and others responded.

Focus on your ability to achieve success over stress (skill 3). This will help you maintain a more even keel so you can remain more stable even when a losing streak overwhelms others. Remind others of their need for perspective when events seem to go the wrong way.

Point out how the tendency to get angry at one's self or lash out does not change what has happened. Focus people on how to use the energy exerted on a heated response to take action that makes a difference.

Consider a well-crafted energizer when people become lethargic or seem to have lost their spirit. A motivational quote may be just what people need. One of my favorites comes from Adlai Stevenson: "Since we have come so far, who shall be rash enough to set limits on our future progress? Who shall say, since we have gone so far, we can go no further?"

Endnotes

1. John Bowe, Marisa Bowe, and Sabin Streeter, *Gig: Americans Talk about Their Jobs at the Turn of the Millennium* (New York: Crown, 2000).

12

Freedom Is Fulfilling

reedom comes first when we recognize, or "re-*cognize*," who we are. Greater freedom comes when we realize what we can become. Everyone has the freedom to master the 108 skills and to earn the attribution "natural born leader." The process requires regular and consistent effort over a long period of time. Exceptional leaders take the journey with enthusiasm and a clear recognition of the challenges.

The Foundational Skill Challenge: Constant Attention

The foundational skills require consistent care. Consider the faces on Mount Rushmore. Workers regularly rappel down the majestic presidential facades to patch a nose, fill in a cheek, or reinforce an eye because the rock keeps cracking. Without constant reinforcement, the massive stone visages would crumble away. Exceptional leaders give the foundational natural born leader skills the same ongoing attention.

Your pursuit of self-awareness must be lifelong. Master leaders regularly and silently search deeply within to scrutinize their thoughts, feelings, beliefs, and values. You can consistently ascertain your current state of awareness to validate that you function from a value-added place: one of positivity, openness, and nonjudgmental observation. Many methods of mindfulness are described in Chapter 3. Whatever method you find comfortable, use it to access that most transcendental, deepest aspect of yourself. From there, perform action.

Your search for successful working relationships requires constant nurturing. In today's fierce competitive markets, cutthroat tactics can crush the finest feeling level within even the most stalwart and sturdy. You can systematically build rapport through common ground and "make me feel good about myself" (MMFG-AM) skills to heal those wounds. Cultivating greater trust and respect will shape your relationships in a positive way to support your search for willing followers.

Expectations need to be constantly clarified between yourself and those you want to lead. Followers need to know what to do, especially when new forces arise or uncertainty rears its head. You can find out what people expect and share your expectations to create mutually acceptable expectations and maintain willing followers.

The Leadership Direction Skill Challenge: Change and Information Overload

The need to lead has never been more important. Change bombards us every day. Unpredictability, which is always present, now exists "24/7" and affects us in radical and explosive ways. Consider that in 1980, the computer industry did not really exist. Recognize that up until 1990, the Cold War dominated our thinking about the "world family."

To lead, you must never assume you have it all figured out. Today's environment demands constant "finding out" behavior. A clear path in response to Generation X does not yet exist, and now we find Generation Y upon us. You can continually map all aspects of the changing mosaic to identify hidden problems and the solutions to them. You can recognize unforeseen opportunities and how to exploit them.

Any course of leadership action you take requires risk. The

stakes increase in times of upheaval. You can chart a course through the risk and upheaval with a clear sense of purpose and willingness to be decisive.

Your organization, all organizations, need more and better leaders at every level. Developing others requires more time and consumes more energy than ever. You can invest yourself in others to maximize leadership throughout their organization. You can sit with someone today and offer your energy to help her improve a leadership skill.

Leadership Influence Skill Challenge: Complexity and Diversity

The ability to gain commitment and keep your followers loyal becomes more complex as access to power becomes more fierce and credibility becomes harder to maintain. You can model your commitment and share your power to enhance others' growth and progress. Such action enhances your capacity to gain and maintain followers.

New information streams and more rapid access to choices make it difficult to even capture followers' attention, much less gain their overt support. More information offered in more "infotaining" ways creates a challenge for even the most gifted and compelling speakers. You can meet followers at their level and lead them in the direction you want them to go. You can craft your message to meet the needs that matter to followers.

The importance of a motivating environment has never been greater as people seek more than just money or a job. No company has a lock on perfection. Each year companies move up and down, off and on the *Fortune* "100 Best Companies to Work For" list. You can create an environment that energizes and excites people. You can behave as a unit of motivational power with every action you take every day and attract willing followers.

The realities and challenges on the path to natural born leader status may make the ideal seem far away. There is no need to be discouraged. The distance represents your measure of potential, not your imperfections.

Our Olympian record-setting athletes and gold medal winners spontaneously respond to the question "Who was your role model?" with the name of someone who inspired them to continue against all odds. Find a model of behavior that reflects your goals and ambitions and stay focused on results. A clear line of sight toward your goals allows you to accomplish them more easily.

The Secret Skill: Number 109

One additional skill defines the natural born leader phenomenon: the capacity to identify additional skills that help meet new leadership challenges. Master leaders constantly seek new behaviors and variations of behaviors that refine leadership effectiveness.

John Gardner gave the commencement address at my 1970 college graduation. Gardner, then chairman of the National Urban Coalition, described the human tendency to believe that a finite goal exists for our life. He explained that we expect to get to a place where we have "arrived." Gardner challenged this notion. He said, "Life is not a summit, it is the mountain that has no real summit, no final goal or ultimate end point."

Leading and leadership development have no summit, either. Leaders take on today's challenges and overcome them so they can be ready for the next challenges. They complete the puzzle of today's uncertainty to help recognize the next arena of incompleteness. They play today's game to learn how to play another game. The continuous tension between action and achievement and the need for additional action make leadership the most fascinating human activity.

Gardner claimed that life is a process and the meaning is in the process. Leadership development also occurs as a process whose meaning is the process. To lead means to live where the action is. Its importance lies in doing the leading and enjoying the process of leading. We don't begin a dance because we want to end it or read a book just to finish it. True leaders lead because the leading matters and the leading motivates.

Gardner clarified that "commencement" means a beginning. He said, "The really important tasks are never finished." Leading never ends. Although master leaders must set up intermediary end-lines, periodic signposts, and progress markers, they use these signals to gauge progress and spur themselves on to the next step. The journey defines the leadership.

Your completion of this book marks the beginning. It signals the starting place to your next level of leadership development. It defines the initiation of your high adventure toward more complete natural born leader status. I thank you for your desire to improve your leadership by reading this book. I honor you for caring enough about yourself and others to find ways to make a more positive difference.

Gardner concluded his address saying he would not offer the traditional wish for our success. That would be too easy. He wished us something harder to come by—meaning in our life. I offer the same wish for you: to nurture that place within yourself where, first and foremost, taking the lead means something to you and thereby creates meaning for those you seek as followers.

Meaning, Gardner related, is not something one stumbles across. We build meaning into our life as we move through the easy and the difficult parts of life. We build meaning by learning from our past. We create meaning in the life experiences we share with others. We demonstrate meaning by applying our talents. We fulfill our life's meaning through the continuous, constant, and great concern we show to create dignity, enjoyment, and enlightenment for all.

Skill 109, then, reminds us that leadership development occurs as the endless unfoldment of desire. Desire then translates into action. Action results in achievement. Achievement becomes the experience of fulfillment. Fulfillment sets the stage for another desire to emerge and begin the cycle again. Leadership development occurs as the continuous process of self-discovery. It involves the endless, unpredictable interaction between the multifaceted circumstances that life offers each day and our individual potentialities to learn, sense, wonder and wander, understand, love, and aspire.

To borrow from Adlai Stevenson, true leaders, "animated by the destiny of greatness can think, and act, and do greatly." We all have the capacity to lead because we can provide direction and gain willing followers. Everyone is born with preferences, strengths, and limitations. We all can improve, learn, develop and grow to think and act and do leadership greatly.

You will hear the words, "You're a natural born leader," more often when you develop the skills in this book. That attribution sets you free to represent your deepest ideals. It allows you to bring to life the highest aspirations within yourself and within the members in a small group, of those who work for an entire company, or of those who live within a community, state, or country. The journey never ends. The journey sets you free.

Appendix: The 108 Natural Born Leader Skills

Foundational Skills

Expand Self-Awareness

1. Get Quiet and Listen
2. Live with Passion and Direct It with Precision
3. Achieve Success over Stress
4. Leverage Time
5. Juggle Professional and Personal Demands
6. Remain Flexible in the Face of Difficulty
7. Use Failure as a Growth Tool
8. Focus on Lifelong Learning
9. Seek 360-Degree Feedback
10. Use Your Whole Brain
11. Know Your Personality Gene Code
12. Be an Ocean

Build Rapport

13. Establish Common Ground
14. Walk in Another's Shoes

15. Listen with Active Ears
16. Be Accessible and Approachable
17. Develop Remote Leadership Capacity
18. Size People Up
19. Apply the Platinum Rule
20. Tune in to MMFG-AM
21. Display a Sense of Humor
22. Demonstrate Rock-Solid Integrity
23. Build Trust

Clarify Expectations

24. Establish Mutually Agreed-On Expectations
25. Root Out Limiting Expectations
26. Explain Organizational Expectations
27. Use Fact-Based Thinking
28. Name the Game
29. Work the Grapevine
30. "Netware" Your Expectations
31. Unravel Rumors
32. Clarify the Action-Results Connection
33. Display Unsinkable Optimism
34. Throw Light on Organizational Shadows
35. Expect the Unexpected

Leadership Direction Skills

Map the Territory: Identify the Need for Leadership Direction

36. Go into the GAP: Gain Another Perspective
37. Work Like Walton: Talk to Everybody
38. Use Bifocal Consciousness
39. Recognize Trends
40. Monitor the Forces of Change
41. Use Strategic Eyesight

42. Recognize Root Causes
43. Sense Possibilities
44. Display Refined Business Acumen
45. Be a Quick Study

Chart a Course of Leadership Action

46. Break the Symmetry—Create a New Symmetry
47. Lead Boldly Where None Dare
48. Take the Highest First Action
49. Create a Vision, Mission, and Values
50. Develop Scenarios
51. Chart Local Action to Support the Big Picture
52. Focus on Customers First
53. Chart a Course in Response to Change
54. Demonstrate Political Savvy
55. Shape and Mirror
56. Demonstrate Good Citizenship
57. Know When to Hold 'Em and Know When to Fold 'Em
58. Step Up and Act: Be Decisive

Develop Others as Leaders

59. Attract Rising Stars
60. Use "World Class" as the Standard
61. Coach and Train
62. Polish the Whole Diamond
63. Appraise Continuously
64. Empower for Results
65. Teach Situational Wisdom in the Action Continuum
66. Push Constant Preparation
67. Use Diversity as a Strength
68. Differentiate between Can't and Don't
69. Be an M&M: Model and Motivate Excellence
70. Pace the Marathon Race
71. Be First Follower Ready
72. Lead Up to Formalize Leader Development

Leadership Influence Skills

Build the Base to Gain Commitment

73. Build Credibility
74. Establish a Core Cadre of the Committed
75. Position for Power
76. Share the Power
77. Champion and Shield
78. Adapt to the Follower Continuum
79. Wear Multiple Hats
80. Model Commitment
81. Form Alliances

Influence Others to Willingly Follow

82. Show Others What's in It for Them: WII-FM
83. Stay on Message
84. Use Precise Speech
85. Use Statistics, Stories, Symbols, and Metaphors
86. Build the Message
87. Communicate Confidence, Conviction, and Enthusiasm
88. Speak the Follower's Language
89. Communicate with Congruence
90. Reframe to Motivate
91. Work through the Resistance
92. Bounce Back When People Won't Follow
93. Work the Web
94. Focus on First Followers First
95. Write for the Front Page

Create a Motivating Environment

96. Establish a Core Identity
97. Mold a Strong and Adaptive Culture
98. Create Action Scorecards

99. Position the Players
100. Put Everybody in Charge
101. Foster Open Communication
102. Maximize Decision Participation
103. Forge Feedback Loops
104. Melt Conflict Icebergs
105. Begin with a Win
106. Use the Entire Arsenal of Incentives
107. Set the Ethical Edge
108. Be the Thermostat

Bibliography

Ailes, Roger. *You Are the Message: Getting What You Want by Being Who You Are*. New York: Doubleday Books, 1989.

"America's Most Admired Companies." *Fortune* (September 29, 2000).

American Society for Training and Development. "State of the Industry." *Training* (1999).

Arndt, Michael. "The Industry Will Pay for United's Deal with Pilots." *BusinessWeek* (September 18, 2000), p. 52.

Blanchard, Ken, and Spencer Johnson. *The One Minute Manager*. New York: William Morrow and Company, Inc., 1982.

Blank, Warren. *The Nine Natural Laws of Leadership*. New York: AMACOM, 1995.

Bowe, John, Marisa Bowe, and Sabin Streeter. *Gig: Americans Talk about Their Jobs at the Turn of the Millennium*. New York: Crown, 2000.

Brinkerhoff, Robert O., and Stephen Gill. *The Learning Alliance: Systems Thinking in Human Resource Development*. New York: Jossey-Bass, 1994.

Buckingham, Marcus, and Curt Coffman. *First, Break All the Rules*. New York: Simon and Schuster, 1999.

Byrnes, Nanette. "The New Calling." *BusinessWeek* (September 18, 2000), pp. 137–148.

Charon, Ram, and Geoffrey Colvin. "Why CEOs Fail." *Fortune* (June 21, 1999), pp. 68–71.

Collins, James. "Built to Flip." *Fast Company* (March 2000), pp. 131–143.

Collins, James C., and Jerry I. Porras. *Built to Last*. New York: Harper-Business, 1994.

Colvin, Geoffrey. "CEO Super Bowl." *Fortune* (August 2, 1999).

Douillard, John. *Body, Mind, and Sport*. New York: Crown, 1995.

"Fast Pack 2000." *Fast Company* (March 2000), pp. 234–254.

Fishman, Charles. "Whole Foods Is All Teams." *Fast Company* (April–May 1996).

Ganguly, Meenakshi. "Speaking Her Mind." *Time* (April–May 2000).

Gardner, Howard. *Frames of Mind*. New York: Basic Books, 1985.

Golden, Frederic. "A Century of Heroes." *Time* (April–May 2000).

Grover, Ronald, and David Polek. "Millionaire Buys Disney Time." *BusinessWeek* (June 26, 2000), pp. 141–144.

Hackman, J. Richard, and J. Lloyd Suttle. *Improving Life at Work: Behavioral Science Approaches to Organizational Change*. Santa Monica, CA: Goodyear Publishing, 1977.

Hamel, Gary. *Leading the Revolution*. Boston: Harvard Business School Press, August 2000.

Hamer, Dean, and Peter Copeland. *Living with Our Genes*. New York: Doubleday Books. 1998.

Hamilton, Martha McNeil. "Blockbuster Branches Out." *Washington Post* (September 19, 2000), pp. E1, E7.

Keltner, Dacher. "Reading Their Lips." *Psychology Today* (September–October 2000), pp. 52–53.

Klein, Gary. *Sources of Power: How People Make Decisions*. Boston: MIT Press, 1998.

LeBoeuf, Michael. *How to Win Customers and Keep Them for Life*. New York: Berkley Publishing Group, March 1989.

Lemann, Nicholas. "The Word Lab." *The New Yorker* (October 16 and 23, 2000), pp. 100–112.

Maruca, Regina Fazio. "Voices." *Fast Company* (September 2000), pp. 105–144.

Masie, Elliott. "Time to Walk in the Shoes of e-Learners!" Online. *TechLearn Trends #188* (October 16, 2000), www.techlearn.com/trends/.

Masie, Elliott. *TechLearn Trends* (October 19, 2000).

Meredith, Gail. "Breaking Down Barriers." *iQ*, pp. 510–514.

Merritt, Jennifer. "Uncle Sam Wants You—And So Does Pepsi." *BusinessWeek* (September 4, 2000), p. 52.

Mintzberg, Henry. "Planning on the Left Side and Managing on the Right." *Harvard Business Review* (July–August 1976).

Naisbitt, John, and Patricia Aburdene. *Megatrends 2000: Ten New Directions for the 1990s.* New York: William Morrow & Co., 1990.

Nocera, Joseph. "I Remember Microsoft." *Fortune* (July 10, 2000).

Okrent, Daniel. "Happily Ever After?" *Time* (January 24, 2000), pp. 39–43.

Oppenheimer, Jerry. *Martha Stewart—Just Desserts: The Unauthorized Biography.* New York: William Morrow and Co., 1997.

Peters, Tom. *The Circle of Innovation.* New York: Alfred A. Knopf, Inc., 1997.

Peters, Tom, and Nancy Austin. *A Passion for Excellence.* New York: Warner Books, Inc., 1989.

Peterson, Christopher, and Fiona Lee. "Reading Between the Lines." *Psychology Today* (September–October 2000), pp. 50–51.

Popcorn, Faith. *Clicking.* New York: HarperCollins, 1996.

Ramo, Joshua Cooper. "A Two-Man Network." *Time* (January 24, 2000), pp. 46–50.

Riley, Pat. *The Winner Within.* New York: Berkley Publishing Group, 1994.

Russell, Peter. *The Brain Book.* New York: E. P. Dutton, 1979.

Sellers, Patricia. "These Women Rule." *Fortune* (October 25, 1999), pp. 94–123.

The Motivational Manager. Ragan Communications, Inc., Newsletter.

Thompson, Charles. *What a Great Idea!* New York: HarperCollins Publishers, 1992.

Ward, Barbara. *The Rich Nations and the Poor Nations.* New York: W. W. Norton & Co., 1962.

Welch, David. *BusinessWeek* (September 4, 2000), p. 50.

Index